Send Out Your SPIRIT

LEADER'S MANUAL

Send Out Your SPIRIT

LEADER'S MANUAL

Preparing Teens for Confirmation

Michael Amodei

ave maria press   Notre Dame, Indiana

The Ad Hoc Committee to Oversee the Use of the Catechism, United States Catholic Conference of Bishops, has found the doctrinal content of this catechist manual, copyright 2003, to be in conformity with the *Catechism of the Catholic Church.*

Nihil Obstat: Reverend Michael Henitz

Imprimatur: Most Reverend John M. D'Arcy
                Bishop of Diocese of Fort Wayne-South Bend

Given at Fort Wayne, IN on 27 August 2002.

Scripture texts in this work are taken from the *New American Bible with Revised New Testament and Revised Psalms* © 1991, 1986, 1970 Confraternity of Christian Doctrine, Washington, D.C. and are used by permission of the copyright owner. All Rights Reserved. No part of the *New American Bible* may be reproduced without permission in writing from the copyright owner.

English translation of the *Catechism of the Catholic Church* for the United States of America copyright © 1994, United States Catholic Conference, Inc.— Libreria Editrice Vaticana. Used with permission.

Some of the lessons in this book has been adapted from the *Developing Faith* series, Kieran Sawyer, S.S.N.D., general editor, copyright © 1996-1998 by Ave Maria Press, Notre Dame, Indiana.

Special thanks and appreciation to the teens and catechists at:
St. Monica Catholic Church, Santa Monica, California (1979-1993)
Old Mission Catholic Church, San Luis Obispo, California (1991-1993)
St. Joseph Catholic Church, South Bend, Indiana (1993-)

Dedicated to:
Notre Dame du Lac

International Standard Book Number: 0-87793-951-9

Cover and text design by Brian C. Conley

Printed and bound in the United States of America.

Contents

Foreword

Send Out Your Spirit most effectively fills a gap in the catechetical resources available for the formation of youth, specifically a Confirmation Handbook for candidates in their teen years.

One of the continuous concerns I have had as a Bishop celebrating the sacrament of Confirmation is that the teen's knowledge of their faith is lacking. Attention to the main articles of faith pales in comparison to their participation in social and service aspects of Confirmation preparation.

I believe that the task of acquiring a strong knowledge of faith certainly needs more attention without sacrificing other elements of the program. *Send Out Your Spirit* provides a comprehensive Candidate's Handbook to assist teens in acquiring an appreciation and thorough understanding of faith in the context of Confirmation and the seven-fold gifts of the Holy Spirit.

While the Leader's Manual provides several workable models for a conducting a Confirmation program, the much-needed information is contained in the Candidate's Handbook. The narrative style of the Handbook presents the faith as applicable to a teen's own age and experience. The narrative style continues in the exposition of the teachings of the faith and provides vital continuity and development. The focus on the goal remains clear throughout: to prepare candidates adequately in the knowledge and practice of the faith and their vocation as witnesses to Christ in the Church.

The central theme of *Send Out Your Spirit* allows candidates to see the primary place of the sacraments of initiation in the life of the Church and in the lives of faithful Catholics. The text explores in varied and successive ways the primary importance of Baptism, Confirmation, and Eucharist to establish and intensify our relationship to the Trinity: Father, Son, and Holy Spirit. *Send Out Your Spirit* presents a sound Trinitarian theology and spirituality.

Scripture usage fits expertly into the text and narratives and invites candidates to explore further the Word of God.

The practice of prayer receives ongoing attention through the inclusion of interesting stories of prayerful people and an appealing section of prayers highlighted through the text.

The Appendix has helpful suggestions for a number of sample service projects the Candidates may complete in preparation for Confirmation. A set of 50 Questions summarizing the key points of the text along with a lexicon of terms are also included in the Appendix.

Send Out Your Spirit: A Confirmation Candidate's Handbook for Faith finds a right balance between the various reading levels of teens. It will challenge some teenage readers to improve their reading skills in the process of preparation for Confirmation.

Catechists, as always, are the key in being teachers of the faith—whatever the text or program that is used. I anticipate that the *Send Out Your Spirit Leader's Manual* will prove an invaluable tool for catechists to lead their Confirmation candidates to a solid knowledge of their faith appropriate to the candidate's age and related to the sacrament itself. At the same time, this program will serve as a foundation and incentive for the continuous learning required of adult witnesses to Christ and the Church. These newly confirmed Catholics will then, in their own way, follow Christ growing in wisdom, age, and grace as they continue their journey of faith.

THE VERY REVEREND SYLVESTER D. RYAN
BISHOP OF MONTEREY

Send Out Your Spirit Preparing Teens for Confirmation

Every baptized person should receive the sacrament of Confirmation. Without the sacraments of Confirmation and Eucharist, Baptism is still valid and efficacious, but Christian initiation remains incomplete.

Traditionally, in the Roman Catholic Church, the custom has been for Confirmation to take place at the "age of discretion," around age seven. In 2001, the United States Catholic bishops determined that the age for children baptized in infancy to be confirmed should be sometime between the ages of seven and sixteen.

Confirmation is also known as "the sacrament of Christian maturity." Confirmation is an important step in a Christian's faith journey that not only stresses maturity, but also commitment, knowledge, freedom, and active participation.

Send Out Your Spirit is most appropriate for Catholic teenagers preparing for and receiving the sacrament of Confirmation during the years of senior high school. Depending on the maturity of your group, it may also be adapted for adolescents in the junior high grades.

Catechesis for Confirmation preparation should be appropriate to this age. Ideally, it should include the following elements:

- performance standards for Church membership (e.g., Mass and course attendance);
- a certain amount of community service;
- a letter of request for Confirmation and an interview with the parish pastor;
- a formational program of catechesis over an extended amount of time;
- the use of catechists, parents, and sponsors from among adult parishioners.

Also, a Confirmation preparation program must take place within a parish community. For teenagers, this often means coming together with fellow parishioners from different schools and different levels of catechetical and religious formation.

In the program itself, the intimate relationship between Baptism, Confirmation, and Eucharist must be stressed. Sacramental catechesis is different from other courses in religious education. It is meant to prepare the candidate and the Church community for a meaningful celebration of the liturgy and a deeper commitment to Christ and the Church. With more detail the *Catechism of the Catholic Church* teaches:

> *Preparation* for Confirmation should aim at leading the Christian toward a more intimate union with Christ and a more living familiarity with the Holy Spirit—his actions, his gifts, and his biddings—in order to be more capable of assuming the apostolic responsibilities of Christian life. To this end catechesis for Confirmation should strive to awaken a sense of belonging to the Church of Jesus Christ, the universal Church as well as the parish community. The latter bears special responsibility for the preparation of confirmands (1309).

Finally, besides the requirement of already being baptized, to be confirmed a candidate must be in a state of grace. He or she should receive the sacrament of Penance prior to Confirmation and engage in more intense prayer in order to receive the gifts of the Holy Spirit with the courage and readiness to act on them.

PRINCIPLES OF INITIATORY CATECHESIS

For adolescents, catechesis for the preparation of the sacrament of Confirmation is intended to prepare them for a full, conscious, and active participation not only in the rite of Confirmation, but in the life of the Church. This preparation is intended to examine the specific aspects of mission, discipleship, Spirit, and witness in the adolescent's life and in the overall life of the Church.

Further, initiatory catechesis, in which preparation for the sacrament of Confirmation is included, has certain necessary characteristics according to the *General Directory for Catechesis*.

First, initiatory catechesis is comprehensive and structured. It looks to and covers what is "common" for the Christian, that is, the main tenets of our faith.

Second, this catechesis is more than instruction: "it is an apprenticeship of the entire Christian life," promoting discipleship in Christ, education in the knowledge of the faith and the life of faith so that the person feels deeply enriched in the word of God. Such catechesis helps the person fulfill his or her baptismal responsibilities and profess faith from the heart.

Third, initiatory catechesis is a basic and essential formation of the Christian person. But it is also only a beginning. Preparation for the sacraments of initiation, whether all at once or at separate times, serves to encourage the initiated Christian to seek more solid nourishment of his or her faith in the life of the Church.

In this specific case, a teenager's preparation for and reception of the sacrament of Confirmation should not in any way be understood as a "graduation" from formal religious education or, in worse cases, the time the now fully initiated can begin the spiral toward eventually abandoning the faith altogether.

Send Out Your Spirit highlights the essential process intended by the Rite of Baptism for Children: that Baptism is to be followed by a lengthy faith formation that allows a person to make a personal commitment to the Christian faith.

How *Send Out Your Spirit* Incorporates the Characteristics of Initiatory Catechesis

The three primary characteristics of initiatory catechesis are a central part of the *Send Out Your Spirit* Confirmation program, especially in the following ways:

1. *Send Out Your Spirit* is comprehensive and structured. The content of the material is arranged to help the teens to understand initial requirements for Church membership (Chapter 1) leading to a further presentation of the foundational elements of our faith: God (Holy Trinity), Christology and the life of Jesus, the place of scripture in the life of the Church, ecclesiology and Church history (with special emphasis on lives of exemplary Christians), liturgy and sacraments, morality (including the Ten Commandments and Beatitudes), and the Church's social teaching. Chapter 9 focuses on Confirmation as the sacrament of the Holy Spirit, delving into a deeper presentation of life in the Spirit, including the gifts of the Spirit. The basic rite of Confirmation is explained near the time of the actual reception of the sacrament.

2. *Send Out Your Spirit* offers an apprenticeship of the entire Christian life. The program includes a combination of prayer experiences, community service suggestions, and faith-sharing activities interspersed within the content of each of the faith themes.

3. *Send Out Your Spirit* encourages the further development of a teen's faith life. Expanding the definition of Confirmation as a sacrament of maturity, *Send Out Your Spirit* helps the teens to understand the sacrament as one step in their *maturing faith*. The process of faith education

does not end with reception of the sacrament. Concretely, the newly confirmed teen is challenged to consider and fill adult roles within the Church. Chapter 10, specifically, asks the teens to project themselves into several adult Christian vocations.

CONFIRMATION PREPARATION PARTICIPANTS

This Confirmation preparation program can be conducted with any number of teenagers. Given that the teens themselves are in possession of the main catechetical content in the Candidate's Handbook, the material can be presented in many different ways, not the least of which requires the teens to read the material on their own and be evaluated through oral and written questioning by a catechist, sponsor, or parent.

However, given the necessity of participation by the local parish community in preparing teens for the sacrament of Confirmation, it is most appropriate for many different adults to participate in the program along with the candidates. They include, but are not limited to, those in the following roles (more than one role may be taken by the same person):

Pastor. Together with the local bishop, the pastor determines the basic requirements for reception of the sacrament of Confirmation for the parish. These may include the length of the preparation time, the types and number of courses, and the age of the Confirmation candidates. The pastor will also serve as an occasional catechist during the preparation sessions.

Director of Religious Education. The DRE coordinates how immediate preparation for Confirmation fits within the whole of the parish's religious education program. For example, the DRE determines what prerequisites (e.g., courses, terms enrolled in religious ed.) a teen will need before being enrolled in Confirmation preparation.

Coordinator of Youth Ministry. Adolescent catechesis, and in this specific case, Confirmation catechesis, may be the intersection of the responsibilities of the DRE and the CYM. Whereas the DRE's task is to fit Confirmation within the entire scope of ongoing religious education, the CYM coordinates how Confirmation preparation is part of the entire offering of total youth ministry in a parish: i.e., amidst other social, service, and worship opportunities.

Confirmation Leader. This person organizes the program in conjunction with the pastor, DRE, and CYM. He or she gets the program started by contacting adult volunteers and potential candidates, setting a calendar based on the model chosen (see pages 16-18), arranging for meeting space, and leading an introductory meeting for candidates and parents.

Catechists. Catechists are responsible for teaching the material for all or parts of particular sessions. The "teaching" is done in several ways; but especially by summarizing and enriching the material covered in the Candidate's Handbook. Catechists should be trained as part of regular formational programs in the parish or diocese.

Sponsors. The sponsor is ideally the same sponsor (godparent) from Baptism. A sponsor assists the candidate by sharing in a close way his or her faith journey and preparation for Confirmation and helping the candidate live as a true witness of Christ. To be a sponsor, Church law requires that the person be a confirmed Catholic who has received Eucharist and is leading a life of faith. The sponsor cannot be a parent of the candidate. Besides attending the rite of Confirmation itself, the sponsor may attend some sessions, meet with the candidate on a regular basis outside of class, participate in community service projects, and attend a retreat with the candidate.

Parents. Parents are the primary educators of their children, especially in their life of faith. Much of this education takes place in their loving example, exhibited in their relationship to their spouse, to their children, and to God. However, this model is strengthened when parents "comment on the more methodical catechesis which their children later receive in the Christian community and help them to appropriate it" (*GDC*, 226). Confirmation preparation is a definite time for parents to verse themselves in the content of material being presented to better help their children receive the sacrament worthily. Parents should be encouraged to read and discuss the material from the Candidate's Handbook with their sons and daughters. Also, parents are expected to attend an Introductory Meeting. They are also expected to participate at liturgy with their children and to easily facilitate their children's participation in the program in other ways: e.g., aiding in Christian service work, driving to group sessions. As a reminder to their children that Christian catechesis is ongoing, parents should also take it on themselves to enroll in an adult education course at the parish, attend a workshop, audit a course at a local Catholic college, or participate in a retreat. Finally, parents can help with many of the hospitality tasks of Confirmation preparation, like arranging for refreshments, scheduling car pools, and the like.

Parishioners. As the candidates are being initiated into a Church represented by the local parish, parishioners should know of and be involved in the preparation. This can be done in several ways. For example, parishioners can participate in community service events with the teens and serve as "prayer partners" (praying for individual candidates by name throughout the time leading to Confirmation). More importantly, the candidates should participate more fully in parish worship and ministries.

Candidates. As determined by regulations from the diocesan bishop and the parish pastor, candidates for this program should be baptized teenagers who meet the other requirements as determined by many of the adults listed above. Once accepted into the program, the candidates must be responsible for things like attending sessions, reading the material in the Candidate's Handbook, meeting with their sponsors, doing community service, and participating in Eucharist.

COMPONENTS OF THIS PROGRAM

Send Out Your Spirit consists of the following components:
1. Candidate's Handbook
2. Leader's Manual

The Candidate's Handbook provides a thorough introduction to key teachings and topics of our faith (see Catechetical Themes, pages 13-14). The main content of this Confirmation preparation program is found in the Candidate's Handbook.

The format for each chapter of the Candidate's Handbook revolves around introducing a topic with a relevant story or short lesson. The main content material for each chapter is organized in three or four main sections, with other subsections in each. Each main section includes discussion or journaling questions. The chapters also include one or two personal interest features, quotations from the scripture or writings of the saints (Word of God), and traditional prayers. All of these elements are related to the main topic of the chapter.

Also in the Candidate's Handbook is an Appendix with a Glossary of Selected Terms, Sample Service Project Ideas, and 50 Questions the candidates are to record answers for at home and return to class.

The Leader's Manual is closely connected to the material in the Candidate's Handbook. The Leader's Manual provides several "how to use" tips for catechists and other adult leaders to break open the material lessons intended for either large or small groups.

Each chapter offers an introductory overview of the important content. Several lesson ideas are listed related to each main section of the Candidate's Handbook. Completing every one of the lessons while covering the material in the Candidate's Handbook is not required; rather, more than one suggestion per section is offered to allow for freedom to adapt the material as suited to the time and setting of the session. Also, Warm-Up/Breaktime ideas are offered for each chapter. These are meant to serve as session icebreakers and short activities to used in between lessons. Assignment and lesson suggestions are also given to correspond with the Feature and Word of God material. At least two short Prayer Experience ideas are also included with each chapter.

Lesson Planning Models for each chapter provide suggestions for lessons based on three different program models. These Lesson Planning Models are explained in more detail on page 16.

Suggested directions are also given in this Manual for assignments related to the words in the Glossary of Selected Terms (pages 225-235), the Sample Service Project Ideas (pages 237-241), and the 50 Questions (pages 243-247).

CATECHETICAL THEMES OF *SEND OUT YOUR SPIRIT*

As catechesis for Confirmation is intended to lead a candidate to a deeper union with Christ, more familiarity with the Holy Spirit, and a sense of belonging to the Church, the scope and sequence of *Send Out Your Spirit* has been arranged to that end. *Send Out Your Spirit* addresses issues of Church membership, highlights the core teaching of our faith related to the doctrine of the Blessed Trinity, leads the candidates to understand the intimate union between Christ and the Church, and calls them to see that their life as a Christian is a participation in Christ's Paschal mystery. *Send Out Your Spirit* also specifically shares the actions, gifts, and calling of the Holy Spirit in relation to the sacrament of Confirmation. Finally, *Send Out Your Spirit* encourages the teenagers to reflect—with the help of the Holy Spirit—on their adult, Christian vocation.

Building on the understanding of the United States Bishop's document on youth ministry, *Renewing the Vision: A Framework for Catholic Youth Ministry* that "catechesis with adolescents recognizes that faith development is lifelong," *Send Out Your Spirit* presents the following catechetical themes with the understanding that the teenagers preparing for Confirmation have been previously introduced to these topics prior and will continue to investigate them further and incorporate them more fully after reception of the sacrament.

Sequence

The chapter titles and sections appear below to provide a brief overview of the sequence of the catechetical themes in *Send Out Your Spirit*. The chapter introductions in this Manual offer an overview of the scope of each chapter.

1 Belonging
  Christian Initiation: Back to the Beginning
  Two Rites of Initiation
  Baptism: The Essential Sacrament

2 God
  Who Is God?
  The Nature of God
  The Holy Trinity

3 Jesus Christ
  Who Is Jesus?
  Jesus, True God and True Man
  The Life of Christ
  Jesus' Passion, Death, and Resurrection

SUGGESTIONS FOR USING THE CANDIDATE'S HANDBOOK

The *Send Out Your Spirit* Candidate's Handbook is a digest of the main catechetical content needed by a teenager who is preparing for the sacrament of Confirmation.

It is recommended that the candidate be given the Candidate's Handbook prior to the first session, preferably at the Introductory Meeting.

The candidate should be encouraged to read the entire book at his or her own pace, but with special focus on particular chapters or sections within specific chapters that will be discussed at upcoming sessions. For example, Chapter 1, Belonging, might be the focus for the month of September and Chapter 9, Holy Spirit and Confirmation, could be the focus of May or any month directly approaching the time the candidates will receive Confirmation.

The exploration of the contents of the Candidate's Handbook can be expanded during catechetical sessions, one-to-one meetings between candidates and sponsors, and enrichment assignments that include asking the candidates to find references in the scriptures and Church documents. Other features of the Candidate's Handbook lend themselves to individual and group assignments related to an overall preparation for Confirmation. These are explained in the next subsections.

Discussion/Journal Writing

In-text questions are offered at the end of each chapter section. These can be used for small group discussions among the candidates at a session. Or, they can be used as discussion starters for one-to-one meetings between candidates and sponsors.

It is recommended that the candidates keep a journal during this time of immediate preparation for the sacrament of Confirmation. Many of the in-text questions can be used as journal entry starters.

A journal can also be used to record more personal thoughts, feelings, and prayers. Encourage these types of entries as well. If any adult will be "checking" the candidate's journal, let the teens know that in advance and suggest that they star or paper-clip any page with material of a personal nature so that it is sure to remain private.

Glossary of Selected Terms

A Glossary of Selected Terms is included on pages 225-235 of the Candidate's Handbook. There are several options for assignments related to the terms in this glossary. For example:

- Assign a selected number of terms each month. Quiz the candidates on their spelling and meaning.
- Ask the candidates to work individually or in small groups to create crossword puzzles, word mazes, and the like using the glossary terms. Make copies of their projects and distribute them to the rest of the candidates.
- Play games pitting one team against another. For example, call one candidate forward, give a term, and ask him or her to provide the definition. If correct, award a point. If incorrect, call on a representative from the other team. Continue to a "winning score" or until everyone has had a chance to come forward.
- Have the candidates make flash cards of the terms and work in pairs to quiz each other on their meanings.

Sample Service Project Ideas

Ongoing service to the parish, local neighborhood community, and world at large is a key lesson candidates should learn and enact both during and beyond the time of Confirmation preparation.

It is best when service projects are undertaken with the help of adults, preferably Confirmation sponsors and others connected with the Confirmation program. Requirements for service are often stated in terms of "hours" (e.g. twenty hours prior to Confirmation, twenty hours after Confirmation), though it may be a more significant lesson to stress the quality of the service and its ongoing and lasting nature.

One suggestion is to require each candidate to participate in one service event in each of the areas listed above and on pages 237-241 of the Candidate's Handbook.

For the purposes of accountability, ask the candidates to provide a short oral or written report on their service experience, focusing especially on these items:

1. description of the project
2. his/her role in the project
3. date and hours spent on the project
4. how the project relates to the ministry of Jesus and the Church
5. a lesson he/she learned from participating

50 Questions

Pages 243-247 of the Candidate's Handbook lists 50 Questions that, when completed, offer a brief synopsis of *Send Out Your Spirit's* catechetical content. The candidates should review the text, as applicable, and write answers to each question. Some of the questions must be researched from other sources. For other questions, the candidates will have to interview people in the parish for the answers. The 50 Questions may be assigned in a number of ways:

1. Assign five to ten questions at a time as ongoing homework. You can choose to assign a specific set related to a particular chapter, or you can assign them randomly.
2. Candidates and sponsors can read and research answers to the questions together. The candidates can record the answers and keep them for accountability.
3. Assign the entire list of 50 Questions as a long-term assignment at the Introductory Meeting with the due date being the last session prior to Confirmation.
4. Play any number of quiz games using the questions within sessions. For example, play a game of "baseball" with two teams. A correct answer merits a trip to first base. An answer to a harder question may merit a double or a home run. Three incorrect answers gives the other team a chance at bat. Keep track of total runs to determine the winning team.

Answers to the 50 Questions are on pages 213-219. Many of the questions allow for much more depth of response than is provided on those pages.

MODELS FOR SCHEDULING CONFIRMATION PREPARATION

There are many ways to cover the content of the material from the Candidate's Handbook. The most appropriate ways involve the candidates meeting together for regularly scheduled sessions over the course of weeks, months, or years.

Most parish Confirmation programs require participation in at least one year of religious education classes prior to immediate preparation for the sacrament itself. Given that supposition, offered below are three different models for one year of immediate preparation based on an eleven-month calendar (typically August to June). In each model, the first month is reserved for an introductory meeting (see pages 18-19), the first candidate session(s) are held in the second month, and the final session ("Your Christian Vocation," Chapter 10) may take place after reception of the sacrament of Confirmation to help the newly confirmed transition into more adult-level participation in the parish.

For each model listed below, individual home assignments and sponsor/candidate activity suggestions are offered within each chapter.

Model I: Focused Preparation (Ten 3-Hour Sessions)

This model is designed for the candidates to meet once per month in a three hour session.

The advantage to Model 1 is that there will be more extended time with sessions to include community-building activities, discussions, opportunities for journal writing, prayer experiences, and solid catechetical lessons.

The content from one entire chapter of the Candidate's Handbook is addressed in each three hour session. Each main section of the chapter, as outlined in the sequence of catechetical themes on pages 13-14, is covered by a separate lesson. Within each lesson a variety of catechetical approaches are offered. A sample schedule with time breakdowns is:

Warm-Up	20 minutes
Lesson 1	30 minutes
Lesson 2	25 minutes
Breaktime (Lesson 2 continuation)	25 minutes
Lesson 3	35 minutes
Lesson 4	30 minutes
Conclusion/Prayer Experience	15 minutes

Model 2: Extended Small or Large Group Preparation (Twenty 1-Hour Sessions)

Model 2 is designed for the candidates to meet twice per month in two one-hour sessions. One or both sessions may be with the entire large group of candidates. Or, one session can be for a small group (up to eight candidates) and the other can be with the entire group.

The advantage for meeting two times in one month is that at least one of the sessions can often be combined with other parish activities—including Mass, youth group, and the like. Piggy-backing two sessions per month on activities of these kind helps to increase attendance and participation at each.

The content from one entire chapter of the Candidate's Handbook is covered over the two sessions. A sample time framework for the two sessions is:

Session 1

Warm-Up	10 minutes
Lesson	20 minutes
Breaktime	5 minutes
Lesson	20 minutes
Conclusion/Prayer Experience	5 minutes

Session 2

Prayer Experience	15 minutes
Lesson	15 minutes
Breaktime	10 minutes
Lesson	15 minutes
Conclusion	5 minutes

Model 3: Concentrated Small Group Preparation (Ten 90-Minute Sessions)

Model 3 is designed for small groups of candidates (up to eight) to meet once per month in ten 90 minute sessions. The same session should be offered on a variety of days, at a variety of times, and, possibly, in a variety of locations (homes and parish) to allow busy teens the opportunity to choose a session date that fits their schedule.

The small group format is an advantage because it allows for more focused time between the catechist and candidates as well as more interaction between the candidates. The challenge for this model is to recruit and train enough catechists to be able to staff each session.

The content from one entire chapter of the Candidate's Handbook is covered over one session. A sample time framework for the session is:

Warm-Up	15 minutes
Lesson	40 minutes
Breaktime	5 minutes
Lesson	20 minutes
Prayer Experience/Conclusion	10 minutes

CATECHETICAL STRATEGIES AND METHODS

The *General Directory of Catechesis* notes that the methods of catechesis require adaptability to the "particular circumstances of the faithful to whom the catechesis is being addressed" (149).

The lesson suggestions in the *Send Out Your Spirit* Leader's Manual employ a number of learning strategies and methods that work especially well with adolescents. Some of these are:

- *Presentations.* Catechists give short presentations on the content that highlight and enrich the key points. These presentations avoid the tone of classroom lectures, relying more on making connections to the teen's culture and world today as well as offering regular opportunities for questioning and feedback.
- *Discussions. Send Out Your Spirit* offers several opportunities for the candidates to interact with one another in a small group setting or on a one-to-one basis. Catechists ask some questions that merely check knowledge of a particular section of catechetical content, and others that help the teens apply what they have learned to their own lives of faith.
- *Videos.* The Leader's Manual offers many suggestions for videos that relate to a given topic. It is usually not necessary to show an entire full length video presentation; rather, preview the video to find a five- to ten-minute segment that connects well with the lesson theme.
- *Panels.* Choose four or five teens to sit before the rest of the group on a panel. Working from a defined set of questions, ask one person on the panel a question. Then ask a second person on the panel to offer a follow-up. Continue with a second question in the same format, choosing a new person to begin each time.
- *Guest Speakers.* In a lesson on Church, for example, consider inviting a long-time parishioner to address the group on his or her remembrances of the living history of the parish, including how the parish adapted to the changes called for by the Second Vatican Council. Guest speakers work well for virtually any topic as long as the person is well-versed in the overall structure of the session, the content you wish them to cover, and the amount of time (maximum 15 minutes) you wish them to share. Guests may also be invited as panelists for a panel discussion similar to the one described above. The catechist could collect teens' questions ahead of time or teens could direct their questions to the panelist of their choice. Again, panelists must be well prepared for the topic to be covered.
- *Community Building Activities.* Part of the task of Confirmation preparation is to involve the adolescents more fully in the life of the parish. Activities which enhance feelings of belonging among the teens themselves (e.g., icebreakers, games) are a first step toward enhancing teens' comfort levels in the parish and the worldwide Church. Several community building activities are offered in each chapter of the Leader's Manual.

SETTINGS

Large group meetings should be held at the parish with the entire group comfortably seated on chairs, cushions, or a carpeted floor close to the presentation area (video screen, board). There should also be separate meeting areas for candidates (with adults) to use for small group discussion and activities.

Small group meetings may be held at the parish or in the homes of the catechists or one of the candidates. Similarly, there should be ample space for eight candidates to sit comfortably in one meeting space (e.g. on a living room floor or around a kitchen table).

INTRODUCTORY MEETING

An introductory meeting for parents and candidates is helpful for providing a brief understanding of the sacrament of Confirmation as well as the requirements for participating in the Confirmation program. The meeting is typically held in the month prior to the first session. As the meeting may also serve as the teen's first introduction to the other participants in the program, the tone of the meeting should be hospitable and warm, and the duration should be no longer than one hour.

Consider including some or all of the following elements:

1. Name tags for all participants.
2. An opening scripture reading. Solicit and prepare a teen who recently made his or her Confirmation to lead a short reading (e.g. 1 Cor 12:1-11).
3. A welcome by the pastor. The pastor may also offer a short homily on the scripture reading related to Confirmation.
4. A short talk on the history of Confirmation related to how the sacrament is understood and celebrated today.
5. An icebreaker that allows for interaction between teens.
6. A presentation on the program model and the candidate requirements (e.g., attendance at sessions, Christian service projects, retreat attendance).
7. An explanation on the requirements for a Confirmation sponsor in your program (see page 11).
8. An explanation on the role of parents in the Confirmation program (see page 12).
9. An opportunity to hear and answer questions from the candidates and parents.
10. Distribution of the Candidate's Handbooks. Also, assign a general reading plan for covering the material. For example, if the first session will be on "Belonging," assign Chapter 1 for reading prior to the session date.

End the meeting by praying the traditional "Come, Holy Spirit" (also on pages 201-202 of the Candidate's Handbook):

> Come, Holy Spirit, fill the hearts of your faithful
> and kindle in them the fire of your love.
> Send forth your Spirit, and they shall be created:
> and you will renew the face of the earth.
> O God,
> on the first Pentecost
> you instructed the hearts of those who believed in you
> by the light of the Holy Spirit:
> under the inspiration of the same Spirit,
> give us a taste for what is right and true
> and a continuing sense of his joy-bringing presence
> and power,
> through Jesus Christ our Lord.
> Amen.

IDEAS FOR CANDIDATE AND SPONSOR MEETINGS

Sponsors and candidates should meet regularly through the Confirmation preparation time. It is recommended that they get together in person or talk on the phone at least once per month. Some ideas for monthly meetings of sponsors with candidates are:

- Discuss the content of the material being covered in the Candidate's Handbook and in the class sessions. (The candidates should bring their Candidate's Handbook to each meeting with their sponsors.)
- Attend Sunday Mass together. Go out for breakfast or lunch and discuss the scripture readings of the day.
- Plan and carry out a Christian service project together (see pages 237-241 of the Candidate's Handbook).
- Go to a movie or some other social outing together.

Retreat

The Confirmation preparation time should include a retreat experience. The retreat is a time for deepened prayer, activities to further bond the candidates into a close group of faith, a chance to be away from the usual people and places, and an opportunity for informal celebrations of the sacraments of Penance and Eucharist.

An overnight retreat off parish grounds is recommended, but if that is too difficult, a Saturday all-day retreat on parish grounds would also be acceptable. In either case, make sure to reserve the date and the facility well in advance and inform the candidates and their parents as soon as possible.

As to the time placement of the retreat, one held at the beginning of the preparation time is beneficial because it will serve as a way to quickly forge community among the group that will last through the rest of the program. However, a retreat held just prior to the rite of Confirmation will serve as a great culmination to the program and will find the candidates better versed in the program's catechetical content.

Remember, the timing is not the most important issue. Rather, it's finding a way to have a retreat at any time.

There are many excellent resources for Confirmation retreats on the market. Two of the best are by Sr. Kieran Sawyer, SSND. They are:

   Time Out!: Resources for Teen Retreats (Ave Maria Press, 1998)
   The Faith Difference: Prayers, Lessons, Activities, and Games for Teens (Ave Maria Press, 2001)

Letter of Request for Confirmation/Interview with Pastor or Confirmation Coordinator

Prior to reception of the sacrament of Confirmation, the candidate should write a letter to the pastor explaining his or her desire for Confirmation. The letter could also include the following points:

1. The highlights of the Confirmation preparation for the candidate.
2. How the candidate's life has changed since beginning the program.
3. What ways the person sees himself or herself being involved with the parish after receiving Confirmation.
4. How the candidate intends to learn more about the faith after Confirmation.

One or more interviews with the pastor or Confirmation coordinator should also be held. If the interview is held at the beginning of the program, questions should focus on why the person wants to be confirmed, the talents and gifts the person brings to the group, and their hopes for what kind of Catholic they would like to become in the future. If the interview is held at the end of the program, it can be a response to the issues raised in the candidate's letter of request for Confirmation. Questions can also be taken from the issues raised in the Confirmation Survey (page 38 of this Manual).

Belonging

(see pages 11-29 of the Candidate's Handbook)

BACKGROUND

The foundation of Christian life is laid by the sacraments of initiation—Baptism, Confirmation, and Eucharist. These three bring about a change that, in many ways, is similar to birth itself, giving us a share in the life of God through the graces offered by Christ. Pope Paul VI compared this new birth in the sacraments of initiation to the "origin, development, and nourishing of natural life."

Through Baptism a person is *incorporated* into Christ and the Church. The baptized is configured to Christ and given an indelible spiritual character of his or her belonging to Christ. This character, or mark, can never be erased, even if sin prevents the graces of Baptism from leading the person to salvation. "To incorporate" means to include or make apart of. Baptism makes a person a member of the Church and enables and commits them to serve God by participating in the Church, especially in the liturgy.

Confirmation is a sacrament that celebrates the special outpouring of the Holy Spirit on the baptized, in the same way that the Spirit once came to the apostles at Pentecost. Confirmation "completes" Baptism in that it, too, imprints an indelible spiritual mark on the soul. Confirmation brings about an increase and deepening of baptismal grace.

It is Eucharist that completes Christian initiation. As the *Catechism of the Catholic Church* teaches, "Those who have been raised to the dignity of the royal priesthood by Baptism and configured more deeply to Christ by Confirmation participate with the whole community in the Lord's own sacrifice by means of the Eucharist" (1322).

A sometimes confusing area for Catholics concerning initiation is that the Church has two rites for initiation. The Rite of Christian Initiation for Adults is modeled on the early Church's catechumenate, a process whereby adult converts prepared for and received the sacraments of initiation sometimes over the course of several years.

Most teenagers preparing for Confirmation are initiated beginning with the Rite of Baptism for Children. They were baptized as infants, received first Eucharist about the age of seven, and are now readying for Confirmation. More recently, in an attempt to maintain the original order of the sacraments of initiation—Baptism, Confirmation, and Eucharist—some children baptized as infants may be confirmed near the time of their First Communion.

All of this information concerning the Church's rites of initiation is important for teens to learn and decipher, all the while knowing that their belonging to Christ and his Church is only dependent on God's grace given to them at Baptism.

Sample Schedules
Model I: Focused Preparation (one 3-hour session)
Suggested Session Plan

Warm-Up (20 minutes)
Refer to pages 11-14 of the Candidate's Handbook.
- Use Warm-Up/Breaktime Exercise "A" (page 30).
- Also, referring to Warm-Up/Breaktime Exercises "D" and "E," offer a detailed account of your parish's confirmation requirements (see pages 30-31).

Lesson 1: Christian Initiation: Back to the Beginning (30 minutes)
Refer to pages 14-17 of the Candidate's Handbook.
- Use Christian Initiation: Back to the Beginning "B" (page 31).
- *Note:* Also invite a parish leader who is part of the RCIA team to address the teens. Make sure the presentation addresses specific ways your parish supports catechumens preparing for initiation (see page 17 of the Candidate's Handbook).
- Ask the teens to offer opinions on whether or not Tom (from the opening story on pages 11-14) should be confirmed.

Lesson 2: Two Rites of Initiation (25 minutes)
Refer to pages 17-21 of the Candidate's Handbook.
- Use Two Rites of Initiation "E" (page 33).
  Follow-up: Discuss with the teens their own Baptisms. Ask where they were baptized, who their godparents were, the date of their baptism, and the significance of their name.

Breaktime/Lesson 3 Introduction (25 minutes)
Refer to pages 21-22 of the Candidate's Handbook.
- Allow time for a short break. Then have the teens return to the large group discussion area.
- Use Warm-Up/Breaktime Exercise "C" (page 30). Call on more than one volunteer to share responses to the questions listed.
- Have the candidates do the preparation for either Baptism: The Essential Sacrament "A" or "C" (page 33).

Lesson 3: Baptism the Essential Sacrament (35 minutes)
Refer to pages 21-24 of the Candidate's Handbook.
- Allow enough time for the candidates to view each other's symbols or skits as a transition to Lesson 3 (see above).
- Use Baptism: The Essential Sacrament "F" (page 34). If possible, arrange for each teen to have his or her own copy of the Bible.
  Discussion: Ask the teens what it means for them to be "configured to Christ" (see page 24 of the Candidate's Handbook).

Lesson 4: More on Baptism and Confirmation (30 minutes)
Refer to pages 26-28 of the Candidate's Handbook.
- To gauge more of the teen's readiness for Confirmation, ask them to complete the Confirmation Survey (page 38) individually. Schedule one-to-one interviews with the pastor (see page 20) as appropriate.

- Use Features "B" (page 36).
  Note: If you will be using the same meeting space throughout the preparation period, try to find ways for the teens to decorate and personalize the space.

Conclusion/Prayer Experience (20 minutes)
Refer to pages 28-29 of the Candidate's Handbook.
- Assign Features "C" (page 36).
- Use either Prayer Experience "A" or "B" (page 36).

Individual Home Assignments
- Have the teens research and report on a) Blandina; b) any other Christian martyr; or c) the meaning of a baptism of blood.
- Assign questions related to the topic from the "50 Questions" (page 243-247 of the Candidate's Handbook). Questions 1-5 are specifically relevant.
- Assign for journal writing some or all of the reflection questions from Chapter 1 of the Candidate's Handbook that were not covered as part of the class session.

Sponsor/Candidate Activities
- Review together the FAQs from pages 26-27 of the Candidate's Handbook.
- Attend together an RCIA session or a dismissal rite for Eucharist. Participate in the faith sharing with the catechumens.
- Attend Sunday Mass together. Discuss reasons the candidate has chosen to prepare for confirmation in an informal meeting after Sunday Mass.

MODEL 2: EXTENDED PREPARATION (TWO 1-HOUR SESSIONS)
Suggested Session 1 Plan

Warm-Up (10 minutes)
Refer to pages 11-14 of the Candidate's Handbook.
- Offer some chance for the candidates to introduce themselves and learn each other's names. Adapt Warm-Up/Breaktime Exercise "A" (page 30) to use as a way for the candidates to learn each other's names.
- Briefly overview the contents of the Candidate's Handbook, referring especially to the Introduction, pages 7-8.

Lesson: Christian Initiation: Back to the Beginning (25 minutes)
Refer to pages 14-17 of the Candidate's Handbook.
- Treat the question of Church membership, asking questions like "Who belongs to the Church?" and "How does a person become a member of the Catholic Church?" Also use the format and questions from Warm-Up/Breaktime Exercise "B" (page 30).
- Discuss the various requirements for Confirmation based on the opening story in the Candidate's Handbook involving Tom (pages 11-14). Refer to Warm-Up/Breaktime Exercise "E" (page 31).
- Summarize the history of Christian initiation, focusing on initiation in the early Church. Using Bibles, examine the controversy on Church membership detailed in the Acts of the Apostles (see Christian Initiation: Back to the Beginning "A", page 31).

Breaktime (5 minutes)
- Use the breaktime to distribute any information or registration forms the candidates will need related to their participation in the preparation program.

Lesson: Two Rites of Initiation (15 minutes)
Refer to pages 17-21 of the Candidate's Handbook.
- Briefly outline the two rites for Christian initiation, the Rite of Initiation for Adults and the Rite of Baptism for Children.
- Focus on infant Baptism. Invite a parent who recently had a child baptized to share something of the preparation and experience of the sacrament with the candidates. See Two Rites of Initiation, "A," page 32.

Prayer (5 minutes)
- Have the candidates stand. With the rest of the adult team of catechists (and sponsors), extend your hands over the candidates. Pray Pope John Paul's "For Our Children" (page 29 of the Candidate's Handbook).

Individual Home Assignments
- Ask the teens to complete and return the "Confirmation Survey" (page 38).
- Assign the feature "I Am a Christian: With Us, Nothing Evil Happens" (pages 27-28 of the Candidate's Handbook). Ask the candidates to answer the question on page 28 in their journal.
- Assign questions 1-2 from the "50 Questions," page 243 of the Candidate's Handbook

Sponsor/Candidate Activities
- For a first meeting, suggest that the candidates attend Mass with their sponsors and meet afterwards for a brief conversation over breakfast or lunch.
- Ask the teens to re-cap the first session for their sponsors.
- As a point of discussion, refer the sponsors to the FAQs on pages 26-27 of the Candidate's Handbook.

Suggested Session 2 Plan

Prayer Experience (10 minutes)
- To open the session, have the candidates renew their baptismal promises. Use the format suggested in Prayer Experiences "A" on page 36.
- *Optional:* Sing the refrain "We Believe" by Christopher Walker (OCP).

Lesson: Baptism: the Essential Sacrament (25 minutes)
Refer to pages 21-24 of the Candidate's Handbook.
- Offer a presentation on Baptism as a sacrament of belonging (see Baptism: The Essential Sacrament, "B").
- Show the video *Baptism: Sacrament of Belonging* (see "E", page 34).
- Discuss water as the essential sign used at Baptism. Have the candidates share some examples of waters destructive and life giving nature.

Breaktime (5 minutes)
- During the break, collect and/or discuss the "Confirmation Survey."

Lesson: Baptism: the Essential Sacrament, continued (15 minutes)
Refer to pages 21-24 of the Candidate's Handbook.
- Divide the class into small groups. Distribute candles and art media. Have the groups decorate baptismal candles for families of children who are about to be baptized.
- If there is time left, ask the teens to discuss the origins of their own names (see "G," page 34).

Conclusion (5 minutes)
- Go around the group and ask the teens to share one piece of new information they learned about Baptism or Confirmation in these two sessions.

Individual Assignments
- Assign some of discussion questions from Chapter 1 of the Candidate's Handbook as journal assignments.
- Have the candidates research more about the "baptism of blood" and Christians who were martyred before being baptized with water.
- Assign questions 3-5 from the "50 Questions" on page 243 of the Candidate's Handbook.

Sponsor/ Candidate Activities
- Have the candidates research and review the origins of their name and share with their sponsor.
- Ask the sponsors to share remembrances of their own confirmation name and why it is important to them.

Model 3: Concentrated Preparation (one 90-minute session)
Suggested Session Plan

Warm-Up (20 minutes)
Refer to pages 11-14 of the Candidate's Handbook.
- Begin by offering a detailed presentation on your parish's requirements for Confirmation preparation. See Warm-Up/Breaktime Exercise "E," page 31.
- Choose a person to be "on the spot" and answer questions about why they belong to the Catholic church, what it means to be Catholic, and the like. Other questions are included in Warm-up/Breaktime Exercise "C," page 30. After a time, choose other candidates to be on the spot.
- Allow a chance for the candidates to mingle and introduce themselves to one another. Then call the group together. Go around the circle and have the candidates introduce the person to their right.

Lesson Plan (40 minutes)
Refer to pages 14-24 of the Candidate's Handbook.
- Prepare a talk on the two rites for Christian initiation, the Rite of Christian Initiation for Adults and the Rite of Baptism for Children.
- Call on the candidates to share remembrances of their own Baptisms, including who their godparents are, where they were baptized, and the significance of their given name.
- Play all or part of a video that introduces the RCIA process (see Christian Initiation: Back to the Beginning "C" on page 31) or invite a person who has recently been initiated into the Church through RCIA to address the group (Lesson Idea "B" page 31).

- Use Baptism: The Essential Sacrament "C" on page 33. Have the teens spend some time prior to the break preparing their skits.

Breaktime (10 minutes)
- Do a condensed version of the icebreaker listed under Warm-Up/Breaktime Exercise "A" on page 30. Choose one or two of the items to list on the nametags rather than all four items.

Lesson Plan continued (15 minutes)
Refer to pages 14-24 of the Candidate's Handbook.
- Allow the candidates to present their small group skits to the entire class. Connect the theme of belonging with the sacrament of Baptism.
- Explain the rites of the sacrament of Baptism (see page 00 of the Candidate's Handbook).

Conclusion/Prayer (5 minutes)
- Use Prayer Experience "B" (page 36) as a concluding prayer.

Individual Assignments
- Assign the "Confirmation Survey" (page 38). Have the candidates return it at the next session.
- Assign questions 1-5 from the "50 Questions," page 243 of the Candidate's Handbook.
- Have the candidates write an essay explaining why they belong to the Church and what type of Catholic they imagine themselves being as an adult.
- Assign for journal writing some of the discussion questions in Chapter 1.

Sponsor/Candidate Activities

- Meet together for a Sunday Mass. Share some time together after Mass to discuss the content of the first session and the requirements of the Confirmation preparation program.
- Review together the FAQs from pages 26-27 of the Candidate's Handbook.
- Encourage the sponsor and candidate to recall as much as possible about their own Baptisms, including who their godparents were.
- For fun, do something together water related: e.g., go to a water park with friends, share a day at the beach or pool, or "walk on water" at the local ice rink.

INTRODUCTION
Warm-up/Breaktime Exercises

A Pass out blank nametags and markers. Ask the teens to print their names somewhere on the nametag but to leave room for other information about themselves. Then ask them to include the following:

- an animal that symbolizes their personality,
- their favorite month of the year,
- their middle name in scrambled letters (e.g., Edward=rddeaw),
- the name of someone they admire.

Have the teens add other information at your discretion. Then have them wander around the room asking each other about the information on the nametags. Finally, call the teens one at a time to the front (or at least a sampling of the teens). Ask the group to explain the information on the person's nametag.

B Present to the teens the question "Why do you belong to the Church?" Write on the board: **What are some of the reasons a person might be Catholic?** Ask the participants to share "good" and "bad" reasons. For example:

- My parents are Catholic.
- I go to a Catholic school.
- Because that's the way I was raised.
- I believe in Jesus.
- I was baptized without having a choice in it.
- I'm a Notre Dame football fan.
- All my friends are Catholic.
- I want to go to heaven.

Write the responses on the board. Place a "+" next to what they consider to be good reasons and a "–" next to what they consider to be bad reasons. Next, have them choose three reasons that best describe why they are Catholic. Have them pair up with a partner to explain their reasons. Allow a few minutes for sharing.

C Call on a volunteer to come before the group. Interview the person about why they belong to the Church, what it means to be Catholic, what they like about being Catholic, etc. Ask questions like the following:

- What are some things you like about being Catholic? What are some beliefs or practices which you find challenging or difficult?
- What kind of Catholic do you envision yourself being ten years from now? Twenty years from now?
- When are you most proud to be a Catholic?
- What differentiates you as a Catholic from peers who are not Catholic?
- What do you think is the Church's most important mission today?
- When do you think the Church is at its best? at its worst?
- Why do you want to continue being Catholic?
- How do you come to know Jesus in the Church?

D Share specific information about various requirements for Confirmation programs at parishes in your local diocese as well as around the nation. Much of this information can be gleaned from parish websites. You may want to make copies of the requirements and distribute them. Make general comparisons between the various parishes' requirements. Call on the participants to comment on the similarities and differences.

E In a detailed presentation, offer your parish's requirements for Confirmation preparation. Include information about required participation at meetings, liturgies, retreats, service work. Also provide information about the Church's requirements for the sacrament (see CCC, 1306-1311).

CHRISTIAN INITIATION: BACK TO THE BEGINNING/LESSON IDEAS

A Examine the Acts of the Apostles to point out the differences in how the Jewish authorities treated St. Stephen and Sts. Peter and John. For example point out the differences in punishment received by Stephen (Acts 6:8–7:60) and Peter and John (Acts 4:1-21). All had been brought to the Jewish Sanhedrin and accused of preaching the gospel of Jesus Christ. Peter and John were flogged, ordered to stop preaching (they disobeyed this ruling), and released. Stephen was condemned to death and eventually became the first Christian martyr when he was stoned to death. The reason for the difference between punishments was that Stephen was a Hellenist (that is, a Jew influenced by Greek culture and practice) while Peter and John were Jews referred to in the New Testament as "Hebrews," that is, those who wished to maintain the purity of Judaism even within the "New Way."

The Council of Jerusalem decided that Gentile converts to Christianity did not have to keep the entire Jewish Law, but only those specific laws which had been first given to Noah, including marriage laws. Have the participants read the text describing the Council of Jerusalem from Acts 15:1-29.

Conduct a mock trial with teens serving as defendants accused of violating the following "rules":
1. dressing inappropriately at church,
2. missing Sunday Mass,
3. publicly disagreeing with the Church's position on premarital sex,
4. not abstaining from meat on the Fridays of Lent.

Assign the defendants a lawyer. Call witnesses for the "defense" and "prosecution." Allow the rest of the group to serve as jury, deciding on the punishment for each of the offenses if found "guilty." Discuss with the teens the relative seriousness of each offense.

B Invite a person who has recently been initiated into the Catholic Church through the RCIA process to address the group. Ask the person to explain how each step in the process aided in his or her spiritual formation. Allow opportunities for questions and answers from the teens to the speaker.

C Play all or part of a video that introduces the RCIA process; for example, *RCIA, An Invitation to New Life* (Paulist Press) or *This Is the Night* (Liturgy Training Publications at www.ltp.org).

D Re-enact with the teens part of a service held on Holy Thursday evening. It is preferable if the service is held near dusk. Bring the teens to the front steps of the church. Pray together the Apostle's Creed. Then, have the teens sit on the church steps facing the west and its oncoming darkness. Call on each teen to tell of his or her love and desire for Christ. After the person has spoken, he or she should turn to the East, the place of the rising sun and hope for eternal life. After all have spoken, call on a qualified cantor/musician to lead the singing of an appropriate song (e.g., "I Want to Praise Your Name" by Bob Hurd, OCP, 1984).

E Show all or part of the documentary *Pillars of Faith: Martyrs to Christianity* (Billy J.W. Mitchell, Kultur International, 1998; available at www.kultur.com). It tells the story of Christian martyrs from the time of Christ to the present. The entire presentation is 48 minutes.

TWO RITES OF INITIATION/LESSON IDEAS

A Invite parents who recently had an infant baptized to speak with the Confirmation candidates, telling why they chose to have their child baptized. Ask them to share information about the preparation that took place and some of the ways they plan to instruct their child in faith. If possible, have the parents bring the child to the meeting. At the end of the presentation, have the teens come forward and mark the child's forehead with the sign of the cross.

B On the chalkboard, print the words: "**The World Is Evil**." Then ask the teens to come to the board and print words all over that tell specifically how this is so (e.g., murders, child abuse, abortion, illness, famine, etc.). After they have written many examples, draw a stick figure of a child in the middle of all the "mess." Ask the teens:

- What effect does the evil have on the child's life?
- How does the evil become part of the child's life?
- How can the child escape the evil of this world?

Explain the doctrine of original sin, a sin that has to do with our *origins* as humans. As with all sin, the original sin was rooted in a disobedience of God. Tempted by the devil, our first parents abused their God-given freedom by disobeying his commandment. In essence, the original sin was that "man *preferred* himself to God and by that very act scorned him" (*CCC*, 398). Adam and Eve were destined to become like God in glory; they chose to be like God *without* God and contrary to his will.

Also help the candidates to understand the ramifications of original sin. Original sin deprives us our spiritual control over our body; tensions arise in the union between man and woman; harmony with creation is broken; and worst of all, death enters human history.

Point out why it is crucial for us to understand the doctrine of the original sin: without understanding the doctrine of original sin the mystery of Christ is undermined. When we understand that we all come into the world as sinners, we realize that we need and are assured the grace of salvation that comes to us through Jesus Christ.

To continue to clarify, draw a circle of "stick people" around the child. Point out that God protects the child from evil by working through a community of people—the Church, all of whom are dedicated to keeping sin and evil out of their lives and the lives of their children. It is the grace God gives the Church through the sacrament of Baptism that "wipes away" original sin.

C Play the video, *This Sacred Place* (Twenty-Third Publications, 18 minutes; available at www.twentythirdpublications.com). It tells the story of Ellen, inspired by Eddie, who has become a catechumen in her parish's RCIA program. She is growing in both her understanding and commitment to faith, but is still aware of how much more she needs to learn. Another option is to play the classic video *Godparent Gussie* (part of *The Changing Sacraments* series; available from St. Anthony Messenger Press at www.americancatholic.org). In cartoon form, it covers the historical development of the sacraments of initiation.

D Invite the pastor or pastoral associate responsible for RCIA in the parish to speak with the teens about how the different stages of the RCIA process (pages 18-19 in the Candidate's Handbook) are adapted at the parish.

E Neatly gift-wrap a cross or bible (any symbol to represent "faith") inside a box. Call the box "the gift of faith." Conduct a demonstration. Choose two teens to represent the parents of an infant being baptized, and two other teens to represent the child's godparents. The rest of the group represents the Church. Explain that, at Baptism, the child is given "the gift of faith" and then gradually, during the formative years this gift is opened with the help of parents, godparents, and the community to uncover the depth and breadth of faith. Pass out the worksheet "The Gift of Faith" (page 37 of this Manual). Ask the teens to print in the margins of the worksheet several things parents, godparents, and the Church at large can do to help a child uncover the gift of faith from birth to sixteen years (e.g., take them to church, read or tell stories from the Bible, teach them bedtime or meal prayers, take them along to serve meals at a soup kitchen, etc.). After they have written, discuss ideas for each age: preschool, age seven, age twelve, and age sixteen. After discussing each level, allow the teens to gradually open the gift box so that by age sixteen it is completely open and the cross, bible, or other symbol is revealed.

Baptism: The Essential Sacrament/Lesson Ideas

A Have the teens bring a photo of themselves. Provide many other art supplies (e.g., poster board, markers, paints, yarn, magazines, glue, scissors). Ask them to create an artistic rendering symbolizing how they have "put on Christ" or are "configured to Christ."

B Read the conversation between Jesus and the rich man and Jesus' subsequent teaching from Mark 10:17-31. Discuss its context: many early Christians were persecuted and shunned by their families and friends for becoming a follower of Jesus. Ask the teens to reflect on the following questions: What does it mean to you to 'put on Christ'? How important is it for you to be a disciple of Christ? Call on volunteers to respond.

This is also a good opportunity to gauge the teens' readiness for Confirmation preparation. Ask the teens to complete the Confirmation Survey (page 38 individually. Follow-up on their responses in one-to-one interviews (see page 20).

C Open a discussion on belonging by asking the teens to name different groups they belong to and some of the things they had to do to be part of the group (e.g., audition for a role in a school play, try out for a team sport, etc.). Divide the class into four groups and have them each develop a skit that explores the theme of belonging. For each skit, the central character should attempt to join the described group. The group members tell what has to be done in order to be a part of the group (e.g., rituals, behaviors, following of rules, etc.). After the small groups practice their skits, have them perform them in front of the entire group.

Skit Themes:
- New student at school tries to be part of popular group.
- New player joins a team.
- New worker starts at fast food restaurant.
- New parishioner comes to youth ministry for first time.

D Display a fish bowl with a living goldfish. Talk with the teens about the living nature of water while you change the water in the fishbowl. The lesson will come to life dramatically as the water is removed and then replaced in the fish tank.

Belonging

E Show the video *Baptism: Sacrament of Belonging* (Franciscan Communications, 15 minutes, available at www.americancatholic.org). The video tells the story of Alfredo, a young Mexican boy orphaned by a tragic fire. He wanders the villages of Mexico in search of acceptance and family. Physically and emotionally scarred by the fire that robbed him of his family, he is welcomed into the loving home and family of the orphanage of Our Little Brothers and Sisters. His story parallels Baptism as the sacrament of welcome into God's family.

F Refer to the following scripture passages dealing with water: Genesis 6–8 (the Great Flood), Exodus 14 (the Red Sea), and Luke 3:21-22 (Jesus' baptism in the Jordan River). Show how each represented a transition from death to life. Ask the teens to share other life-giving examples of water, from both the Bible and contemporary life.

G Assign one or more of the following exercises related to symbols used in Baptism:
- Use a bible concordance to find and explain many uses of oil in the scriptures.
- Write about the significance of the white garment you wore at Baptism.
- Design a baptismal candle for the family of a child who is about to be baptized.
- Find out the Christian origins of the names of at least five teens in your Confirmation group.

REFERENCES/FAQ

References from the *Catechism of the Catholic Church* for the Frequently Asked Questions include:

Who can baptize? (CCC, 1256)
The normal ministers of the sacrament of Baptism are the bishop, priest, or deacon. However, in an emergency (like the imminent death of an newborn) any person—even a non-baptized person—can baptize another as long as he or she has the right intention, uses water, and recites the Trinitarian formula: "I baptize you in the name of the Father, and of the Son, and of the Holy Spirit."

Who can receive Baptism? (CCC, 1246-1255)
Any person who has not yet been baptized can receive Baptism. This means that when the Church welcomes a convert from another Christian denomination, that person's Baptism in his or her original church will usually be accepted. The Church confesses in its creed that it believes in one Baptism for the forgiveness of sins."

Can a non-Catholic be a godparent at Baptism? (CCC, 1255; also canon 874, §1, 3o)
A Catholic, who has been confirmed and has received the Eucharist, must be the baptismal sponsor. A baptized person who is not Catholic may serve as a witness with the Catholic sponsor.

What happens to children who die without Baptism?(CCC,1261)
The Church trusts these children to God's mercy and recalls Jesus' words, "Let the children come to me" as a sign of hope that children who have died without Baptism will be saved. Still, the Church recognizes the urgency to welcome children to Christ through Baptism.

Someone told me I have to be "born again" in order to be saved. Is that true? (CCC, 977-980, 1262-1266, 1272-1274)
The phrase "born again" comes from a translation of John 3:3-5 where Jesus tells the Pharisee Nicodemus that "No one can enter the kingdom of God without being born of water and Spirit." Some Christians believe that the phrase "born again" refers to a personal conversion experience that guarantees the person salvation. Catholics understand "born again" to mean the spiritual rebirth that takes place at Baptism. So, if you have been baptized, you can respond that you have already been "born again."

Shouldn't a person be able to choose whether or not he or she wants to be baptized? (CCC, 1250-1252).
This brings up the issue of infant Baptism. Remember, no person chooses his or her salvation. This is an event of God's initiative, of God's unconditional love, and God's election. God chooses the time and place to bring a person to salvation. (More response to this question on pages 21-22 of the Candidate's Handbook.)

FEATURES/LESSON IDEAS

A Martyrdom has long been associated with a "baptism of blood," while taking two forms. The first form is of catechumens who were put to death before being baptized. The Church teaches that their martyrdom is equivalent to baptism. The second form is martyrdom of those who have been baptized. For them, the martyrdom is like a "second baptism" that renews and consummates the effects of the first Baptism.

Assign the candidates to research and write a short report detailing the life of one of the martyrs of the second century, including the martyrs of Lyons of which St. Blandina was a part.

B Ask the teens to bring blank, light-colored t-shirts. Provide fabric paints and/or markers. Ask them to decorate their shirts with faith statements that proclaim their belief in Jesus. Or, post large pieces of newsprint on the walls of your meeting space. Ask the participants to write faith statements or print symbols that speak of their faith to model the graffiti found in the catacombs.

C Have the teens write a letter to themselves that consoles them over the death of their "old life" and offers them hope in their new life in Christ.

Prayer Experiences

A Have the teens renew their baptismal promises during a short prayer service. Use this simple format, or one like it:

1. Light the Christ candle.
2. Read Romans 6:3-6. Discuss how Christ brings us new life.
3. Read Matthew 28:18-20. Discuss how we are called to teach and baptize.
4. Have the teens renew their baptismal promises by answering "I do" to the following questions:
   - Do you reject Satan?
   - And all his works?
   - And all his empty promises?
   - Do you reject sin, so as to live in the freedom of God's children?
   - Do you reject the glamour of evil, and refuse to be mastered by sin?
   - Do you reject Satan, father of sin and prince of darkness?
   - Do you believe in God, the Father almighty, creator of heaven and earth?
   - Do you believe in Jesus Christ, his only Son, our Lord, who was born of the Virgin Mary, was crucified, died, and was buried, rose from the dead, and is now seated at the right hand of the Father?
   - Do you believe in the Holy Spirit, the holy catholic Church, the communion of saints, the forgiveness of sins, the resurrection of the body, and life everlasting?

Then say: "This is our faith. This is the faith of the Church. We are proud to profess it, in Christ Jesus our Lord. R: Amen.

5. To conclude, recite together the conclusion of the Baptism Rite (page 28 in Candidate's Handbook).

B Incorporate the symbol of water into a prayer service. For example, display a large bowl of water or several bowls depending on the size of your group. Use a short prayer to ask God to bless the water in the bowl or bowls and make it holy. Have the teens dip their right hand into the water and take turns blessing one another by making the sign of the cross over each other's head, eyes, mouth, and heart while reciting the prayer, "God Be in My Head" (page 29 of the Candidate's Handbook).

NAME _____

THE GIFT OF FAITH

*How can parents, godparents, and the entire Church help a child break open
the gift of faith given at Baptism?*

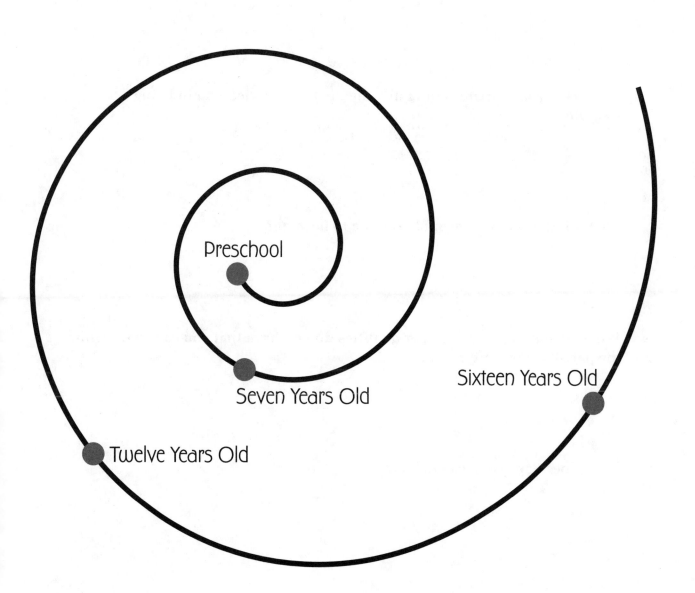

Preschool

Seven Years Old

Twelve Years Old

Sixteen Years Old

NAME _____

CONFIRMATION SURVEY

What motivated you to enter the Confirmation preparation process?

How have your parents and family members supported you in being Catholic?

What kind of Catholic would you like to become?

What talents, gifts, abilities, or qualities do you have that you can share with the parish community?

What does Baptism mean to you?

2 God

(see pages 31-49 of the Candidate's Handbook)

BACKGROUND

Teenagers are at a time in life when they are beginning to ask some of life's deep questions. For example, "Why was I born? What is the meaning of suffering and death? What is the purpose of my life?"

Inevitably, these questions will lead a person to ask "Is there really a God?" and "If so, what is God like?" and finally, "How can I know God?"

Most people believe that there is some type of deity. Even people with no formal religious experience can express some type of belief in God. Also, most cultures throughout history have believed in and worshipped a higher being. Today, all of the major world religions express faith in some type of invisible, all-knowing reality whom we may understand as God. There are different ways of understanding the divine. Hindus, for example, believe in many gods. Jews believe the one, true God is Yahweh ("I Am, Who Am") who has been revealed throughout their history. Christians and Moslems both trace their faith to the Jewish patriarch Abraham. Christianity and Islam share with Jews a faith in one God. Moslems refer to this God as Allah and believe that Mohammed was Allah's greatest prophet.

"I believe in God," is the first and most fundamental affirmation of the Apostles' Creed. The Catholic creeds include the Church's central beliefs about God, beliefs that when studied, pondered, and prayed over, can help us to learn more about the mystery of God.

The lessons related to God are based on the main sections of Chapter 2 of the Candidate's Handbook. They will help the teens to understand who God is, beginning with our creedal beliefs that there is one God, that God is Creator, not created, that God is almighty, and that God is Trinitarian.

Additionally, the teens will explore several ways they can come to know God. God has revealed himself progressively and under different names throughout the years. Ultimately, God is love, a truth that God has given humans the capacity to understand and experience.

Christianity also understands the one God as having three distinct Persons—Father, Son, and Holy Spirit. The lessons that follow present the Church's primary dogmas about the Trinity: that the Trinity is One, that the three Persons are distinct from one another, and that the divine persons are related to one another. An explanation of the theology of the Trinity in terms of immanent Trinity and salvific or economic Trinity is also offered.

Finally, Christians are privileged to call God "Father" because Jesus did. In doing so, we are better able to understand the unconditional love that our Father has for us.

SAMPLE SCHEDULES

MODEL I: FOCUSED PREPARATION (ONE 3-HOUR SESSION)
Suggested Session Plan

Warm-Up (30 minutes)
Refer to pages 31-32 of the Candidate's Handbook.

- As the candidates arrive, begin with an adaptation of Warm-Up/Breaktime Exercise "A" (page 46). On the board, write **"Who Is My God?"** Have the candidates write a short essay that answers the question and keep it for later discussion.
- Once everyone has arrived, do Warm-Up/Breaktime Exercise "B" (page 46).
- Return to the essays the teens completed. Do the opening of the exercise ("A") comparing our different understandings of people to our different understandings of God. Then call on several candidates to read their essays to the group.

Lesson 1: Who Is God? (25 minutes)
Refer to pages 32-36 of the Candidate's Handbook.

- Use Who Is God? "C" (page 47). Write each point on the board or overhead. Make sure the teens understand each point before moving on to the next.
- Allow the teens to work with partners to develop a brief argument for God's existence. Call on volunteers to share.
- Ask: "How do you know God?" Call on candidates to share examples, especially from the areas listed on pages 35-36 of the Candidate's Handbook.

Breaktime (20 minutes)
- Allow at least the first 10 minutes for the teens to stretch and move around. If you wish to provide a light snack and/or drink, this would be an appropriate time for that as well.
- Divide the group into two teams. Play the game described in Warm-Up/Breaktime Exercise "E" (page 46).

Lesson 2: The Nature of God (45 minutes)
Refer to pages 36-39 of the Candidate's Handbook.

- Following up on how we encounter God, do the demonstration with the pizza suggested in The Nature of God "C" (pages 48-49). Make sure to discuss ways that we can fully involve our entire beings in encountering God.
- After allowing time for the teens to share the pizza, play one segment of the PBS "Searching for God in America Series" (see "E," page 49).

Lesson 3: The Holy Trinity (35 minutes)
Refer to pages 40-43 of the Candidate's Handbook.

- To introduce the mystery of the Holy Trinity use some or all of the "creative ways" described in The Holy Trinity "E" (page 50).
- Provide information about the Church's teaching of the *immanent Trinity* and the *salvific Trinity* or *economic Trinity*. See pages 41-42 of the Candidate's Handbook and also The Holy Trinity "C" (page 50).
- *Optional*: Use Features/Lesson Ideas "C" page 52.

Prayer Experience (20 minutes)

- Use Prayer Experience "B" (page 52). Another option is to have the candidates write short personal notes to fellow candidates telling how God can be seen in them. The notes can be placed in lunch bags labeled with each person's name, set up around the room. Be sure each bag has at least a few notes in it before giving the bags back to the candidates.

Conclusion (5 minutes)

- Review the session. Write on the board and ask the teens to comment on the following:
  - **Their favorite part of the session.**
  - **New ways they learned to understand God.**
  - **Concrete ways they will practice for developing their relationship with God.**

Individual Home Assignments

- Assign the material in the Features section of the text. Ask the teens either to write a poem in the same theme as "I Am" or to develop creative ways for describing the Holy Trinity.
- Assign questions 6-10 from the "50 Questions" (pages 243-244 of the Candidate's Handbook).
- Assign for journal writing at least three of the discussion questions included in Chapter 2.

Sponsor/Candidate Activities

- Have the teens work on the "Imagining God" resource (page 53 of this Manual). With their sponsor, they should research and write quotations from other sources and come up with their own words that speak of God.
- Review together the FAQs from pages 44-45 of the Candidate's Handbook.
- Take a silent walk together in either a natural or city setting. Then stop to talk about how they witnessed God's presence while on the walk.

MODEL 2: EXTENDED PREPARATION (TWO 1-HOUR SESSIONS)
Suggested Session 1 Plan

Warm-Up (10 minutes)
Refer to pages 31-32 of the Candidate's Handbook.
- Do Warm-Up/Breaktime Exercise "C" (page 46). After sharing part of the story, discuss with the candidates the following two questions (write on the board): **Who is God? How can I know God?** Write a sampling of the responses on the board.

Lesson: Who Is God? (30 minutes)
Refer to pages 32-36 of the Candidate's Handbook.
- Use Who Is God? "B" (page 47). Have the candidates write their responses to the discussion questions after playing the video. If possible, connect the discussion to current events involving an Islamic understanding of God.
- Present several ways that people can "come to know God" from the text.

Breaktime (10 minutes)
- Provide art media and ask the candidates to depict a scene from nature that reminds them of God or helps lead them to God. Display the works around the room.

Prayer Experience (10 minutes)
- Use the art projects the candidates have created and, if possible, a slide show of other nature scenes (see Who Is God? "A", page 47) as part of a prayer service. In conclusion, call on a candidate to read the poem, "I Am" (pages 45-46 of the Candidate's Handbook).

Individual Home Assignments
- Ask the teens to read Ephesians 5:18-20 and 2 Corinthians 13:13 and to write a summary of what each passage teaches about the Trinity.
- Assign for focused reading pages 36-39 of the Candidate's Handbook, beginning with "The Nature of God." For journal writing, assign the second two questions on page 39.
- Assign questions 6-8 from the "50 Questions," pages 243-244 of the Candidate's Handbook.

Sponsor/Candidate Activities
- Give a copy of the resource "Imagining God" (page 53) of this Manual to each candidate and have them work through the activity with their sponsor.
- Suggest a nature walk during which the sponsor and candidate take time to reflect on the nature of God.

Suggested Session 2 Plan

Lesson: The Nature of God (25 minutes)
Refer to pages 36-39 of the Candidate's Handbook.
- Do The Nature of God "A" (page 48). Allow time at the end of the discussion to clean up the ice cream.
- Summarize the attributes of God found on page 37 of the Candidate's Handbook. See also The Nature of God "B" (page 48).

Breaktime/Lesson: The Holy Trinity (25 minutes)
Refer to pages 40-43 of the Candidate's Handbook.
- Display several symbols of the Holy Trinity (see both The Holy Trinity "A" and "E") for the teens to observe first-hand while on a five-minute stretch break.
- Do The Holy Trinity "C" (page 50). Conclude with a detailed presentation on the immanent Trinity and salvific (economic) Trinity (see pages 41-42 of the Candidate's Handbook).

Conclusion/Prayer (10 minutes)
Refer to pages 44-48 of the Candidate's Handbook.
- Use the references from the *Catechism of the Catholic Church* to delve more deeply into the Frequently Asked Questions (FAQ). Read and discuss with the candidates. Call on teens to write other questions they have on a slip of paper. Collect and answer at a future session.
- Pray the "Prayer of Blessed Elizabeth of the Trinity" (page 48 of the Candidate's Handbook) to conclude the session.

Individual Home Assignments
- Assign an essay titled "The Christian Belief in God." Ask the candidates to summarize some of the material covered in Chapter 2 of the Candidate's Handbook.
- Ask the candidates to research and share other dramatic stories (like the story of Lt. Col. Mike Couillard) that portray the human desire for and dependence on God.

Sponsor/Candidate Activities
- Ask the teens to explain their understanding of the doctrine of the Holy Trinity to their sponsors. Encourage them to use any models or symbols of the doctrine they have learned or created themselves in this explanation.
- Remind the teens to work on a service project (see pages 237-241 of the Candidate's Handbook) and to discuss the work with their sponsors.

MODEL 3: CONCENTRATED PREPARATION (ONE 90-MINUTE SESSION)
Suggested Session Plan

Warm-Up (20 minutes)
Refer to pages 31-36 of the Candidate's Handbook.

- Distribute the resource "Imagining God" (page 53 of this Manual). After a brief time for reflection, have the teens write their own quotations about God. Then ask them to go around the room and share their quotations with other candidates and to write some of their favorites on their sheet. See Warm-Up/Breaktime Exercise "D" (page 46).
- Prior to beginning the lesson, play the game described in Warm-Up/Breaktime Exercise "E" (page 46) using as many or as few of the quotations as you have time for.

Lesson Plan (30 minutes)
Refer to pages 36-40 of the Candidate's Handbook.

- Begin with The Nature of God "D" (page 49). Print on the board or newsprint several ways teens say they can encounter God in the world.
- Highlight several of the terms and concepts presented in the Candidate's Handbook including *monotheism*, *polytheism*, and *pantheism*. Focus on the New Testament readings suggested in The Nature of God "B" (page 48). Ask the teens to explain how these readings show the importance of the Christian's belief in one God.
- Share the quotation from St. Augustine (Who Is God?, "D", page 47). Call one teen to the front to be "on the spot." Ask the person to describe a time he or she has been "restless for God." If there is time, call more teens forward one at a time.

Breaktime (10 minutes)

- Set up a display of ways for explaining the Holy Trinity (see The Holy Trinity "A," page 49).
- If possible, run a slide show of scenes from nature while the teens are on break.

Lesson Plan continued (25 minutes)
Refer to pages 40-43 of the Candidate's Handbook.

- Explain the doctrine of the Holy Trinity first by using some of the creative ways you have set up during the break to share the idea of "three in one." Allow the teens to develop their own models of explanation as suggested in "A" (page 49).
- Play all of the video *Jesus BC* (The Holy Trinity, "D", page 50). Allow the teens the opportunity to express their reactions.
- Conclude with a fuller exposition of the theology of the Holy Trinity from the material in the Candidate's Handbook, pages 41-42.

Prayer (5 minutes)

- Stand and recite together "A Spirit to Know You" from page 48 of the Candidate's Handbook.

Individual Assignments

- Ask the teens to research and report on the understanding of God by four religions (e.g., Islam, Hinduism, Buddhism, Sikhism) other than Christianity.
- Ask the teens to write a letter to God explaining why they would like to make their Confirmation. Then have them write a letter from God in response.
- Assign questions 6-10 from the "50 Questions," pages 243-244 of the Candidate's Handbook.
- Assign for journal writing some of the discussion questions in Chapter 2.

Sponsor/Candidate Activities

- Have the candidates ask their sponsor to explain the meaning of the Holy Trinity. After the sponsors attempt a reply, the candidates should explain more about the Trinity from their own understanding.
- Visit an art museum together, commenting on how God's nature is revealed in the pieces of artwork.
- Review together the FAQs from pages 44-45 of the Candidate's Handbook.

INTRODUCTION
Warm-up/Breaktime Exercises

A Print a teen's name on the board, for example, "**Mark**." Discuss with the participants the difference between how the following people know Mark: his dad, his mom, his best friend, his girlfriend, his teacher. Point out that though Mark is one person, each person knows Mark a little differently and has a different experience of him. Even so, in essence, Mark remains the same person no matter how others view him.

Compare this experience to God. God does not change or become different even though different people have different perceptions of him.

Have the teens write a short essay entitled "Who Is My God?" describing God, what he is like, how they know him, etc. Call on some of the teens to read their essays to the class.

B Give each person a strip of scrap paper. On one side of the scrap paper have them print a question they have *for* God. For example, "God, how is it that you always were?" or "God, what is heaven like?" or "God, why do you allow wars?"

Collect the papers and randomly pass them out again, making sure no one gets his or her own question. On the back of the slip, the teens should take the voice of God and attempt to answer the question.

Collect the scraps again and read some of the questions and answers. Add to "God's answers" with information of your own. Save the especially difficult questions and answers for discussion during the coverage of the rest of the material on pages 32-36 of the Candidate's Handbook.

C Read selections from *Miracle on the Mountain*, the story of the experience of Lt. Col. Mike Couillard and his son Matthew, lost on mountaintop in Turkey in 1995. (This story is summarized on pages 31-32 of the Candidate's Handbook.)

D The reality of God is always deeper and fuller than we can describe. Distribute the resource "Imagining God" (page 53 of this Manual). Read the quotation of Thomas Merton. Ask the teens, "What does this quotation tell us about God and our understanding of God?"

The teens should also share this quotation with their sponsors and research and write quotations from other sources and of their own invention that speak of God.

E Choose one of the scripture passages below or any others that you choose. Vertically print the first letter of each word down the chalkboard. Gradually fill in the other letters of the words, prepositions and shorter words first. The first person who guesses the passage exactly wins.

Sample Passages
Come, follow me. (Mark 10:21)
Love your enemies, do good to those who hate you. (Luke 6:27)
The last will be first, the first will be last. (Matthew 20:16)
Love your neighbor as yourself. (Matthew 19:19)
Prepare the way of the Lord. (Mark 1:3)

Who Is God?/Lesson Ideas

A Prepare a slide show that helps the teens to experience God and the work of God. The slides can be of beautiful scenes in nature, or of people of all ages and nationalities. For each slide call on the teens to share what the picture tells about God or to say a short prayer suggested by the picture.

B Explore with the teens more about the different understandings of God among the major world religions. In Islam, for example, it is said that every child is born Muslim by nature: he has the belief in his heart of one God. The Time-Life video *Islam: There Is No God But God* (part of "The Long Search Series", available from www.ambrosevideo.com), explores the Islamic experience in the oasis of an Egyptian village 50 miles from Cairo, at a wedding, in the market town of El Fayoum for dawn prayers, and in Cairo itself. The video is 22 minutes in length. After the presentation, ask the teens to comment on how they think the people in the video imagine God. Ask: "How is their understanding of God different than yours? the same?" *Optional:* View another video from the "Long Search Series" on Hinduism. It is titled *Hinduism: 330 Million Gods* and runs 52 minutes.

C St. Anslem (1033-1109), the archbishop of Canterbury, is well-known for his motto *"Credo ut intelligam,"* that is, "I believe in order to understand." Anselm also is well-known for his *ontological* (the branch of metaphysics that deals with the nature of being) argument for the existence of God. Share the eight points of the argument with the teens. Help them to follow this simplified version point by point:

1. God is defined as the being in which none greater is possible.
2. It is true that the notion of God exists in the understanding (your mind).
3. And that God may exist in reality (it is *possible* that God exists).
4. If God *only* exists in the mind, and *may* have existed, then God might have been greater than he is.
5. Then, God might have been greater than he is (if he existed in reality).
6. Therefore, God is a being in which a greater is possible.
7. This is not possible, for God is a being in which a greater is impossible.
8. Therefore God exists in reality as well as in the mind.

D The *Catechism of the Catholic Church* offers two ways of approaching God from creation (see *CCC*, 31-35): 1) The physical world: "starting from movement, becoming, contingency, and the world's order and beauty, one can come to knowledge of God as the origin and end of the universe" (*CCC*, 32); 2) The human person: "With his openness to truth and beauty, his sense of moral goodness, his freedom and the voice of his conscience, with his longings for the infinite and for happiness, man questions himself about God's existence. In all this he discerns signs of his spiritual soul" (*CCC*, 33).

Print the famous quotation from St. Augustine on the board:

> **"You are great, O Lord, and greatly to be praised: great is your power and your wisdom is without measure. . . . You yourself encourage us to delight in your praise, for you have made us for yourself, and our heart is restless until it rests in you."**

Ask the teens to write or discuss what it means for their hearts to be "restless for God". Ask them to describe a time when their own hearts have been restless for God.

THE NATURE OF GOD/LESSON IDEAS

A Have the group sit in one large circle. Print the following words on the board (or newsprint): **evil, discouragement, frustration, sadness, suffering**. Go around the circle and have the teens talk about an experience from their own lives or an incident from the recent news that elicits one of these feelings. After everyone has shared, print these words on the board: **goodness, courage, hope, joy, love**.

Pass out plastic spoons to all the participants. Place a half-gallon (or two) of ice cream on a table in the center of the circle. Say: "We believe in a good God. We believe in a God who gives us the grace of courage to overcome the dark times that befall us and the world around us. We live in hope for the everlasting joy of the eternal kingdom when all of our tears will be wiped away. We believe in a God who loves us more than life itself. In fact, "God" and "love" are synonymous."

Now have the teens talk about an experience from their own lives or an incident from the recent news that exemplifies one of the words on the board. Say, "It is God that sweetens our world with goodness, courage, hope, joy, and love. After you tell your story, have a spoonful of the sweet tasting ice cream."

Continue around the circle, sharing stories and ice cream.

B Present some more information on the theological terms described on pages 36-37 of the Candidate's Handbook.

The *monotheism* of the Old Testament affirms that the being and power that acts on behalf of the people of Israel is not just *a* God but *the* God of Abraham and all the patriarchs. Monotheism also acknowledges the possibility of communication between God and his creation. This is the anticipation of the Christian doctrine of *grace*. Christianity comfortably adopted the Jewish understanding of "one" God and it became the foundation of the Christian faith.

Optional: Assign the teens to read Mark 12:29, John 17:3, and 1 Corinthians 8:5-6 for evidence of how belief in one God is central to Christian belief.

Polytheism, the belief in many gods, was prevalent in the cultures that interacted with the Hebrews, and the Israelites sometimes lapsed into belief in "other gods." There are even some similarities between the Genesis account of creation and the Babylonian epic, *Enuma Elish*, for example. But they part company when *Enuma Elish* describes the final episode of the creation of the world as the battle between two camps of gods. In the Hebrew account, God is "in the beginning"—he is before all else and has no family tree.

Pantheism alleges that "God" is one comprehensive term for the world, and the world is viewed as the complete manifestation of God. Pantheism is false, however, because God is an infinite, unchanging, and permanent being while things of nature change and disappear.

C How do we encounter God? Try this demonstration with the teens:

Bring a freshly warmed pizza (or slice of pizza) in a box. Set it before the group.

Explain that one way we encounter something is through the sense of smell. Pass the box under the noses of the teens.

Then open the box. Say: "Another way we encounter something is through the sense of sight." Again, pass the open box around the room.

The best way to "encounter" pizza is to put all the senses together and really taste it. (If you have enough pizza, share it now.)

Then make the point that really encountering God involves all of the physical senses as well as our intellect, emotions, and imagination.

Discuss with the participants ways they can involve their entire beings in more fully encountering God.

D Share the following story with the teens. It is called "The Little Fish." It was originally published by Gujarat Sahitya Prakash and is excerpted from *The Song of the Bird* by Anthony deMello (Loyola University Press).

"Excuse me," said one ocean fish to another. "You are older and more experienced that I, and will probably be able to help me. Tell me: where can I find this thing they call the Ocean? I've been searching for it everywhere to no avail."

"The Ocean," said the older fish, "is what you are swimming in now."

"Oh this? But this is only water. What I am searching for is the Ocean," said the young fish, feeling quite disappointed as he swam away to search elsewhere.

Ask the teens to explain what the story tells them about ways they should go about looking for God in the world. Have them brainstorm a list of many different ways they can "encounter" God in our world.

E The "Search for God in America Series" is a production of the Public Broadcasting System and is available at www.shop.pbs.org. The series features conversations with some respected and provocative people in America as they discuss God and how to find him. Among the people interviewed: Charles Colson, Roberta Hestenes, Fr. Thomas Keating, Rabbi Harold Kushner, the Dalai Lama, Elder Neal Maxwell, Cecil Murray, and Seyyed Nasr. Each segment is 30 minutes long. Choose parts of some or all to share with the teens.

THE HOLY TRINITY/LESSON IDEAS

A Display some traditional symbols of the Holy Trinity as a help in explaining it. For example, the equilateral triangle symbolizes the equality in nature of the three Persons of God. The joining of the sides points to the one and inseparable nature of God. In the same way, three interlocking circles displays both the unity and distinctness of the three divine Persons. The shamrock (three leaves but one flower) was used by St. Patrick to communicate the mystery of the Trinity. Print the analogy used by St. John Damascus to describe the Trinity on the board or newsprint:

Think of the Father as a root, of the Son as a branch, and of the Spirit as a fruit, for the substance of these is one. Or, the Father is a sun with the Son as rays and the Holy Spirit as heat.

Pass out various forms of art media (markers, poster paper, paints, old magazines, etc.) and have the teens work individually or in groups to illustrate one of the symbols of the Trinity described above or create their own symbol of the Trinity.

B Two of the earliest Christian understandings of the Trinity are found in Ephesians 5:18-20 and 2 Corinthians 13:13. Read and discuss these passages with the teens.

C Call a teen to the front of the group. Have him or her write three positive adjectives or descriptions of himself or herself. Ask a second teen to write three positive adjectives or descriptions of the teen who is in front. For example, "athlete, quiet, tall." Compare both lists of words. Explain: "The way we see ourselves and the way others see us is sometimes the same, but usually at least a little different."

Repeat the demonstration with other teens. Then connect its lesson with the Church's teaching on the *immanent Trinity* (how God exists in God) and the *salvific Trinity* or *economic Trinity* (how humans put into words the mystery of the Trinity).

See pages 41-42 of the Candidate's Handbook for a further exposition of the theology of the Holy Trinity.

D Play all or part of the video presentation *Jesus BC* from the Insight Series (Paulist Press, available from www.paulistpress.com). This video presents an interesting look at the relationship between the persons of the Trinity and their actions on behalf of humankind. Ask the teens how the depiction of the Trinity and the divine Persons compares with their own understanding.

E Share some other creative ways for explaining the Holy Trinity. For example,

- Crack an egg in a bowl. Point out that though there are three parts (shell, yolk, white) it is only one egg.
- Make a quart of punch. Mix water, sugar, and drink mix. Again point out how the three parts make the whole.
- Show three versions of the same type of soft drink (e.g., regular, diet, caffeine free). Point out they they are all technically "cola."
- Show a portrait of three generations of family members (grandfather, son, grandson). Point out how a man can be a son to his father, a dad to his son, and a husband to his wife, but he is still one person.

Call on the teens to develop creative ways to explain the Trinity. Divide the class into groups of three with the following roles:

1. Teacher (uses creative way to explain the mystery of the Trinity to a child)

2. Child (listens to the explanation and asks followup question)

3. Theologian (attempts to answer the child's followup question)

F The good news of Christianity is that we can have an intimate, personal relationship with God. The powerful God described in the Old Testament is revealed by Jesus to be a loving Father, "Abba" or "Daddy" as he is called by Jesus. And by knowing Jesus, we can also know the Father (Jn 14:7).

Summarize or assign for reading the *Catechism of the Catholic Church*, #232-260 on the Holy Trinity.

References/FAQ

References from the *Catechism of the Catholic Church* for the Frequently Asked Questions include:

Does God have a body? (CCC, 370)
No. As Jesus explained, "God is Spirit, and those who worship him must worship in spirit and truth" (Jn 4:24).

If God is good, why is there evil, suffering, and death? (CCC, 272, 309-314)
This is one of the most challenging and perplexing questions that humans have ever faced. With Job who wondered as much, we are ultimately resigned to the fact that God's ways are much higher than our own and that we will never have a complete answer to this question while on earth. However, we do know that God is in no way, directly or indirectly, the cause of any moral evil. God permits evil, suffering, and death, because he respects human freedom and, mysteriously, knows how to derive good from them. From our human experience, we know that pain often brings perfection and satisfaction. Consider the athlete who puts in months and months of painful weightlifting and running in order to achieve a satisfying season. Ultimately, we only have to look to the greatest moral evil ever committed—the Passion and death of God's only Son—and the subsequent good (Christ's resurrection and our redemption) that came from it. However, even for all that, evil itself never becomes a good.

What is a soul? (CCC, 362-368)
The soul refers to the innermost part of a person. It is the spiritual part of the person. Every soul is created immediately by God. It is not produced by parents. The soul is immortal. It does not perish with the body at death. At the final resurrection it will be reunited with the body.

Does God know all things?(CCC, 269-271)
Yes. God is omniscient, meaning "all knowing." God knows even our most secret thoughts, words, and actions.

If God knows everything about us, how can we really be free? (CCC, 302-314)
God gives us the gifts of intellect and free will, allowing us to make choices. Also, God created a world with natural laws (e.g., the law of gravity) with which he rarely interferes. To God, everything about your life—beginning to end—is happening now. It's something like standing over and watching an ant trail from the ant's hole in the ground to a source of water. You can see an individual ant's past, present, and future. But you don't interfere with the ant's freedom to choose the route from point A to point B.

Since we can't see God, how do we know God exists? (CCC, 26-67)
We know God exists because he reveals himself, most perfectly in Jesus Christ. We see the effects of God's existence. In the same way, we would not know that there was wind unless we saw and felt its effects.

Features/Lesson Ideas

A Building on St. Augustine's words "our heart is restless until it rests in you" and the poem, "I Am" by Marly Elizabeth Sink (see pages 45-46 of the Candidate's Handbook), have the teens name and describe at least five key people, events, or experiences that have been occasions of personal growth in faith.

B Invite a recently confirmed teen to speak to the group about his or her relationship with God and how the preparation process for Confirmation enhanced his or her faith. *Optional*: Ask one of the adult Confirmation sponsors to give the same talk.

C Fill an old laundry bag with many odd items (e.g., a shoe, cooking utensils, a ball). Divide the class into small groups. Call on a representative from each group to come forward, reach in, and pick an item. Assign each group to develop an explanation of the Trinity that uses the item they have chosen.

D Christians enjoy new life and a new relationship with God because of the Spirit's presence within them. This new relationship allows us to address God as "Abba, Father." As a cross reference to Galatians 4:4-7 (see page 47 of the Candidate's Handbook), have the teens read Romans 8:14-17. Ask the participants to develop contrasting lists for what it means to be a "slave" of God versus a "child" of God.

PRAYER EXPERIENCES

A Have the teens sit in a large circle. Place a large lit candle in the center of the circle. Give each teen an unlit taper. Go around the circle, with each person offering thanks for a person who has been influential in his or her faith life. For example, "Thank you, Lord, for my parents who first brought me to the Church for Baptism." Or, "Thank you, God, for my grandmother who has influenced me by her simple way of loving you." After each teen has prayed aloud, he or she should light the taper from the large candle. In conclusion, pray one of the prayers on pages 47-48 of the Candidate's Handbook.

B Play a song with lyrics that talk of discovering God in the people and events around us. One example, is "Anthem" by Tom Conry ("We are called, we are chosen. We are Christ for one another.") Talk about ways that we can find God in each other. Then have the participants sit in pairs, silently facing their partner. Continue to softly play some instrumental music. After a time, return the group to a circle. Go around the circle and have the teens tell "how they recognized God" in their partner, describing more than the person's physical appearance, but their actions, demeanor, and way of being.

NAME _____

IMAGINING GOD

Since God cannot be imagined, anything our imagination tells us about him is ultimately misleading. And therefore we cannot know him as he really is unless we pass beyond everything that can be imagined and enter into an obscurity without images and without the likeness of any created thing.

—THOMAS MERTON (*NEW SEEDS OF CONTEMPLATION*)

With your sponsor, write how you and your sponsor imagine God. Also, if possible, find other quotations that describe God and our understanding of God.

Jesus Christ

(see pages 51-67 of Candidate's Handbook)

BACKGROUND

Who are we without Jesus? Jesus is at the heart and center of our faith. As the *Catechism of the Catholic Church* states, "The transmission of the Christian faith consists primarily in proclaiming Jesus Christ in order to lead others to faith in him" (*CCC*, 425). We believe that the Jesus of history—the Jewish infant born of Mary, raised in Nazareth, who died in Jerusalem under the sentence of the Roman governor Pontius Pilate—is the eternal Son of God.

It is important to place Jesus in the historical context of first century Palestine. He was raised Jewish and came to understand himself in the mode of one of the great Hebrew prophets. His mission as the "Messiah" was gradually revealed; in Mark's gospel he tells his disciples three times that he must be handed over to the gentiles, suffer, and be put to death for he "did not come to be served but to serve" (Mk 10:45).

After Jesus' resurrection, the "Christ of faith" took on new significance. The Church grew in its understanding of Jesus' true identity, as one equal with God, as God's only Son. From the beginning, the first disciples burned with their desire to share the good news of Christ. This remains the charge of today's disciples. To do this, catechesis attempts to put—in the words of *Catecheis Tradendae*—"people . . . in communion . . . with Jesus Christ: only he can lead us to the love of the Father in the Spirit and make us share in the life of the Holy Trinity." (5)

At Confirmation, there is an increase and deepening of baptismal grace, uniting us more firmly to Christ. This unification occurs also as the confirmandi prepare to receive the sacrament. As the *Catechism* points out, "Preparation for Confirmation should aim at leading the Christian toward a more intimate union with Christ" as well as a more "lively familiarity with the Holy Spirit" (*CCC*, 1309).

Sample Schedules
Model I: Focused Preparation (one 3-hour session)
Suggested Session Plan

Warm-Up (20 minutes)
Refer to pages 51-52 of the Candidate's Handbook.
- Use Warm-Up/Breaktime Exercise "A" (page 62)
  Option: Rather than a panel, choose one teen with a dramatic story of encountering Christ to share his or her witness with the group.

Lesson 1: Who Is Jesus? (30 minutes)
Refer to pages 52-53 of the Candidate's Handbook.
- Use Who Is Jesus? "A" (page 62)
  Have the teens work in small groups. When they have finished, discuss Jesus' names and titles and the things they reveal about him. Which title are you most comfortable expressing your belief in? (see page 53 of the Candidate's Handbook for more questions)
- Use Who Is Jesus? "C" (page 63)
  Mark 10:45 is the pinnacle of Mark's gospel as it clearly expresses Jesus' mission and reveals the messianic secret. Make sure the candidates can explain why this is so.

Lesson 2: Jesus, True God and True Man (25 minutes)
Refer to pages 53-55 of the Candidate's Handbook.
- Begin with Jesus, True God and True Man "B" (page 64)
  Explain how the Nicene Creed answered the heresies described (see pages 54-55 of the Candidate's Handbook).
- Use Jesus, True God and True Man "A" (page 63)
  Optional: Have the candidates create an art project using one or more mediums to depict all or part of the prologue to John's gospel (1:1-18).

Breaktime/Lesson 2 continued (30 minutes)
- Use Warm-Up/Breaktime Exercise "B" (page 62)
- Use Jesus, True God and True Man "C" (page 64)

Lesson 3: Life of Christ (30 minutes)
Refer to pages 56-58 of the Candidate's Handbook.
- Use Life of Christ "A" (page 64) and margin notes on the infancy narratives in the gospels of Matthew and Luke from *The New American Bible* to supplement the information found in the Candidate's Handbook.
- Combine Life of Christ "B" and Life of Christ "D" (page 65) to do a study of the parables with a focused emphasis on parables in which Jesus describes what the kingdom of God is like. Have the candidates write responses to the question, "What are the characteristics of God's Kingdom?" (see the Candidate's Handbook, page 58).

Lesson 4: Jesus' Passion, Death, and Resurrection (30 minutes)
Refer to pages 58-61 of the Candidate's Handbook.
- Use Jesus' Passion, Death, and Resurrection "A" (pages 65-66). Following the lesson, make sure the candidates can articulate a response to the question "Why did Jesus have to die?" from each of the three perspectives discussed in the lesson.

- Assign the Stations of Cross (Jesus' Passion, Death, and Resurrection "B", page 66) for journal or notebook writing. If the candidates do not have time to finish the work in class, have them continue to work on the assignment at home.

Conclusion/Prayer Experience (10 minutes)

Refer to pages 62-66 of the Candidate's Handbook.

1. Use Prayer Experience "B" on page 70. Call on volunteers to share their ideas for how Jesus has made a difference to their lives.
2. Conclude with a common recitation of a traditional prayer (see Prayer Experiences "A," page 70).

Individual Home Assignments

- Assign questions 11-15 from the "50 Questions," page 244 of the Candidate's Handbook.
- Assign the feature "They Said Yes" (pages 63-64 of the Candidate's Handbook). Have the candidates do a written report on any other Christian martyr—contemporary or ancient. *Option*: Read and report on the book *She Said Yes* by Misty Bernall.
- Assign for journal writing some or all of the reflection questions from Chapter 3 of the Candidate's Handbook that were not covered as part of the class session.

Sponsor/Candidate Activities

- Review together the FAQs from pages 62-63 of the Candidate's Handbook.
- Rent at least one part of the video series *Jesus of Nazareth*. Watch together and discuss the unity and any discrepancies between what is in the video and what is in the gospels.
- Attend a communal devotional service at the parish or pray the Stations of the Cross together.

MODEL 2: EXTENDED PREPARATION (TWO 1-HOUR SESSIONS)
Suggested Session 1 Plan

Warm-Up (10 minutes)
Refer to pages 51-52 of the Candidate's Handbook.
- Call on the participants to share a favorite story about Jesus. In conjunction with the discussion, play a game of "Jesus' Charades" (Warm-Up/Breaktime Exercise "B", page 62).

Lesson: Who Is Jesus? (20 minutes)
Refer to pages 52-53 of Candidate's Handbook.
- Focus a presentation on the meaning of the different names and titles for Jesus. Ask the teens to write or share what each name or title reveals about Jesus.
- Play a game using copies of the worksheet "More Names for Jesus" (page 71). Divide the group into teams of three to five participants. Give each team a bible. Call out a passage on the resource (e.g., Mt 1:23). Award a point to the first team who is able to tell the title or name for Jesus that appears in that passage.
- Delve into the "messianic secret" expressed in the gospel of Mark. Use the introduction and notes for Mark from the *New American Bible*. See Who Is Jesus? "C" on page 63.

Breaktime (5 minutes)
- Play an extra round of "Jesus' Charades."

Lesson: Jesus, True God and True Man (20 minutes)
Refer to pages 53-55 of Candidate's Handbook.
- The lesson focuses on clearly delineating for the teens that Jesus Christ is both true God and true man. Refer the teens to John's gospel, especially the prologue (1:1-18). See Jesus, True God and True Man "A" on page 63.
- Briefly summarize some of the heresies involving Jesus' divinity/humanity (see Jesus, True God and True Man, "B", page 64). Ask the candidates how the Nicene Creed clearly answers the truth of the Church's teaching on Jesus' divinity and humanity.

Conclusion/Prayer Experience (5 minutes)
- Pray the Lord's Prayer with the teens using Jesus' words as quoted in one of the gospels: Matthew 6:9-15; Luke 11:1-4.

Individual Home Assignments
- Assign as journal entries one or more of the questions on pages 53 and 55 of the Candidate's Handbook.
- Assign for reading "One Solitary Life" (pages 64-65 of the Candidate's Handbook). Ask the teens to write their own similar descriptions of Jesus as an essay or journal entry.
- Assign some questions from the "50 Questions," pages 243-247 of the Candidate's Handbook.

Sponsor/Candidate Activities
- Work together on the resource "More Names for Jesus" (page 71).
- Develop an art or media image to describe Jesus' humanity and divinity.
- Recap the material covered in the Candidate's Handbook (pages 51-55) as well as the applicable FAQs (page 62).

Suggested Session 2 Plan

Prayer Experience (15 minutes)

- Adapt Prayer Experience "B" (page 70) to the timeframe for this lesson. Emphasize in the prayer how Jesus, the light of the world, overcomes all darkness in the world and in our personal lives.

Lesson: The Life of Christ (15 minutes)

Refer to pages 56-58 of the Candidate's Handbook.

- Develop a chronology of Jesus' earthly life. Summarize the text on pages 56-58 of the Candidate's Handbook.
- Explain the term "kingdom of God." See Life of Christ "D" on page 65. Assign the participants to choose one favorite parable that describes what the kingdom of God is like. Also, allow time for them to write their own metaphors for God's kingdom.
- Ask the teens to develop a profile for a contemporary, teenage Jesus. Have the candidates write and/or share what Jesus would observe if he was in their peer group, student body, family and what he would say or do if faced with some of the same situations faced by teens today.

Breaktime (10 minutes)

- Adapt Warm-up/Breaktime Exercise "A" (page 62) to fit a ten-minute period. For example, invite one or two older teens to briefly address the meaning Jesus holds for their lives.

Lesson: Jesus' Passion, Death, and Resurrection (15 minutes)

Refer to pages 58-61 of the Candidate's Handbook.

- Base a lesson on answering the question "Why did Jesus have to die?" See Jesus' Passion, Death, and Resurrection Lesson Idea "A" (pages 65-66) for more information.
- Assign the feature "They Said Yes" (pages 63-64 of the Candidate's Handbook). Ask the candidates to comment on the dramatic witness of Rachel Scott and what it means to them to "put on Jesus Christ."

Conclusion (5 minutes)

- Go around the room and ask the teens to share one thing they will do in the coming week to improve their relationship with Christ.

Individual Assignments

- Assign some or all of the questions on pages 53, 55, 58, and 61 of the Candidate's Handbook for journal writing.
- Have the candidates do a report on a Christian martyr.
- Assign the pertinent questions from the "50 Questions" (pages 243-247 of the Candidate's Handbook).

Sponsor/Candidate Activities

- Together, pray the Stations of the Cross. Provide the sponsor and candidate pairs with scripture passages related to each station (see page 66).
- Review the entire chapter on Jesus, pages 51-66 of the Candidate's Handbook.

MODEL 3: CONCENTRATED PREPARATION (ONE 90-MINUTE SESSION)
Suggested Session Plan

Warm-Up (30 minutes)
- Use Warm-Up/Breaktime Exercise "C" (page 62). If the group is large, have the candidates share their responses in triads. Then call on two or three candidates to share a few of their responses with the entire group.
- In small groups or with the entire group of candidates, use Warm-Up/Breaktime Exercise "D" (page 62).

Lesson Plan: Who Is Jesus? (50 minutes)
Refer to Chapter 3, "Jesus," on pages 51-56 of Candidate's Handbook.
- Identify Jesus as the "Messiah." Read or have the candidates read Matthew 11:5 to see Jesus' response to John's question about his identity. Point out other titles Jesus is known (e.g., Good Shepherd, bread of life). See Who Is Jesus? "B" and "C", page 63.
- Present information on the two natures of Christ: divine and human. As time permits, include in the presentation how the Church's creeds answered the various heresies that denied either Christ's divinity or humanity. See Jesus, True God and True Man "B" on page 64.
- If not shown previously, show all or part of the video *Jesus: BC* (see Jesus, True God and True Man "C" on page 64). If shown in part, include the scene in which Father, Son, and Holy Spirit first appear together.
- Read or summarize the material in the "Life of Christ" and "Jesus' Passion, Death, and Resurrection" sections of the Candidate's Handbook, pages 56-61. Use the reflection questions at the end of each section to initiate a class discussion.
- Review the material covered in the section by covering the FAQs on pages 62-63 of the Candidate's Handbook. As time permits, have the candidates write other questions they have about Jesus on small slips of paper and present them to you. Answer the questions at this session or another, or have all the questions typed and copied and distributed as a home or sponsor assignment.

Prayer Experience (10 minutes)
- Adapt Prayer Experience "B" (page 70) to fit the time frame. For example, go around the circle only once sharing how Jesus brings light to the world.

Individual Home Assignments
- Assign the worksheet "Breaking Down the Parables" (page 73).
- Continue assigning questions from the "50 Questions," pages 243-247 of the Candidate's Handbook.
- Have the candidates read "One Solitary Life" (pages 64-65 of the Candidate's Handbook). Ask them to write their own descriptions of Jesus as an essay or journal entry.
- Read the entire gospel of Mark. Answer the questions: "Who is Jesus?" and "What is the meaning of discipleship?"
- Assign as journal entries some or all of the reflection questions included in Chapter 3 of the Candidate's Handbook.

Sponsor/Candidate Activities

- Review together the FAQs from pages 62-63 of the Candidate's Handbook. Share and discuss any questions the candidate has about Jesus.
- Organize and/or attend a parish Bible Study with other candidates and sponsors. Choose several parables of Jesus to read and discuss.
- Attend a communal devotional service at the parish or pray the Stations of the Cross together.

INTRODUCTION
Warm-Up/Breaktime Exercises

A Invite a panel of older teens—those who have already received the sacrament of Confirmation—to address the group about the meaning of Jesus in their lives. Ask them to share how Jesus has made a difference in their lives in real, practical ways. Ask them to tell about ways they first came to "really know" Jesus, and how they have maintained a relationship with Jesus (e.g., scripture reading, prayer, worship, service). Allow time for the class to ask questions of the panel.

B Play a game of "Jesus' Charades." Divide the class into small teams. Prepare a stack of phrase cards with separate phrases about the life of Jesus. For example,

Jesus walks on water

Jesus feeds the 5,000

Jesus heals the paralytic

Jesus calms the storm

Jesus drives Satan into the herd of swine

Jesus carries his cross

Jesus welcomes the criminal into paradise

Jesus lets Thomas probe his wounds

Jesus ascends into heaven

Call on a representative from one group to choose a phrase from the stack (without looking) to be acted out silently until someone from another team guesses the event. Take turns, calling on a new team and representative each time.

C Go around the room and have each participant share either their favorite gospel story about Jesus or a question they have about Jesus.

D Ask the participants if anyone has ever asked them whether or not they are a Christian or if they believe in Jesus Christ. How did they respond?

WHO IS JESUS?/ LESSON IDEAS

A Assign the worksheet, "More Names for Jesus" (page 71). Have the participants look up each scripture passage and list the title/name for Jesus. Answers (from *The New American Bible with Revised New Testament*) are listed below:

Answers

1. Matthew 1:23	(Emmanuel)
2. Matthew 2:6	(Ruler and Shepherd)
3. Matthew 3:17	(beloved Son)
4. Matthew 13:27	(Master)
5. Mark 1:24	(Holy One of God)
6. Mark 6:4	(prophet)
7. Luke 1:78	(Daybreak)
8. John 1:29	(Lamb of God)
9. John 4:14	(spring of water)

10. John 6:35	(bread of life)
11. John 10:11	(Good Shepherd)
12. John 11:25	(resurrection and life)
13. Eph 1:22	(head of the Church)
14. 1 Pet 5:4	(chief Shepherd)
15. Rev 19:16	(King of kings, Lord of lords)

Have the participants work individually or in small groups. Correct the answers with the class. *Optional*: Have them research other titles and names for Jesus from the scriptures.

B Ask the participants to read Matthew 11:5 (Jesus' response when John the Baptist's asks about whether or not he is the Messiah). Then have them look up passages from Isaiah 26:19, 29:18-19, 35:5-6, and 61:1 to show how Jesus' answer fulfills these passages from the Old Testament.

C Have the participants read the three times Jesus predictions of Jesus' coming passion and death in Mark 8:27-38, 9:30-37, and 10:32-45 and note the reaction to each of these predictions. Ask the participants to chart the disciples growing understanding of Jesus' mission. (By the third prediction, even though James and John misunderstand Jesus' definition of the kingdom and ask to sit at his right and left hand, the other disciples become indignant with them, showing that they are beginning to understand that Jesus' kingdom is one of service, not of being served.)

JESUS, TRUE GOD AND TRUE MAN/ LESSON IDEAS

A Focus on the organization of the gospel of John. Have the participants recognize the following main sections:

I. Prologue (1:1-18)

II. The Book of Signs (1:19–12:50)

III. The Book of Glory (13:1–20:31)

IV. Epilogue: Resurrection Appearance in Galilee (21:1-25)

The prologue highlights Jesus' divinity and states the main themes in the gospel: life, light, truth, world, testimony, and the pre-existence of Jesus as the incarnate Logos. Call on the participants to read John 1:1-18 replacing "the word" with "Jesus."

The Book of Signs contains seven "signs" or miracles of Jesus, beginning with the wedding at Cana and ending with the raising of Lazarus. Each of the signs is followed by a teaching. Have the participants find and identify each sign and the main teaching expressed after each.

The entire gospel is meant to reveal Jesus' glory. In the Book of Glory Jesus' hour arrives and he explains the meaning of the passion, death, and resurrection in the dialogue that takes place in the Upper Room. Ask participants to research the meaning of these events as explained in John's gospel.

Finally, the gospel ends with the resurrection appearances. Ask the participants to note the differences between Jesus' newly resurrected body and his former one (e.g., he appears in locked rooms).

B Provide a summary of the heresies that denied some part of Jesus' true divinity and/or true humanity:

Gnostic Docetism. Christ did not come to the earth in the flesh, but in a ghost-like appearance; from apostolic times the Church had believed in the true incarnation of Christ.

Arianism. Held that the Son of God came "from another substance" than that of the Father. Rather, the Council of Nicea confessed that the Son of God is "begotten, not made, of the same substance (*homoousios*) as the Father."

Nestorianism. False belief that Jesus was two persons—one human and one divine. Rather, Jesus is one divine person with two natures, human and divine. This makes Mary truly the Mother of God.

Monophystism. Held that Jesus has only "one nature." Again, the Council of Chalcedon affirmed that Jesus is one divine person with a divine nature and a human nature.

C If not shown previously, play the video *Jesus BC* (available from www.paulistpress.com). In the video, sin has entered the world. God, in the persons of the Trinity, comes up with the ultimate plan of redemption: the Son will take human form to be the Savior of the World. In the video, God the Father is known as "Dad," God the Son as "Chris," and the Holy Spirit is "Grace." After playing the video, discuss the following questions with the class:

Who were Norman and the maid? (angels)

How did God attempt to reconcile the world before the Incarnation? (through prophets and the law)

How is the Son portrayed as "begotten, not made?" (He was always present with the Father.)

How does the video compare with your understanding of Trinity?

LIFE OF CHRIST/ LESSON IDEAS

A Using the worksheet "Comparing Infancy Narratives" (page 72) have the participants compare the infancy narratives in Matthew and Luke. Mention these points before the participants do their own investigation:

- The genealogy of Jesus is placed at the beginning of Matthew's gospel to show Jesus' connection with the people of Israel, all the way back to the patriarchs. Luke places the genealogy of Jesus just before the beginning of his ministry and extends his family tree all the way back to Adam and God to underscore Jesus' divinity and to be inclusive of all people, Gentiles and Jews, in the family of Jesus.
- The announcement of Jesus' birth is to Joseph in Matthew's gospel and to Mary in Luke's gospel. (In both gospels, Jesus' ancestry is traced through Joseph who was from the family of King David.)
- Matthew mentions the flight of the Holy Family to Egypt and the massacre of infant boys in Bethlehem. Both of these incidents parallel events that happened at the time of Moses and the Exodus.
- Luke's gospel emphasizes Jesus' relationship with the poor and lowly. This theme is highlighted at the time of Jesus' birth when the shepherds are singled out for God's blessing. The theme is extended when Jesus is presented in the Temple and his parents use the exception to the requirement for bringing a lamb to sacrifice because they are poor. Instead, they are permitted to bring two turtledoves or two pigeons.

B Do a study of Jesus' parables. Point out that a parable is a very unique form of storytelling in which the person tells a story that includes common experiences that most everyone can understand. For example, Jesus did not use angels or space aliens or Cyclops as central characters. He used people, settings, materials, and situations that people around him understood. The parables also lead to a single teaching point, and conclude with an unexpected twist or surprise. Parables also call on the listener to make a decision for himself or herself. How would he or she have acted if presented with the situation in the parable? After you have explained the meaning of parables, assign the worksheet "Breaking Down the Parables" (page 73).

C The miracle stories of Jesus, retold in the gospels, typically follow a three-fold pattern: First, there is a problem. Second, Jesus solves the problem with a miraculous action. Third, people react to the miracle. For example, in the healing of the two blind men (Mt 20:29-34), the problem is obvious: the men were blind. Jesus touches their eyes and they are healed. Their reaction after receiving their sight was then to follow Jesus. Give the participants a list of several other miracle stories and have them name this three-fold pattern. For example,

The cure of Simon's mother-in-law (Mk 1:29-31)
The cleansing of the leper (Mk 1:40-45)
The feeding of the five thousand (Lk 9:10-17)
The healing of a boy with a demon (Lk 9:37-43)

D The "kingdom of God" is a term with origins in the Old Testament. The Jews had understood the kingdom of God as a political kingdom that God would establish on earth. Jesus' revised the definition and preached that the kingdom of God was already present at his coming and among all people who repented, turned their lives around, and followed him. Jesus' parables ("The kingdom of God is like . . .") help to explain the meaning of the kingdom of God. The Church itself is described as the "new kingdom" though the kingdom of God is not identical to the Church. Rather, it is the duty of the Church to help to continue to usher in the kingdom of God that is already at hand. Have the participants look up several parables in which Jesus describes what the kingdom of God is like (e.g., Lk 13:18-19; 20-21).

JESUS' PASSION, DEATH, AND RESURRECTION/ LESSON IDEAS

A The question "Why did Jesus have to die?" is often asked. The answer can be looked at from three perspectives. First, "Why did Jesus' accept his death?" The answer can be found in several places in scripture (e.g., Jn 8:21-30; 12:23-24; 16:7-11). Jesus does what is pleasing to the Father. He is like the grain of wheat that must die in order to bring new life. Jesus desires to return to the Father. At Gethsemane on the night before he died, Jesus voices his fears about pain and death. He does not want to die, but he will accept pain and death if it is the Father's will (Lk 22:41-42). The second question is "Why did some people wish to put Jesus to death?" These reasons vary from greed (Judas), to political expediency (Pilate), to false obedience to superiors (the soldiers who arrested Jesus and carried out his crucifixion). Finally, the third perspective is "Why did God the Father permit Jesus to die?" This question is best answered in Hebrews 5:7-10:

> In the days when [Jesus] was in the flesh, he offered prayers and supplications with loud cries and tears to the one who was able to save him from death, and he was heard because of his reverence. Son though he was, he learned obedience from what he suffered; and when he was made perfect, he became the source of eternal salvation for all who obey him, declared by God high priest according to the order of Melchizedek.

Jesus Christ

In other words, God's motivation for allowing Jesus to die was salvation for all humankind. All three of these plans and motivations (Jesus', his opponent's, and God the Father's) worked together to form one plan of salvation. Salvation is the permanent union between God and all who love God.

B Pray the Stations of the Cross with the class. Or, have the participants write their own reflections for the eight scriptural stations listed below. First, have them read a scripture passage related to the station, then answer the accompanying questions in a journal or notebook.

Station 1   Agony in the Garden   Luke 22:39-46
List several emotions besides fear that Jesus experienced. When are times you have been afraid?

Station 2   The Arrest of Jesus   Luke 22:47-53
Imagine Jesus' thoughts about those who arrested him. When was a time you were falsely accused of something?

Station 3   Peter's Denial   Luke 22:54-62
What's the problem with gossip? When was a time you denied—by words or actions—that you know Jesus?

Station 4   Jesus Is Sentenced to Death   Matthew 27:20-26
If you could describe in one sentence what Jesus did that got him to this point, what would it be?

Station 5   Jesus Is Mocked   Matthew 27:27-31
Jesus just took it. He did not fight back against his tormentors. When have you done something like that? What happened to you when you did?

Station 6   Simon of Cyrene Helps Jesus   Matthew 27:32
Do you think Simon thought he was helping a winner or a loser? Have you ever had to help someone you didn't necessarily want to help?

Station 7   Jesus Is Crucified   Luke 23:33-43
Describe a time you know of when an innocent person took the punishment for those who were guilty.

Station 8   Jesus Dies on the Cross   Luke 23:44-46
Picture yourself at the foot of the cross. What are you thinking? What do you tell Jesus?

C Choose a participant to play the part of a talk show guest. Pretend you are Jesus, the host of a television talk show and that the participant is your guest. Interview your guest using some or all of the questions below. Also create your own questions. Choose more than one participant be on the show.

Why are you preparing for Confirmation?

How well do you think you know me?

What is one question you would like to ask me?

We used to be better friends. What do you think has happened to our relationship recently?

What do your friends think about me? What do your family members think about me?

Who has taught you the most about me?

Sometimes I see you pay lots of attention to me at Mass, other times not. Who or what helps you to stay focused?

What do you think is the biggest problem in our Church?

How well do you think my followers have gotten the good news out about me and my Father?

Are you afraid to die? How can I help you be less afraid?

Jesus Christ

References/FAQ

References from the *Catechism of the Catholic Church* for the Frequently Asked Questions include:

Is Jesus God? (CCC, 202, 241, 422-451)
Yes. Jesus Christ is true God and true man. He became truly man while remaining truly God. Jesus is one person, the Second Person of the Trinity, with two natures, human and divine. He is the Word Made Flesh.

Was Jesus really human in the same way I am human? (CCC, 456-478)
Jesus was a real person who lived and walked on this earth. He lived in Nazareth, a town in Israel, nearly 2,000 years ago. Jesus is like us in everything but sin. He was able to grow in "wisdom, age, and grace."

Did Jesus know he was God? (CCC, 470-478)
The union of the human and divine is a mystery that is hard to comprehend. Most theologians recognize that since Jesus had a human nature, he came to understand his divine nature in that context. This means the three-year-old toddler did not likely tell his mother all there is to know about God or predict the future. Rather, as he developed as a human, he was able to express more clearly his identity and mission as God.

Did Jesus have brothers and sisters? (CCC, 499-501)
The New Testament does mention "brothers and sisters" of Jesus (e.g., Mark 3:31-35). The Church understands these references to be to children of another Mary, a disciple of Christ. The words brother and sister may also refer to close relations like cousins. The Church holds that Jesus was Mary's only child and that she was ever-virgin, though she is the spiritual mother of all.

Who is responsible for the death of Jesus? (CCC, 598)
Throughout history, the Jews have taken unfair blame for the death of Jesus. The Jews, collectively, must not be held responsible for the death of Jesus. As to the personal sin of participants like Judas, members of the Sanhedrin, and Pilate, it is known to God alone. Rather, the answer to the question is more accurately "all sinners are responsible for the death of Jesus" as our sins affected Christ himself.

Why did Jesus descend into hell? (CCC, 631-635)
In scripture, the place where the dead go was called hell—Sheol in Hebrew or Hades in Greek. When the Apostles' Creed says that Jesus descended into hell, it is teaching that Jesus really died and through his death conquered death. He did not descend into hell to free the unjust or to destroy hell, but to lead the dead who were just to heaven. As the first letter of Peter says: "The gospel was preached even to the dead" (4:6).

When will Jesus come again? (CCC, 668-679)
Since the Ascension of Jesus to heaven, Jesus' Second Coming is imminent, though we do not know the day or hour. We are to live each moment as if Jesus' may come. Before Christ's Second Coming, the Church will pass through a final test that will test the faith of many. At the end of time, all creatures in the universe will acknowledge Christ as Lord.

FEATURES/LESSON IDEAS

A A Christian martyr is someone who freely chooses to give up his or her life for the faith. The word martyr means "witness" in Greek. There have been many martyrs throughout the history of the Church. As a way to recognize martyrs, many have been beatified—the last step before one is declared a saint—or, in fact, canonized saints. In March 2000 Pope John Paul II honored forty-four martyrs. From the time he became Pope in 1978, he beatified or canonized more than 1,200 candidates, about the same number that had been canonized from the early seventeenth century until his papacy. Among the most recently honored martyrs were Vietnam's first martyr, Andre de Phu Yen who was baptized at the age of fifteen in 1641 and beheaded three years later when he refused to renounce his Christianity. The first Christian martyr is traditionally named as St. Stephen, stoned to death as recorded in Acts 6–7. The first three centuries were filled with Christian martyrs as Christianity was illegal and punishable by death in the Roman empire. Catholics believe martyrs have achieved full union and happiness with God in heaven and can be prayed to for intercession. There are daily examples in the news of people who literally give up their life professing their faith in Christ. Several teenagers at Columbine High School in Littleton, Colorado, were forced to answer the question, "Do you believe in God?" with a gun put to their heads. When they answered "yes," they were shot.

B Conduct this exercise. Have the participants carry bibles with their schoolbooks, wear a visible religious medal, or a shirt that proclaims a Christian message. Have them note the reactions—both harsh ones and positive ones—to their public witnessing statements.

C Read the meditative "One Solitary Life" to the participants (also on pages 64-65 of the Candidate's Handbook):

> He was born in an obscure village, the child of a peasant woman. He grew up in another village, where he worked in a carpenter shop til he was thirty. Then for three years he was a traveling preacher. He never wrote a book. He never held an office. He never traveled two hundred miles from the place where he was born. He did none of the things one usually associates with greatness.
>
> He was only thirty-three when the tide of public opinion turned against him. He was turned over to his enemies and went through the mockery of a trial. He was nailed to a cross between two thieves. When he was dead, he was laid in a borrowed grave.
>
> Nineteen centuries have come and gone, and today he is the central figure of the human race and the leader of humanity's progress. All the armies that ever marched, all the navies that ever sailed, all the kings that ever reigned have not affected the life of human persons as that One Solitary Life.
>
> —ANONYMOUS

Ask the participants to lists ways that Jesus has made a difference both to the world at large, and to their own personal lives.

D Have the participants collect and record in their journals quotations by saints, Catholics, other Christians, and non-believers alike about Jesus Christ.

Jesus Christ

PRAYER EXPERIENCES

A Encourage the participants to pray some traditional prayers, including the Prayer of the Criminal ("Jesus, remember me when you come into your kingdom."), the Jesus' Prayer ("Lord Jesus Christ, Son of God, have mercy on me, a sinner."), and the Lord's Prayer.

B Remind the participants that Jesus calls himself "the light of the world" (Jn 8:12). Have the participants write on small slips of paper specific elements of darkness in their own lives (e.g., jealousy, hatred, prejudice, fear, loneliness) and on other slips of paper specific ways Jesus has brought light to their lives (e.g., a special friendship, a caring teacher, a favorite spot in nature, peace through participation in the sacraments, prayer). Have the group sit in a circle with unlit taper candles. Call on one participant to begin by sharing one occasion of darkness from their life. Repeat the process around the rest of the circle with each participants sharing about darkness in darkness. Then repeat the sharing, this time with the participant sharing about how Jesus brings light. Light the first person's candle. After each person has shared, they should light their candle from the preceding person. Conclude with a song (e.g., "I am the Light of the World," Greg Hayakawa, OCP).

MORE NAMES FOR JESUS

Look up each scripture passage. List the name or title for Jesus reflected in each passage.

1. Matthew 1:23 _____

2. Matthew 2:6 _____

3. Matthew 3:17 _____

4. Matthew 13:27 _____

5. Mark 1:24 _____

6. Mark 6:4 _____

7. Luke 1:78 _____

8. John 1:29 _____

9. John 4:14 _____

10. John 6:35 _____

11. John 10:11 _____

12. John 11:25 _____

13. Ephesians 1:22 _____

14. 1 Peter 5:4 _____

15. Revelation 19:16 _____

NAME _____

COMPARING INFANCY NARRATIVES

Listed below are several names and items associated with the Christmas story. Mark an "M" for those found in Matthew 1:18–2:23 and an "L" for those found in Luke 2:1-39. Some items are in both Matthew and Luke.

Mary ___   Joseph ___   Caesar Augustus ___

shepherds ___   massacre of infants ___   inn ___

Bethlehem ___   Nazareth ___   Herod ___

magi ___   angels ___   turtledoves ___

Simeon ___   Quirinius ___   manger ___

Egypt ___   star ___   swaddling clothes ___

Temple ___   Anna ___   gold, frankincense, and myrrh ___

Breaking Down the Parables

1. The Parable of the Sower (Matthew 13:1-9)

    How does the parable use common experiences that most everyone can understand?

    What is surprising about the message of the parable?

    What does the parable mean to you?

2. The Parable of the Lost Sheep (Luke 15:1-7)

    How does the parable use common experiences that most everyone can understand?

    What is surprising about the message of the parable?

    What does the parable mean to you?

3. The Parable of the Persistent Widow (Luke 18:1-8)

    How does the parable use common experiences that most everyone can understand?

    What is surprising about the message of the parable?

    What does the parable mean to you?

4. The Parable of the Talents (Matthew 25:14-30)

    How does the parable use common experiences that most everyone can understand?

    What is surprising about the message of the parable?

    What does the parable mean to you?

Scripture

(see pages 69-89 of the Candidate's Handbook)

Background

In order for God to reveal himself to us, he must speak to us in human words. The sacred scriptures are a source of the word of God, and the Church has always found nourishment and strength in them. In the scriptures, God speaks one single Word to the Church. That Word is his Son, in whom the Father is completely revealed.

For Catholics, the Bible is known as the "Book of the Church." The Bible did not magically appear and was not literally written by God, as some fundamentalist Christians may hold. Many fundamentalist Christians see themselves as belonging to a "Church of the Book." Catholics, on the other hand, understand that it was the Church who was inspired by God to write the word of God. (In the Old Testament, it was the chosen People of God, the Israelites, who were likewise inspired.) It is God's inspiration that makes the Bible true.

For themselves, teens must delve more deeply into the question of "How is the Bible true?" by exploring the different types of truth—scientific truth, moral truth, and religious truth, for example—ultimately coming to an understanding that the Bible is true because God is its author.

To help explain Church teaching on the Bible to non-Catholic friends, teens must also have a good understanding of the equal weight the Church gives to God's revelation through scripture and Tradition. Catholics believe that God did not stop communicating with humankind when the final book of the Bible was written sometime late in the first century. God has continued to inspire the Pope and bishops—the successors of the apostles—to preserve, expound on, and spread God's word to all.

Finally, teens need an overview of the Bible, a large book that is really made up of seventy-three books. They need to understand the particulars about when, how, and by whom the books of the Bible were written, how the canon of the scriptures was formed, and why there are differences in arrangement of the canons of the Old Testament in the Catholic and Protestant Bibles.

Most importantly, teens must recognize and know that it is Jesus Christ who is present throughout the pages of the Bible. The Old Testament sets the stage for Christ's coming and the New Testament tells how Jesus brought salvation to the world. That is why Jesus, the Word of God, is the one unique word of the sacred scriptures.

Sample Schedules
Model 1: Focused Preparation (one 3-hour session)
Suggested Session Plan

Warm-Up (30 minutes)
Refer to pages 69-70 of the Candidate's Handbook.
Note: The candidates should each have a copy of the Bible—preferably the same translation—for this session.
- Use Warm-up/Breaktime Exercise "A" (page 81). For the follow up discussion, conduct the discussion with the entire group or break the group up into small groups of four to six candidates.
- Play the game listed in Warm-up/Breaktime Exercise "C" (pages 81-82).

Lesson 1: Truth and Inspiration (40 minutes)
Refer to pages 70-75 of the Candidate's Handbook.
- Point out the questions on page 70 of the Candidate's Handbook. Ask the candidates how questions like these often confuse the issue of whether or not the Bible is true. Discuss different kinds of truth as presented on page 70-71.
- After the discussion on truth, move on to discuss the meaning of "inspiration" and "divine inspiration." See Truth and Inspiration "A" (page 82).
- Have the teens do the preparation work in pairs for the activity suggested in Truth and Inspiration "C" (pages 82-83). Save the presentation of the role plays for the end of the break.

Breaktime/Continuation of Lesson 1 (20 minutes)
- Allow the first five to ten minutes for a stretch, cold drink, and snack. Then have the group proceed to the large group area.
- Call on several teen pairs to share their role plays based on Truth and Inspiration "C" (pages 82-83).

Lesson 2: The Canon of Scripture (30 minutes)
Refer to pages 76-80 of the Candidate's Handbook.
- Help the candidates to understand the main divisions of the Bible, the styles of writing in the Bible, and how the canon of the Bible was formulated. Use The Canon of Scripture "A."
- Briefly touch on the Old Testament canon. Then move to a discussion of the stages in the development of the New Testament. Pass out the resource sheet "New Testament Timeline" (page 94) and complete the activity suggested in The Canon of Scripture "E"(pages 85-86).

Lesson 3: Scripture in the Life of the Church (20 minutes)
Refer to pages 80-85 of the Candidate's Handbook.
- Use Scripture in the Life of the Church "A" (pages 85-86). Consult with the speaker on the focus of his or her talk. Provide the teens with an introduction of the speaker and the theme prior to the presentation.
- If appropriate, allow time for a brief question and answer session.

Break (5 minutes)
- Allow a short stretch break prior to the continuation of the lesson.

Lesson 3: Scripture in the Life of the Church continued (20 minutes)

- Use Scripture in the Life of the Church "C" (page 87). Have the teens begin work on a short homily based on the week's readings. These may be shared with a family member or their sponsor (see Sponsor/Candidate Activities, below).
- Allow for a sampling of answers based on the week's readings.

Features/Prayer Experience (15 minutes)

- Share some or all of the Feature material on pages 86-89 of the Candidate's Handbook. Next, use Feature "C" (page 91).
- Use Prayer Experience "B" (page 91) as a concluding prayer.

Individual Home Assignments

- Assign the worksheet "Literary Genres in the Bible" (page 93) as homework. The answers can be found with Truth and Inspiration "E" (page 83).
- Have the teens do a survey of the Old Testament, reading and reporting on their favorite stories.
- Make sure the candidates complete the assignment begun in Lesson 3 (see above).

Sponsor/Candidate Activities

- Assign Truth and Inspiration "D" (page 83) which is also on page 75 of the Candidate's Handbook.
- Have the teens share the homily they finished for homework with their sponsors.
- Arrange for the candidates and sponsors to attend a parish or inter-parish Bible study or presentation on scriptures.

MODEL 2: EXTENDED PREPARATION (TWO 1-HOUR SESSIONS)
Suggested Session 1 Plan

Warm-Up (10 minutes)
- Display several different translations of the Bible as the teens arrive. Print a reference to one or two scripture passages. Ask the teens to look up the passages in the various versions and note the differences. See Warm-up/Breaktime Exercise "E" (page 82).
- Offer a brief overview of the topic of Chapter 4 (see pages 69-70 of the Candidate's Handbook), Scripture. As time permits, go around the room and ask the teens to name their favorite Old and New Testament stories.

Lesson: Truth and Inspiration (15 minutes)
Refer to pages 70-75 of the Candidate's Handbook.
- Lead a discussion on the meanings of truth and inspiration. Combine the material in Truth and Inspiration "A" and "B" (page 82).
- Ask the teens to write and share a response to the following questions (write on the board): **What does it mean to say that the Bible is inspired? How is the Bible true?**

Breaktime (5 minutes)
- Display several of the Bible tools suggested in Truth and Inspiration "F" (pages 83-84) Allow the candidates a chance to browse through the display while they take a stretch and have a drink.

Lesson: The Canon of Scripture (20 minutes)
Refer to pages 76-80 of the Candidate's Handbook.
- Use the table of contents of the Bible in connection with The Canon of Scripture "A" (page 84) to introduce the main divisions of the Bible and biblical categories. Refer to the discussion questions on page 80 of the Candidate's Handbook for follow up.
- Use The Canon of Scripture "C" (page 85). Allow time for them to briefly write and then share a personal story as suggested in the lesson idea.

Prayer Experience (10 minutes)
- Use Prayer Experience "A" (page 91). If time is limited, eliminate the opportunity for shared prayer. Instead, focus the remaining time on how the teens can live up to the words expressed in the Philippians passage.

Individual Home Assignments
- Assign the "Bible Survey" (page 92). Collect at the next session.
- Assign the worksheet "Literary Genres in the Bible" (page 93).
- Ask the candidates to develop a personal plan for reading the Bible and to be prepared to discuss the plan at the next session or with their sponsors.

Sponsor/Candidate Activities
- Have the candidates discuss each of the individual home assignments (above) with their sponsors.
- Encourage both sponsors and candidates to share their personal Bibles with one another and any stories of its history in their families.
- Take turns sharing favorite Bible passages and stories with one another.

Suggested Session 2 Plan

Warm-Up (15 minutes)
- Briefly lead a follow up discussion on the individual home assignments. For "Literary Genres in the Bible," check answers from page 83.
- Play one or two of the games suggested in Warm-Up/Breaktime Exercise "B," "C," or "D" (pages 81-82).

Lesson: Scripture in the Life of the Church (20 minutes)
Refer to pages 80-85 of the Candidate's Handbook.
- Use Scripture in the Life of the Church "B" (pages 86-87). Make sure to allow enough time to be able to wrap up the exercise using the concluding points on page 87.

Breaktime/Continuation of Scripture in the Life of the Church lesson (10 minutes)
- Provide one large piece of newsprint and the other media items suggested in Scripture in the Life of the Church "E" (page 88). Allow a brief time for the teens to print their favorite passage. Then display the newsprint in the room

Feature/Prayer (15 minutes)
Refer to pages 87-89 of the Candidate's Handbook.
- Read or have the candidates read "New Holy Words" (pages 87-88). Then provide more information on St. Augustine and St. Jerome (see Features/Lesson Ideas "A," pages 89-90).
- Read or assign a teen to read the passage from Philippians 4:4-8 (page 89 of the Candidate's Handbook) as a closing prayer.

Individual Home Assignments
- Assign the resource "Themes of Sunday Readings" (page 95). Have the candidates work to write their own homily for a coming Sunday's readings.
- Assign the teens to complete one of the assignments connected with Features/Lesson Ideas "A" (pages 89-90).
- Make sure the candidates keep up with the "50 Questions" assignment (pages 243-247 of the Candidate's Handbook). Questions 16-20 relate directly to the scriptures.
- Assign for journal writing some or all of the reflection questions or exercises from Chapter 4 of the Candidate's Handbook that were not covered as part of the class session.

Sponsor Candidate/Activities
- Encourage the teens to share their homily from the individual home assignment with their sponsor.
- Review together the FAQs from pages 86-87 of the Candidate's Handbook.
- Take a trip together to a local bookstore and browse through books written about Christian scripture.

MODEL 3: CONCENTRATED PREPARATION (ONE 90-MINUTE SESSION)
Suggested Session Plan

Warm-Up (15 minutes)
* As the candidates arrive, pass out the "Bible Survey" (page 92 of this Manual) and have them complete it. With the large group, discuss the teen's responses then continue with Warm-up/Breaktime Exercise "A" (page 81).

Lesson Plan (40 minutes)
* Introduce the theme of the lesson by having the teens browse through a Bible, noting the divisions between Old and New Testament, as well as the main classifications of books in the Bible. Discuss the literary genres in the Bible using the material on pages 74-75 of the Candidate's Handbook. Assign the resource "Literary Genres in the Bible" (page 93) to accompany the presentation.
* Briefly present the material on truth and inspiration (see Truth and Inspiration "A" and "B," page 81). As follow-up, assign the role plays described in Truth and Inspiration "C" (pages 81-82). As suggested, call on some volunteers to present their dialogues to the large group.
* Assign individuals to do the exercise suggested in Truth and Inspiration "D" (page 82).

Breaktime (10 minutes)
* Play one of the games suggested in Warm-up/Breaktime Exercise "B," "C," or "D" (pages 81-82).
* Call on volunteers to share their results from the assignment in Truth and Inspiration "D."

Lesson Plan continued (20 minutes)
* Use The Canon of Scripture "B" (page 84). Print the "proclamations of faith" the teens find in the passage on the board.
* Use The Canon of Scripture "E" (pages 85-86).
* Related to the discussion from "E," above, have the candidates complete the assignment suggested in The Canon of Scripture "F" (page 86).

Prayer Experience (5 minutes)
* Use Prayer Experience "B" page 91

Individual Assignments
* Ask the teens to write a short essay on their favorite Old Testament story including information about why it is their favorite and what religious lesson the story teaches.
* Assign The Canon of Scripture "G" (page 86).
* Make sure the candidates continue answering the relevant "50 Questions," especially questions 16-20.

Sponsor/Candidate Activities
* Together, work through "Themes of Sunday Readings" suggested in Scripture in the Life of the Church "C" (page 87).
* Take turns quizzing each other on Bible knowledge (see Features "C," page 91).
* Pray with the Bible. Use the *lectio divina* form explained on pages 83-84 of the Candidate's Handbook.
* Read and discuss the FAQs for this chapter (see pages 86-87).

INTRODUCTION
Warm-up/Breaktime Exercises

A Have each participant fill out the "Bible Survey" worksheet (page 92 of this Manual). When completed, lead a general discussion. Poll the teens on each statement, comparing responses. Then, continue by printing the following queries on the board or newsprint:

> **Name a favorite story from the Old Testament.**
> **Name a favorite person from the Old Testament.**
> **Name a favorite parable or teaching of Jesus.**
> **Name a favorite miracle story of Jesus.**

Allow time for discussion for each statement. The teens can discuss with a partner. Then call on volunteers to share some of what was discussed with the entire group.

B Print the following incomplete scripture passages on the board or newsprint, one at a time. Divide the group in two teams. Call on a representative from one team at a time to attempt to finish the passage (answers in italics). If the person is correct, the team gets five points. If wrong, the passage is read to a representative of the other team. A correct answer merits four points. Continue with the passage back and forth until there is a correct answer, down to a possible one point. Determine ahead of time whether or not to allow conversation among team members, and call on new responders for each round.

Passages
1. "My God, my God *why have you abandoned me.*" (Ps 22:1)
2. God blessed them saying: "Be fertile and *multiply; fill the earth and subdue it.*" (Gn 1:28)
3. Give thanks to the Lord, who is good *whose love endures forever.* (Ps 118:1)
4. The Lord is my shepherd; *there is nothing I lack.* (Ps 23:1)
5. God said to Moses, "Come no nearer! Remove *the sandals from your feet for the place where you stand is holy ground.*" (Ex 3:5)
6. "My Father, if it is possible, *let this cup pass from me.*" (Mt 26:39)
7. "Go, therefore, and make *disciples of all nations.*" (Mt 28:19)
8. "Father, I have sinned against heaven and against you; *I no longer deserve to be called your son.*" (Lk 19:18-19)
9. "Whoever eats my flesh and drinks my blood *has eternal life.*" (Jn 6:54)
10. "Whoever eats my flesh and drinks my blood *remains in me and I in him.*" (Jn 6:56)
11. "As the Father loves me, *so I also love you.*" (Jn 14:9)

C Pass out Bibles to all the teens. Play a game where the teens race to look up particular stories or books in the Bible. The first person who correctly calls out the passage or shows you the page in the Bible wins the round. *Optional:* Play in teams; the first team to answer correctly wins a point.

Sample Items
- The first story of creation (Gn 1)
- "Take and eat, this is my body." (Mt 26:26-30; Mk 14:22-26; Lk 22:14-20; 1 Cor 11:23-25)
- The Ten Commandments (Ex 20)
- The division between the Old Testament and New Testament
- The parable of the prodigal, or lost son (Lk 15:11-32)
- The birth of Jesus (Mt 1:18-25; Lk 2:1-14)

- The Book of Psalms
- The Beatitudes (Mt 5:3-12 or Lk 6:20-23)

D Divide the class into small groups and give each group ten scraps of paper in the shape of flash cards. Have them work together to write ten questions with answers that can be found in the Bible. One side of the card should have the question, the other side the answer with scripture reference. (e.g., Q: "What was the name of the first Christian martyr?" A: "Steven, Acts 7:59-60.")

Collect all the cards, keeping them in sets from each group. Pass a new set to each group. Have the group work through the questions, seeing how many they get correct before checking their answers.

E Bring in a number of different editions and translations of the Bible. Call on different teens to read the same passage from the different Bibles. Note the differences.

TRUTH AND INSPIRATION/LESSON IDEAS

A Discuss with the teens some different understandings of the word *inspiration*. For example:
- a literary work may be viewed as the product of the inspiration of great poets or writers;
- a team may play an inspired game;
- a student may be inspired to complete a project;
- a moving speaker may inspire the audience.

Explain how *divine inspiration* is similar to and different from the examples discussed. As with human forms of inspiration, with divine inspiration there is a spirit and power at work. However, the product of divine inspiration does not have to be moving or compelling. It may even be dull. The definition of divine inspiration is that it means that God has involved himself in a human event and guaranteed his presence in that event.

Ask: "What does it mean to say that the Bible is inspired?" Work with the teens to help them understand that "God is the author of the Sacred Scripture" (CCC, 105) and that God inspired the human authors of the sacred books of the Bible.

B Ask the teens to read the first and second creation stories (Gn 1 and 2) and list some of the religious truth taught in either or both stories. For example:
1. God was present in the beginning.
2. God created heaven and earth from nothing.
3. All creation is created good.
4. One day of the week is for rest and is to be made holy.
5. Human beings, both male and female, are made in God's image.
6. Humans are to be fertile and multiply; have dominion over all living things on earth.
7. In marriage, a man and woman become one.
Optional: Have the teens look up and list ten other examples of religious truth from the Bible.

C Have the teens work in pairs. Each pair should choose one person to play the role of God, the other to take the role of one of the human authors of the sacred scriptures. Have them work together to construct a role play dialogue between God and the author about one of the following topics:
"How I Will Inspire You to Write"
"The Main Truths I Want You to Communicate"
"What Styles of Writing I Would Like You to Use"

After the teens have practiced their dialogues, call on some volunteers to role play the conversation between God and author before the entire group. Then discuss how their role-plays may or may not shed light on the process of inspiration.

D Assign the following exercise (also on page 75 of the Candidate's Handbook):

Read Mark 10:35-45. Compare it with Matthew 20:20-28. What are the differences? What are the reasons for the differences?

Answer: In Mark, James and John ask to sit at Jesus' right hand. In Matthew, it is their mother who asks the question of Jesus. Mark's was the first account written, at least thirty years after the time of Christ. It may have offended the sensibilities of the new Christians who now only knew James and John as great Church leaders, not as disciples who would ask a misguided question. Matthew's assigning the question to the mother of James and John removes most of their culpability.

Optional: Have the teens compare two versions of the Beatitudes (Mt 5:1-12 and Lk 6:20-23). Ask: "Why are the Beatitudes delivered on a mountain in Matthew's gospel and on a plain in Luke's gospel?" *Answer*: As Matthew's gospel was intended for Jewish Christians, it not only includes passages specifically related to Jewish Christians (e.g., Mt 5:17-20; 6:1-8, 16-18) but it also is delivered on a mountain to parallel Moses' reception and deliverance of the commandments on a mountain.

E Distribute the worksheet "Literary Genres in the Bible" (page 93) and a bible to each teen. Ask them to look up the listed passages and write the type of writing found in each passage.

Answers:
1. history
2. love song
3. genealogy
4. letter
5. parable
6. prayer
7. history
8. hymn
9. letter
10. parable
11. genealogy
12. proverb
13. prayer
14. proverb

Have the teens work with a partner to find at least one new example for each of the styles of writing listed above.

F Display for the teens and help them to become familiar with several different helps for reading and studying the Bible. For example:
- a *concordance* that lists all the occurrences of words in the Bible;
- a *biblical commentary* (e.g., *The New Jerome Biblical Commentary*) which offers commentary on particular passages of the Bible. (Many versions of the Bible, itself, have excellent notes with biblical commentary.)

Scripture

- a *Bible atlas* that presents relevant maps of the biblical world from different historical periods in the Old and New Testaments.
- a *Bible dictionary* written like a desk encyclopedia which provides brief background information on places, names, and events in the Bible.

Also, refer the teens to http://www.biblestudytools.net a site offering most of the Bible study tools mentioned above, and more.

G As *Dei Verbum* states: "In the sacred books, the Father who is in heaven comes lovingly to meet his children, and talks with them"[68]. Have the teens write a short prayer to God the Father, thanking him for sending his Son, and for the gift of his holy word in the sacred scriptures

THE CANON OF SCRIPTURE/LESSON IDEAS

A Make seventy-three flash cards, each containing the name of one book of the Bible. Then print the Bible categories (Old and New Testaments) on the board or on larger flash cards taped to the wall. Shuffle the flash cards. Divide the group in two. Call on a player from Team 1 to pick one flash card and tape it under the correct category. If correct, record one point on a scoreboard where all can see. If incorrect, award zero points and return the flashcard to the pile. Call on a representative from Team 2 and continue the process until all the cards have been correctly placed.

Bible categories (from New American Bible)
Old Testament
The Pentateuch
The Historical Books
The Wisdom Books
The Prophetic Books

New Testament
The Gospels
The New Testament Letters
The Catholic Letters

B *Kerygma* is a Greek word for "preaching" or "proclamation." In scripture study, kerygma refers to the central message of the gospel and preached by the apostles. Simply put, the kerygma is "Jesus Christ is Lord. He is risen." The biblical authors began with the kerygma and then worked backwards to fill in other details of his life.

A summary of the kerygma is found in Peter's speech to the Jews in Jerusalem for the feast of Pentecost, Acts 2:14-41. Assign the teens to read this passage from the Bible and list several proclamations of our faith. For example:
- Jesus was commended to us by God (v. 22)
- God raised him up (v. 24, 32)
- Jesus sits at God's right hand (v. 33)
- Jesus received and sent out the gift of the Spirit (v. 33)
- Jesus is both Lord and Messiah (v. 36)
- Repent, be baptized, and receive the gift of the Spirit (v. 38)

C Print on the board or newsprint **September 11, 2001**. Next to that date, print **significant event** and remind the teens of the significance of that day in the United States.

Next, under "significant event," print **reflection**, **interpretation**, and **tell the story**.

Explain that the real significance of September 11, 2001 did not come to light until people could reflect on and interpret what had happened. After that, there were many stories told of heroism, friendship, and the courage of the people who died and those who tried to save them.

Connect this process with how the Bible (especially the Old Testament) was written. Stories about significant events (e.g., Creation or the Great Flood) were likely to be told over hundreds of years. As they were told, they were also reflected on and re-interpreted several times. It was not until the Hebrew people became a nation under King David and King Solomon that a unified movement arose to write the stories down.

Have the teens undertake this process with a significant personal event in their lives (e.g., award, tragedy, move to new area) from at least five years before. Have them write about the story from the perspective of five years of reflection and interpretation.

Then discuss. Ask: "How would you have described this event right after it happened? How is that description different from the one you just wrote?"

D Assign small groups of three or four participants to read and report on some of the key stories of the Old Testament. Assign each group one story from the list below or any others you choose. After they individually read the story, they should discuss it in their group and organize a short presentation for the entire class. Encourage each teen to have a speaking part in the presentation.
1. The Story of Creation (Gn 1 or 2)
2. The Fall of Man (Gn 3)
3. Cain and Abel (Gn 4:1-16)
4. The Great Flood (Gn 6:5–9: 17)
5. The Testing of Abraham (Gn 22:1-19)
6. The Call of Moses (Ex 3:4-22)
7. The Ten Plagues (Ex 7–11)
8. Crossing of the Red Sea (Ex 14)
9. The Covenant at Mount Sinai (Ex 19–20)
10. David and Goliath (1 Sm 17)
11. David's Sin (2 Sm 11–12)
12. Wisdom of Solomon (1 Kgs 3)
13. Ezekiel's Vision of Dry Bones (Ez 37:1-14)
14. Martyrdom of a Mother and Her Sons (2 Mc 7)

E Distribute copies of the worksheet "New Testament Timeline" (page 94) to all the participants. Go over the three stages of gospel formation. At the bottom of the page, ask the participants to write down as many significant world and national events that took place thirty-five to forty years ago as they can. For example,
- the Vietnam war
- the Civil Rights Movement
- the assassinations of John F. Kennedy, Martin Luther King Jr., Robert F. Kennedy
- the first man on the moon
- the break-up of the Beatles

Call on the participants to share their lists. Then ask them to imagine what it would be like if there were no written records, film, or audio of any of these events and if the only way we knew about them was through stories passed on by word of mouth from grandparents, relatives, and parents. Compare this experience to how the gospels were formed and written.

F Choose a recent news story and recap it with the teens. Assign groups of four teens each to write about the news story you described. The teens should write about the event in one of the following styles:

- a letter to a relative overseas describing the event;
- a journal entry with their own personal feelings about the event;
- an historical summary of the event to be preserved for future generations;
- a prayer that mentions the event.

Have them read what they wrote to their groups. Call on random participants to share their writings with the entire group.

Connect the experience with how different styles of writing emerged in the Bible.

G Assign the teens to research and report on some biographical information on one of the four evangelists, Matthew, Mark, Luke, or John, especially by using the introductory notes and commentary for each gospel.

Introduce the assignment by pointing out that biographical information and assigning authentic authorship to each of the gospels is sketchy. For example, it is assumed that the author of Mark was a friend of Peter (see 1 Pt 5:13) or a travelling companion of Paul (see Acts 12:12, 25). There is also a legendary story that Mark was the young man who followed Jesus after he had been arrested and all of the other disciples had fled (see Mk 14:52).

Provide an opportunity for the teens to share what they learn with one another.

SCRIPTURE IN THE LIFE OF THE CHURCH/ LESSON IDEAS

A Invite a guest speaker to share with the group his or her love for scripture. Consider inviting for a speaker a parish priest, high school theology teacher, or any other adult well versed in scripture. Possible topics:

- the Church's changing interest in scripture study,
- current scripture scholarship,
- analysis of a particular book or passage of scripture,
- ways to pray with scripture.

B Have the teens work in small groups of four or five. Give each group a normal, everyday item (e.g., fork, baseball glove, can of soda, CD, transistor radio, dollar bill). Tell the participants they are going to be asked to explain the item they have been given to a group that has never seen or heard of it before. Of course, besides explaining the name, the teens must explain what the item is used for and how it is used. Allow time for each group to develop its presentation. Then call them to share with the entire class. (The rest of the class should act as if they have never before seen the item.) Allow time for questions and answers.

After all of the presentations, place a bible before the group. Hold a general discussion asking the participants how they might go about explaining what the Bible is to a group of people who had never heard of it or of Jesus Christ. After hearing some suggestions, offer the following points in conclusion:

- The Bible contains culturally and historically conditioned words. To better understand the Bible, we have to understand something of the time, place, and culture of those who wrote it.
- Some parts of the Bible are more important than others. For example, Christians believe that the New Testament is more important than the Old Testament, the gospels more important than the epistles.
- The Bible was written by members of the faith community. Their words reflect their experience.
- God inspired the Bible, but he did not "whisper in the ear" of the human authors telling them what he wanted on paper. As believers, they used their human talents and experiences with God's inspiration to form the words of scripture.
- The Church decided which writings to include in the Bible and which to exclude. The books that are included are called the canon of scripture.

C Following up on the second discussion question for this section (page 85 of the Candidate's Handbook) distribute the worksheet, "Themes of Sunday Readings" (page 95 of this Manual) and have the teens look up and read the first readings and the Sunday gospels listed and briefly write on the line below each the common theme of the readings.

Themes:
1. The Messiah is coming. Repent and ready yourselves.
2. The Lord provides for all our needs. Jesus gives water for eternal life.
3. The call of discipleship.
4. Work for food that lasts into eternal life.

Optional Assignments: (1) Have the participants choose one set of readings and write a short homily for them; (2) Have the participants present their short homily (two to three minutes) in front of the entire class.

D Print several passages from the New Testament on the board or newsprint. For example:
- The Beatitudes (Mt 5:1-12)
- The Call of Simon the Fisherman (Lk 5:1-11)
- The Parable of the Persistent Widow (Lk 18:1-8)
- The Wedding at Cana (Jn 2:1-12)
- The Letter of James
- The First Letter of Peter
- The First, Second, and Third Letters of John

Allow the teens to choose one of these passages and go to a separate area of the room with a piece of scrap paper, a pen, and a bible. Have them go through the following steps of Bible study (also on page 83 of the Candidate's Handbook)
1. Choose a passage.
2. Read the passage all the way through, paying special attention to the people and setting.
3. Read the passage again, this time writing down any questions you have about the passage or anything else that draws your attention.
4. Seek answers to your questions as well as more background on this passage from the introduction to the book and from the margin notes in your Bible.
5. Pray over the passage. Listen for a special message God is giving you regarding this passage.

Allow approximately fifteen minutes for study. Follow-up by asking the teens to meet in groups with anyone else who studied the same passage. Instruct the groups to share their questions and answers from the passage and any special insights they received.

Optional: Have the teens dramatize a scripture reading they have read.

E Have the participants decorate the room with their favorite scripture passages. Pass out strips of poster board, colorful markers, and bibles. Tell the teens to look up and print their favorite scripture passages on the poster board, a passage that speaks directly to them and provides a basic theme for their lives. Decorate the walls or a bulletin board with the finished passages.

REFERENCES/FAQ

References from the *Catechism of the Catholic Church* for the Frequently Asked Questions include:

How is God the author of the sacred scripture? (CCC, 105)
God is the author of the sacred Scriptures because all of the divinely revealed truths contained in the Bible have been written under the inspiration of the Holy Spirit. God inspired the human authors of the Bible. It was as true authors that they wrote whatever God wanted written, and no more.

Who wrote the Bible? (CCC, 106)
Several human authors wrote the words of the Bible. Both the Old and New Testaments developed from an oral tradition in which stories were passed by word of mouth over generations. Much of the Hebrew scriptures were recorded during the Babylonian captivity. Originally the first five books of the Hebrew scriptures were attributed to Moses. More accurately, entire communities, under God's inspiration, helped to record the scriptures. A similar process for the New Testament writings also took place. The gospels were written thirty to sixty years after Jesus' death and resurrection.

Why should Christians bother reading the Old Testament? (CCC, 121-123)
The Old Testament is important to Christians for several reasons. The books are divinely inspired. They are heard in liturgy and contain many beautiful prayers. The books of the Old Testament are a testimony to the entire story of our salvation, including a prophecy of the coming of Jesus Christ, our Redeemer.

Is the Bible true? (CCC, 107)
Yes. While there are scientific and historical errors in the Bible according to today's understanding, the Bible teaches primarily religious truth. The Bible teaches the truth God wants to communicate to humankind. As the Second Vatican Council taught, the Bible teaches "firmly, faithfully, and without error that truth which God wanted put into the sacred writings for the sake of our salvation" (*Constitution on Divine Revelation*, 11).

How should we read the Bible? (CCC, 109-119)
Catholics read the Bible contextually. That is, they understand the sacred scriptures in the broad historical, cultural, and geographical context in which they were written. They also examine the styles of literature present. Catholics rely on the Magisterium (Pope and bishops) to help them interpret the meaning of the Bible. Oppositely, a fundamentalist approach at reading the Bible involves taking all the words literally. For example, a fundamentalist would believe that God created the world in six twenty-four hour days.

What is the most important message of the Bible? (CCC, 101-103)
As the *Catechism* points out, Christ is the unique word of the scriptures. The most important message of the scriptures is that Christ—the Word of God—became man and brought salvation to mankind through his life, death, and resurrection.

FEATURES/LESSON IDEAS

A Share some more of the controversy between St. Augustine and St. Jerome concerning the translation of the book of Jonah. Read these parts of the correspondence between Augustine and Jerome to the teens:

From Augustine to Jerome:

> A certain bishop, one of our brethren, having introduced in the Church over which he presides the reading of your version, came upon a word in the book of the prophet Jonah, of which you

have given a very different rendering from that which had been of old familiar to the senses and memory of all the worshippers, and had been chanted for so many generations in the Church. Thereupon arose such a tumult in the congregation, especially among the Greeks, correcting what had been read, and denouncing the translation as false, that the bishop was compelled to ask the testimony of the Jewish residents (it was in the town of Oea). These, whether from ignorance or from spite, answered that the words in the Hebrew manuscript were correctly rendered in the Greek version, and in the Latin one taken from it. What further need I say? The man was compelled to correct your version in that passage as if it had been falsely translated, as he desired not to be left without a congregation—a calamity which he narrowly escaped. From this case we also are led to think that you may be occasionally mistaken. You will also observe how great must have been the difficulty if this had occurred in those writings which cannot be explained by comparing the testimony of languages now in use.

From Jerome to Augustine:

You tell me that I have given a wrong translation of some word in Jonah, and that a worthy bishop narrowly escaped losing his charge through the clamorous tumult of his people, which was caused by the different rendering of this one word. At the same time, you withhold from me what the word was which I have mistranslated; thus taking away the possibility of my saying anything in my own vindication, lest my reply should be fatal to your objection. Perhaps it is the old dispute about the gourd which has been revived, after slumbering for many long years. [An] illustrious man . . . brought against me the charge of giving in my translation the word "ivy" instead of "gourd." I have already given a sufficient answer to this in my commentary on Jonah. At present, I deem it enough to say that passage, where the Septuagint has "gourd," and Aquila and the others have rendered the word "ivy" (*kissos*), the Hebrew manuscript has "*ciceion*," which is in the Syriac tongue, as now spoken, "*ciceia*." It is a kind of shrub having large leaves like a vine, and when planted it quickly springs up to the size of a small tree, standing upright by its own stem, without requiring any support of canes or poles, as both gourds and ivy do. If, therefore, in translating word for word, I had put the word "*ciceia*," no one would know what it meant; if I had used the word "gourd," I would have said what is not found in the Hebrew. I therefore put down "ivy," that I might not differ from all other translators. But if your Jews said, either through malice or ignorance, as you yourself suggest, that the word is in the Hebrew text which is found in the Greek and Latin versions, it is evident that they were either unacquainted with Hebrew, or have been pleased to say what was not true, in order to make sport of the gourd-planters.

Assign the teens to either 1) research and report more about the life of St. Jerome or 2) compare the translations of at least three different versions of a biblical passage by printing them in columns side by side.

B Share some brief biographical information on Fr. Lawrence Jenco:

Fr. Jenco was held hostage by Islamic radicals in Lebanon for eighteen months after being captured on the streets of Beirut in 1985. Fr. Jenco said, "The first thing you do upon being captured is sing. Then you cry. And then you remain silent."

Fr. Jenco faced death several times. On one occasion the captors tied explosives to his body. Another time he saw a chain suspended from the ceiling and he thought he was to be hanged. Though his faith never wavered, Jenco admitted he prayed to God: "I am not Job, I want to go home now."

Fr. Jenco was released in July 1986. He died at age 61 in 1996 after returning to his home in Joliet, Illinois.

Ask the teens to reflect on and share how a particular scripture reading has helped them through a difficult time.

C Assign each teen to write five unique and true statements about the Bible, or about a particular passage of scripture, along with at least three incorrect statements. For example,
- Mark's gospel was the shortest gospel written. (T)
- All of the gospels mention the birth of Jesus. (F)
- The book of Psalms were mostly written by Moses. (F)

When completed, have the participants take turns quizzing each other, keeping score to see how many they get correct. *Optional*: Collect all of the questions and expand to a larger contest, pitting team against team.

PRAYER EXPERIENCES

A St. Paul asks us to think about whatever is **true**, **honorable**, **just**, **pure**, **lovely**, **gracious**, **excellent**, and **worthy of praise**. (See the text of Philippians 4:4-9 from page 89 of the Candidate's Handbook.) Write these words on the board or on newsprint.

Sit in a circle. Go around the circle and ask the participants to offer a prayer of thanks for someone they know who fits one of these descriptions. For example, "Give thanks for my father who is more honorable than anyone I know." Or, "Thank you, God, for my friend Ellen who cheerfully accepts any roadblock that gets in her way."

Continue with a discussion on how the teens can live up to the meaning behind these words.

Read Philippians 4:4-9. Conclude by playing a recording of the song "Rejoice in the Lord Always" by Christopher Walker (OCP) or another song with similar lyrics.

B Say to the teens: "Jesus, the Word, was present with God from the beginning of time. After I read a line from the prologue of the gospel of John, you repeat it back to me. Please stand and pray."

Read the lines from John 1:1-5 one at a time, pausing to allow the teens to repeat them back to you.

> In the beginning was the Word
>   and the Word was with God,
>   and the Word was God.
> He was in the beginning with God.
> All things came to be through him,
>   and without him nothing came to be.
> What came to be through him was life,
>   and this life was the light of the human race;
> the light shines in the darkness,
>   and the darkness has not overcome it.

C Review with the teens the proper responses to the opening and closing of the gospel at Mass and how Catholics make three small Signs of the Cross on their foreheads (thoughts), lips (words), and heart (feelings) prior to listening to the gospel reading at Mass.

NAME _____

BIBLE SURVEY
Check all the statements you agree with.

____ The Bible is the word of God.

____ I have my own personal Bible.

____ I read the Bible at least once a week.

____ I know how many books are in the Bible.

____ I know the meaning of the word testament.

____ I can name the four gospels.

____ I know what both the first and last books of the Bible are.

____ I know what Mt 1:5 means.

____ I want to learn more about the Bible.

____ I have some friends who know more about the Bible than me.

____ I have been approached by someone who wanted to use the Bible to preach to me.

____ I listen carefully to the Bible readings when I go to Mass.

LITERARY GENRES IN THE BIBLE

Look up each passage and write the type of writing found in each passage on the line.

1. 1 Chronicles 5:11-22   _____

2. Song of Songs 4   _____

3. Luke 3:22-38   _____

4. 1 Corinthians 1:1-9   _____

5. Luke 15:1-7   _____

6. Matthew 6:9-13   _____

7. 1 Maccabees 1   _____

8. Psalm 23   _____

9. 1 Peter 5:12-14   _____

10. Matthew 18:21-35   _____

11. Exodus 6:14-27   _____

12. Proverbs 3:13   _____

13. Luke 22:42   _____

14. Sirach 26:1   _____

NAME _____

New Testament Timeline

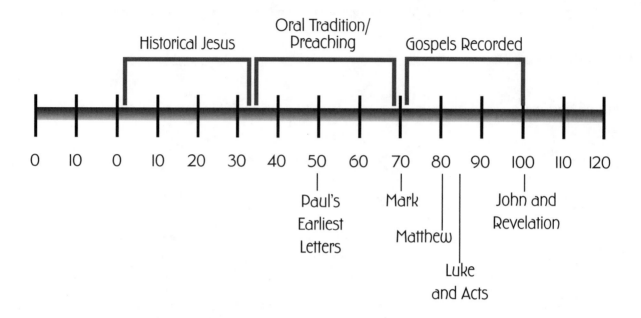

Why the Gospels Were Written

-
-
-
-
-
-

THEMES OF SUNDAY READINGS

Briefly write the common theme of the first reading and gospel for these Sundays.

1. Second Sunday of Advent (A)

First Reading: Isaiah 11:1-10   Gospel: Matthew 3:1-12

2. Third Sunday of Lent (A)

First Reading: Exodus 17:3-7   Gospel: John 4:5-42

3. Second Sunday in Ordinary Time (B)

First Reading: 1 Samuel 3:3b-10, 19   Gospel: John 1:35-42

4. Eighteenth Sunday in Ordinary Time (B)

First Reading: Exodus 16:2-4, 12-15, 31a   Gospel: John 6:24-35

Optional: Write and present a homily based on one set of these readings.

Church

(see pages 91-117 of the Candidate's Handbook)

BACKGROUND

The Nicene Creed lists four marks or signs of the Church: the Church is one, holy, catholic, and apostolic. Yet, while these marks point to the divine elements of the Church, the imperfect human elements remain. That is why many both outside and inside the Church—including teens—characterize the Church as hypocritical whenever it does not seem to live up to these marks.

It is amazing how the divine and human elements of the Church work together side by side. For example, the Church is one because of her source: the Trinity of Persons in one God, the Father, the Son, and the Holy Spirit. Her founder is Jesus Christ, and her soul is the Holy Spirit. This fact is the foundation of the Church's unity, in spite of the disharmony between different Christian denominations and disagreements within the Church itself.

The Church is holy because Christ loved the Church as his bride and joined the Church to himself as his body. Yet the Church is made up of sinners.

The Church is "catholic" or "universal" in a double sense. First, it is Catholic because Christ is present in her. In the Church subsists the fullness of Christ's body united with Christ himself, the head. Secondly, the Church is catholic because Jesus has sent us on a mission to the whole of the human race, to be a new People of God. Yet individual members of the Church often display narrow-mindedness and prejudice even as they attempt to invite others to join the Church.

The Church is apostolic because it is built on the foundation of the apostles, especially St. Peter, the first Pope. The Church continues to hand on the teachings of the apostles and continues to be taught, guided, and made holy by the successors of the apostles, the Pope and bishops, until Christ's return. Again, some within and outside the Church misunderstand and often disobey or deny the Church's legitimate authority.

Using the marks of the Church as a foundation, the lessons within this chapter help teens to understand more about the divine nature of the Church. They emphasize to the candidates that their role is to live these marks and make them more, not less, present in the Church and visible to the world at large. To help them do this, they will reflect on several "success stories" of Christians who have come before them, who by their lives have shown to the world how the Church is one, holy, catholic, and apostolic.

Sample Schedules

Model I: Focused Preparation (one 3-hour session)
Suggested Session Plan

Warm-Up (20 minutes)
Refer to pages 91-92 of the Candidate's Handbook.
- Introduce the topic of the session, the Church, using the material on pages 91-92. Discuss with the teens their level of commitment to the Church for now and for the future. Call for a survey from 1 to 5 with the teens holding up fingers to address their level of commitment: 1 finger being low commitment and 5 fingers being a high level of commitment. While the teens hold up their fingers, call on representatives holding different number(s) of fingers to comment. If necessary, remind the teens not to use their middle fingers to signal a commitment.
- Use Warm-Up/Breaktime Exercise "B" (page 103).

Lesson 1: The Church Is One (20 minutes)
Refer to pages 92-96 of the Candidate's Handbook.
- Use The Church Is One "A" (page 104) as a point of direction for opening discussion.
- Review the unity of the Church using the resource "Major Teachings of the Council of Trent" (page 112) in relation to The Church Is One "D" (page 104).
- *Option:* Use The Church Is One "B" (page 104). If time and schedule permits (e.g., the session is held on a Sunday), arrange for the teens to make a visit to a neighboring parish.

Guest Speaker/Breaktime (40 minutes)
- Use Warm-Up/Breaktime Exercise "C"(page 103). Make sure to discuss topics and time limits with the speaker ahead of time (see page 103). Allow about 20 minutes for the presentation and 5 to 10 minutes more for questions and answers.
- After the speaker's presentation, use Warm-Up/Breaktime Exercise "A" (page 103).
- Allow time for refreshments and a bathroom break before moving on to the next lesson.

Lesson 2: The Church Is Holy (about 20 minutes)
Refer to pages 96-102 of the Candidate's Handbook.
- Use The Church Is Holy "A" (page 104). Besides naming holy people found in the current news, the teens should also name friends and acquaintances from their own lives whom they consider to be holy.
- Assign the final two discussion questions on page 102 of the Candidate's Handbook. Allow time for writing. Then call on volunteers either to share their "game plan" for becoming a saint, or to talk about one of their favorite saints.

Break/Prayer (about 15 minutes)
- Allow time for a stretch.
- Give some brief background on the rosary (see The Church Is Holy, "F," page 105). Use the resource "Praying the Rosary" to pray at least one decade of the rosary with the candidates.

Lesson 3: The Church Is Catholic (about 30 minutes)
Refer to pages 102-107 of the Candidate's Handbook.
- Play the video on St. Thérèse of Lisieux suggested in The Church Is Catholic "D" (page 106). Connect the life of Thérèse, a young woman who spent the majority of her life in one locale, with the Church's mission to spread the gospel to everyone.

- Do a brief version of The Church Is Catholic "A" (page 105). Make the concluding points suggested on comparing school membership with Church membership.

Prayer Experience (about 15 minutes)
- Use Prayer Experience "A" (page 110).

Lesson 4: The Church Is Apostolic (about 20 minutes)
Refer to pages 108-111 of the Candidate's Handbook.
- Provide key background information on the Church's Magisterium, including the name and biographical information on the local ordinary (see The Church Is Apostolic "A" and "C," page 107). *Option:* At this time in the course, you may wish to have the teens write a letter to the bishop who will be confirming them explaining who they are, and why they wish to be confirmed. Arrange for the letters to be mailed once completed.

Individual Assignments
- Adapt The Church Is Holy "C" (page 105) for a home assignment.
- Assign the candidates to write a short report on one of the North American Martyrs (see The Church Is Catholic, "E," pages 106-107).
- Continue answering questions from the "50 Questions" (pages 243-247).

Sponsor/Candidate Activities
- Assign the worksheet "Knowing Our Church" (page 111). The candidates and sponsors should work together to fill in all the information.
- Attend Mass at a parish not your own. Report on the differences and similarities in the liturgy, community, physical setting, etc.
- Rent and watch together *The Mission*. Note the apostolic theme of the presentation.

MODEL 2: EXTENDED PREPARATION (TWO 1-HOUR SESSIONS)
Suggested Session 1 Plan

Warm-Up (about 10 minutes)
Refer to pages 91-92 of the Candidate's Handbook.
- Use Warm-Up/Breaktime Exercise "D" (page 103).

Lesson: The Church Is One (about 25 minutes)
Refer to pages 92-96 of the Candidate's Handbook.
- Begin with a discussion of the teen's personal histories in the Catholic Church. Discuss using Warm-Up/Breaktime Exercise "E" (page 103).
- Show part of a video depicting an overview of Church history. See The Church Is One "C" (page 104).

Breaktime (about 10 minutes)
- Use Warm-Up/Breaktime Exercise "B" (page 103).

Lesson: The Church Is Holy (about 10 minutes)
Refer to pages 96-102 of the Candidate's Handbook.
- Use The Church Is Holy "C" (page 105). Assign the "random act of love" as a home assignment.

Prayer/Conclusion (about 5 minutes)
- Pray the Apostles' Creed (page 00 of the Candidate's Handbook) or conduct Prayer Experience "B" (page 116) as time permits.

Individual Home Assignments
- Participate in a diocesan-sponsored event related to youth. See Features "C" (page 110).
- Compete and report on the "random act of love" assigned during Session 1.

Sponsor/Candidate Activities
- Together, visit a neighboring church of a different denomination. Research some of the information as asked for in The Church Is One "B" (page 104).
- Pray five decades of the rosary together. Choose one set of mysteries, joyful, sorrowful, or glorious, on which to reflect during your prayer time.
- Read and review the FAQs on pages 112-113 of the Candidate's Handbook.

Suggested Session 2 Plan

Feature (about 15 minutes)
Refer to pages 114-116 of the Candidate's Handbook.
- Provide some information on Thomas Merton. Complete Features "A" (page 110). After brainstorming ideas for ways to be a saint, ask the teens to briefly write a short personal plan for "becoming a saint" for their own lives.

Lesson: The Church Is Catholic (about 20 minutes)
Refer to pages 102-107 of the Candidate's Handbook.
- Use The Church Is Catholic "A" (pages 105-106).

- Share a presentation on the North American Martyrs (see The Church Is Catholic "E,"pages 106-107), especially focusing on one of the martyrs listed on page 107. Read the excerpt of the letter from St. Jean de Brébeuf to his superiors prior to his martyrdom.

Breaktime (about 5 minutes)

- Allow time for a stretch. Then play the challenge game suggested in The Church Is Apostolic "B" (page 107).

Lesson: The Church Is Catholic (about 15 minutes)

Refer to pages 102-107 of the Candidate's Handbook.

- *Option:* If possible, arrange for the diocesan ordinary or auxiliary to visit with the candidates and share his thoughts about the sacrament of Confirmation, Confirmation preparation, and the call of all Catholics to be apostolic.
- Summarize the material in this section of the Candidate's Handbook. Use The Church Is Apostolic "C" (pages 107). If there is time, use The Church Is Apostolic "D" (page 108) as well.

Prayer/Conclusion (about 5 minutes)

- Ask the candidates to stand. Pray for the holiness of all people and Blessed Andre Bessette specifically using the prayer on page 108.

Individual Assignment

- Ask the teens to write about the value of the Church having a final arbiter (the Pope) in matters of faith and morals (see The Church Is Apostolic "C," page 107).
- Have the candidates research information on the next or recent World Youth Day. Ask them to interview teens from their parish or local area who have attended a World Youth Day.
- Assign some or all of the discussion questions in Chapter 5 for journal writing.
- Remind the teens to keep up with the "50 Questions" from pages 243-247 of the Candidate's Handbook.

Sponsor/Candidate Activities

- Rent and watch together *Entertaining Angels: The Dorothy Day Story*.
- Share personal reflections on the Prayer of St. Ignatius Loyola (see Prayer Experience "C," page 110).
- Review and discuss the FAQs on pages 112-113 of the Candidate's Handbook.

MODEL 3: CONCENTRATED PREPARATION (ONE 90-MINUTE SESSION)
Suggested Session Plan

Warm-Up (about 20 minutes)
Refer to pages 91-92 of the Candidate's Handbook.
- Introduce the topic of "Church." Remind the teens that the sacrament of Confirmation is a time when they publicly confirm their commitment to the Catholic creeds. Ask the group to stand and recite the Apostles' Creed (page 116 of the Candidate's Handbook).
- Arrange for a guest speaker to tell of the parish's history. See Warm-up/Breaktime Exercise "C" (page 103).

Lesson Plan (about 50 minutes)
Refer to pages 92-111 of the Candidate's Handbook.
- Use The Church Is One "C" (page 104). Choose an approximately 15 minute segment that gives the candidates a flavor of some of the key issues faced in the Church prior to the legality of Christianity in 313 AD.
- Review the Church's teachings formulated at the Council of Trent. See The Church Is One "D" (page 104).
- Discuss the meaning of holiness as a mark of the Church, summarizing the information on pages 96-102 of the Candidate's Handbook.
- Ask the students to move into small table groups of four to six people each before doing The Church Is Holy "B" (page 105). Candidates should write only to the people at their table.

Breaktime (about 5 minutes)
- Have the group stand in place, stretch, and refocus.

Lesson Plan continued (about 15 minutes)
- Present information on the Church's Magisterium. Highlight the material in The Church Is Apostolic "C" (page 107).
- Review the FAQs on pages 112-113 of the Candidate's Handbook. Provide more information as needed from the references to the *Catechism of the Catholic Church* (page 109).

Individual Assignments
- Have each candidate write a report on one of the North American Martyrs. Adapt The Church Is Catholic "E" (pages 106-107).
- Assign the candidates to create a display with either the text of St. Patrick's Breastplate (The Church Is Catholic "C," page 106) or the words of St. Irenaeus (page 116 of the Candidate's Handbook).
- For journal writing, ask the teens to choose at least four of the margin exercises in Chapter 3.
- Remind the candidates to continue working on the "50 Questions" (pages 243-247).

Sponsor/Candidate Activities
- Pray five decades of the rosary together, using either the joyful, sorrowful, or glorious mysteries. (Distribute a copy of the resource "Praying the Rosary, page 113, to all candidates and sponsors.)
- Share together individual plans for "becoming a saint."
- Rent and watch together *Entertaining Angels: The Dorothy Day Story* or *The Mission*.

INTRODUCTION
Warm-up/Breaktime Exercises

A A rather active exercise can be used as a lead-in to help the teens understand that they are literally members of the body of Christ. Divide the class into groups of six to eight participants. Remind them of St. Paul's description of the Church as a body with many parts. Read all or part of 1 Corinthians 12 as a means of introduction.

Within the small groups, assign "parts" of the body. Two people can be "arms," two to four people can be "legs," one person can be a "mouth," and the last person can be the "eyes." The task of the group is to cross from one side of the room to another and to open a closed bible to 1 Corinthians 12.

The challenge is that only the people who are legs can have their feet touching the ground. Only the people who are arms can use their hands. Only the person who is eyes can see (the rest of the group should close their eyes or be blindfolded), and only the mouth can speak.

Basically, it falls to the "legs" to carry the other members of the group across the room and the "eyes" and "mouth" to direct the "arms" to open the bible to the correct page.

The first team that completes the task is the winner. Besides following up on the activity with more discussion of 1 Corinthians 12, this can be a good lead-in to a discussion on the diversity of gifts within the Church and how all must work together.

B Play a game of twenty questions with the teens related to items associated with being Catholic or with a Catholic tradition: for example, rosary beads, a crucifix, a holy card, a parish bulletin, a book about a saint. Hide the item in a paper bag. Divide the group into two teams. Show the item to one team and allow them to field questions from the other team (e.g., "Is it something you wear? Is it something you find in church?"). Score right answers based on how many questions were asked (20 points if guessed after one question to 1 point guessed after 20 questions).

C Invite a longtime adult parishioner to give a presentation to the teens about the history of their parish. Ask the speaker to include some or all of the following elements in the presentation:
- how long he/she has been a member of the parish,
- the cultural and ethnic makeup of the parish in those years,
- any information about the founding of the parish,
- memorable pastors who have served the parish over the years,
- the development of parish traditions (e.g., bazaars, picnics, missions, etc.),
- how the liturgy has changed over the years,
- the reaction of the parish to the changes brought on by the Second Vatican Council,
- the effects of any tragedies on the parish,
- his/her opinion on the future of the parish.

D Assign the teens to work with a partner or in a small group to answer the questions on the worksheet "Knowing Our Church" (page 111). Check the answers and award a round of applause to the team with the most correct answers.

E Ask the teens to trace their own family history as Catholics. Ask: "When did your ancestors become Catholic? How was the Catholic faith first taught to your ancestors?" Have the teens either write this information in a report or share it in a short oral presentation with the entire group.

THE CHURCH IS ONE/LESSON IDEAS

A Discuss differences and similarities the teens have noticed between two or more local parishes. For example, discuss differences in:
- liturgy,
- church design and décor,
- organization of pastoral staff,
- programming (e.g., youth ministry, Confirmation preparation),
- school and religious education,
- cultural, ethnic, and age spectrum of members.

After the discussion on the differences, point out similarities in the above areas, concluding by reminding the teens that all the parishes discussed believe in the same creed, celebrate the sacraments, and are shepherded by the same bishop and Pope.

B Arrange for the teens to visit a neighboring church of a different denomination. Or, invite a minister or other member of the pastoral staff to share information about this particular community with the teens. Arrange with the presenter to share information on some of the following topics:
1. Sunday worship,
2. sacramental preparation,
3. catechetical instruction,
4. teen youth ministry,
5. social service,
6. evangelization.

Leave time for questions and answers following the talk.

C Play all or part of a video that depicts a good overview of Church history or focuses on one period of Church history. *Suggestion: Rome: In the Footsteps of Peter and Paul* (distributed by Harcourt Religion Publishers, www.harcourtreligion.com) focuses on key events in Rome from the first century to the present day.

D Explain to the teens that the Council of Trent (1545-1563) is often called the "Catholic Reformation" as it reaffirmed Catholic teaching and brought renewed confidence to the Church after the Protestant Reformation. Summarize the main teachings of Trent as found on the resource "Major Teachings of the Council of Trent" on page 112. Duplicate and pass out copies to the teens. *Optional:* Have the teens read and research more of the teachings of the Council of Trent. The documents from the council can be found on line at: www.hanover.edu.

E Arrange for the group to collaborate with teens from another parish, Catholic or otherwise, in a social service project or simply in a friendly social gathering. In either case, make sure to allow time for the teens to interact with one another formally and informally as they develop their understanding of their "unity within their diversity."

THE CHURCH IS HOLY/LESSON IDEAS

A Provide a collection of periodicals (newspapers and magazines) that include recent articles profiling news events and feature accounts of how people react and respond to events in the news. Have the teens search out large or small reports of people who they consider to be holy. Call on teens to share the stories they have found with the rest of the group and to explain why they find these people to be holy.

B Have the teens sit in small group circles of four to six. Pass out sheets of paper, pens, and envelopes to each person. Explain that they will be writing a "letter of affirmation" to each person in their group. The letter should be as concrete as possible, telling the person things like:
- what is special and unique about them,
- the special talents and gifts that are observed,
- why he or she is an appreciated part of the class,
- the signs of holiness he or she exhibits.

Each person should write a letter for everyone in the group, seal the letters, and wait until the end of the activity time to "deliver" them. Remind the teens to be constructive and polite, and that they may feel ashamed if they receive letters that have been written with more care than the letters they send.

C The first letter of John (4:7-21) describes the correlation between God and love: a person who loves his brother and sister knows God; one who is without love is without God. Ask the teens to read the passage and to highlight the important truths about God and love they find there. For example,
- God is love.
- It is not that we have loved God; it is that he sent his Son out of love for us.
- When we acknowledge Christ as savior of the world, God remains in us and we in God.
- There is no fear in love.
- Whoever loves God must also love his brother and sister.

Ask the teens to do at least one "random act of love" prior to the next session. This random act of love should be an ordinary act of kindness, mercy, or compassion for another without the expectation of any reward in return. Arrange for a way for the teens to report on or share what they did either in writing or discussion.

D The *What Catholics Believe* video series (Oblate Media, available www.videoswithvalues.org) features Fr. Michael Tueth fielding questions about the Church from theologians and catechists. Play the thirty-minute segment from the series "Mary and the Saints" that includes questions and answers about the role of saints in the Church.

E Share any current information on an ongoing canonization process in the Church today (e.g., Archbishop Fulton J. Sheen, Mother Teresa).

F Pope John Paul II said this about the Rosary:
> The Rosary is marvelous in its simplicity and in its depth. . . . Against the background of the words "Hail Mary" there passes before the eyes of the soul the main episodes in the life of Jesus Christ. They are composed altogether of the joyful, sorrowful, and glorious mysteries, and put us in living communion with Jesus through—we could say—his Mother's heart.

Review and pray at least a decade of the rosary with the teens. The resource "Praying the Rosary" (page 113) offers basic instruction. *Optional:* Have the teens look up and record relevant scripture passages that can be used for reflection with each of the joyful, sorrowful, and glorious mysteries.

THE CHURCH IS CATHOLIC/LESSON IDEAS

A Ask the participants to brainstorm different types of social groups (cliques) that are present in their school (e.g., jocks, druggies, gangs, nerds, brains, etc.) Then present the teens with a potential issue their school would face. For example, "Whether or not to have a closed campus or open campus at lunchtime."

Choose teens to role play before the group stereotypical responses to this issue from each of the cliques mentioned above. Note the differences in opinion on the issue.

Conclude the exercise by pointing out that even though there are many different kinds of students and many differing opinions in one school, *all* the above mentioned are still part of the *one* student body. Also remind the candidates that Jesus would treat all these groups with love and respect and that the teens should do likewise.

Connect the exercise with membership in the Church. Despite differences in language, culture, and belief worldwide, Catholics who are baptized and who believe in and practice the major tenets of faith are all members of the same Church, the body of Christ.

B The classic film *The Mission* (popular release and available and many video rental locations) shows how a bureaucrat and Jesuit priest unite efforts to protect a Brazilian Indian tribe from brutal treatment by colonial empires in the eighteenth century. Show a brief cut from the video (e.g., Rodrigo carrying the heavy armor up the hill) that represents the work and effort that accompanies Jesus' call to share the gospel with all nations. *Optional*: Play all or most of the video if you have time.

C Share this prayer attributed to St. Patrick. It is called "St. Patrick's Breastplate" because it was believed to have been prayed by Patrick for protection in battle.

ST. PATRICK'S BREASTPLATE
Christ, be with me, Christ before me, Christ behind me,
Christ in me, Christ beneath me, Christ above me,
Christ on my right, Christ on my left,
Christ where I lie, Christ where I sit, Christ where I arise,
Christ in the heart of every one who thinks of me,
Christ in the mouth of every one who speaks of me,
Christ in every ear that hears me.
Salvation is of the Lord.
Salvation is of the Lord.
Salvation is of the Christ.
May your salvation, O Lord, be ever with us.

Optional: Provide various kinds of art media for the teens to create a display with the text of St. Patrick's Breastplate.

D *Thérèse Lisieux: My Vocation Is Love* (Pauline Video available at www.catholicshopper.com) is a video that tells the story of St. Thérèse, the Little Flower. It contains footage of her birthplace and childhood home, and the convent at Lisieux. The video is twenty-one minutes ong. Play it in its entirety for the teens.

E Read this letter from St. Jean de Brébeuf to his superior on his impending martyrdom:

We are perhaps upon the point of shedding our blood and of sacrificing our lives in the service of our good Master, Jesus Christ. It seems that His Goodness is willing to accept this sacrifice from me for the expiation of my great innumerable sins, and to crown from this hour forward the past services and the great and ardent desires of all our priests who are here. . . . But we are all grieved over this, that these barbarians, through their own malice, are closing the door to the Gospel and to Grace. . . . Whatever conclusion they reach, and whatever treatment they accord us, we will try, by the Grace of Our Lord, to endure it patiently for His service. It is a singular favor that His Goodness gives us, to allow us to endure something for love of Him . . . (dated October 28, 1637).

Assign the teens to work in groups to research (from Internet or textbook sources) and report on one of the following North American Martyrs:

- Jean De Brébeuf
- Joseph de la Roche Daillon
- Anthony Daniel
- Charles Garnier
- Isaac Jogues
- Rene Goupil
- Noel Chabanel
- Jean de LaLande
- Gabriel Lalemant

THE CHURCH IS APOSTOLIC/LESSON IDEAS

A Share some biographical information on your diocesan ordinary, including his place of birth, date of ordination to the priesthood, and date of ordination to the episcopacy. If an auxiliary bishop will be confirming the teens in your group, share biographical information on him as well. *Options:* 1) Invite a bishop to one of your sessions to share this information himself with the teens; 2) Read the vocation stories of three priests who became bishops from *Extraordinary Lives* by Msgr. Francis Friedl (Ave Maria Press, 1997).

B Divide the class into small groups (three or four teens). Give each group a bible. Play a challenge game. Have the first group open their bible (all other groups keep their bibles closed). Say, "Locate and read a scripture verse that includes Peter's name." Allow thirty seconds. If the group is successful, award a point. Move on to the second group with the same challenge (except that they cannot use the first group's passage). When each group has had a turn, offer ten bonus points for the group that guesses closest to the number of times Peter's name is used in the New Testament (*answer:* 154, *New American Bible*). For an extra bonus of ten points, ask the groups to guess how many times Jesus' name is used in the New Testament (*answer:* 948, *New American Bible*).

C Jesus gave Peter teaching authority (see Mt 16:18-19) which has been passed on to the Pope and bishops. Expand on the definitions of these key concepts on the Church's Magisterium, or teaching authority for the teens:

Magisterial teaching refers to the role of the Pope and bishops to teach authentically, that is "with the authority of Christ" (*CCC*, 2034). Normally this teaching can be found in papal encyclicals (letters), pastoral letters of the bishops, and sermons.

Infallibility refers to the Catholic belief that on essential matters of faith and morals, Church teaching is infallible, or "without error." This teaching is based on Jesus' promise always to remain with the Church and it occurs especially when the world's council of bishops gather and meet with the Pope in an ecumenical council.

Papal infallibility applies to those moments when when the Pope teaches *ex cathedra*, or "from the chair" of St. Peter. To be an *ex cathedra* teaching, it must be a teaching by the Pope in his role as visible head of the Church, be addressed to all Catholics, be a definitive teaching on a matter of faith or morals, and be an unchangeable decision in which the Pope has used full authority.

Ask the teens to write about and then discuss what they perceive to be the value of the Church having a final arbiter (the Pope) in the matter of faith and morals.

D Before the session, write different roles people play in the life of the Church on small scarps of paper, such as: pastor, lector, bishop, eucharistic minister, Pope, catechist, missionary, permanent deacon, nun, cardinal, brother, married person/parent, secular priest, altar server, etc. Try to come up with enough roles for every person in your group, but duplicate them if necessary. Pass out the slips of paper randomly and then ask the group to divide itself; those who are "laity" should move to one corner, those who are not should gather in the opposite corner. Ask the teens to justify their choices until it becomes clear that the term *laity* is understood to mean all the faithful except those who have received Holy Orders, i.e., deacons, priests, and bishops.

E Play the video *Entertaining Angels: The Dorothy Day Story* (110 minutes, Paulist Videos, popular release). The video is rated PG-13. It stars Martin Sheen and Moira Kelly.

F Pray with the teens for the canonization of Blessed André Bessette. The following prayer is from the Brothers of Holy Cross web site:

PRAYER FOR THE CANONIZATION OF BROTHER ANDRÉ BESSETTE

Joseph, we come to pray for the canonization of your friend, Brother André.

You know how humble he was, how he turned away from honors and prestige.
You know that we cannot depend on him to help us in the process of his canonization. . . . He never wished to be recognized publicly as a Saint . . .
Therefore, with great confidence we turn to you.

Must we remind you how much this little Brother loved you, and how during his whole life he talked about your powerful intercession?
But, for him, words were not sufficient. He realized the great dream of his life by building this grand sanctuary: Saint Joseph's Oratory.

Come to our help.
We have the certitude that the canonization of Blessed Brother André will renew the faith of God's people, and thus, by honoring your friend, his outstanding virtues will call us forth to become men and women of God.

Joseph, you who have always been known as the Just Man, into your hands we place our request:
Pray to the Father on our behalf,
so that in the near future He may grant us the favor
of the canonization of your dear friend,
our Blessed Brother André.

References/FAQ

References from the *Catechism of the Catholic Church* for the Frequently Asked Questions include:

Is the Catholic Church really the only true Church? (CCC, 811-819, 2105)
The very name "catholic" means that the Church strives to reach out and include all people—this is the Church's mission. The Church teaches that "one true religion subsists in the catholic and apostolic Church" yet it recognizes that holiness can be found and God's will detected in various other Christian and non-Christian communities and in individuals who through no fault of their own have not been exposed to the Catholic Church.

Is the Church necessary for salvation? (CCC, 846-848)
The answer to this traditional question is "yes" simply because Jesus is necessary for salvation and Jesus remains present in the Church, his body. Those who know and understand that the Church is the Body of Christ, yet reject it, are rejecting salvation. However, this also means that those who never heard of Christ or the Church have not forfeited their chance for salvation.

Do I have to believe everything the Pope says? (CCC, 888-892; especially 891)
The Church believes in the primacy of the bishop of Rome, the Pope. This means that since the time of St. Peter, Christians have been obliged to follow the teachings of the Pope in matters of faith and morals. Of course, this does not extend to matters not concerning faith (e.g., the Pope says "everyone's favorite color must be blue").

What do I tell people who say to me "Catholics worship Mary"? (CCC, 971; 2112-2114)
You can tell them they are wrong. Catholics worship and adore God alone, as required by the first commandment. Worship of any other person or thing would be idolatry, honoring gods other than the one, true Lord. Catholics do venerate or respect Mary and all the saints because of their holiness and faithfulness as disciples of Christ. We revere Mary more than the other saints because she is the Mother of God, the queen of all saints.

How can a Catholic be excommunicated? (CCC, 1463)
To be excommunicated means that a baptized person is no longer "in communion" with the rest of the Catholic faithful. One type of excommunication is automatic and occurs when a Catholic commits a particular sinful action, defined as: desecrating the eucharist, laying hands violently on the Pope, violating the seal of confession (for priests only), giving absolution to an accomplice in sin (for priests only), participating in an abortion, or committing the sins of apostasy, heresy, or schism. The other type of excommunication is imposed by the Church at the discretion of the local bishop for a particular action; for example, pretending to preside at Eucharist although one is not a priest.

What percentage of the world is Roman Catholic? (see CCC 836-845 for related information)
The latest census numbered one billion Roman Catholics worldwide, about 17 percent of the world's total population. There are also an additional one billion Christians of other denominations. Islam is the second largest faith with 1.3 billion adherents (22 percent).

What is necessary for someone to become a canonized saint? (CCC 828, 1173)
The Congregation for the Causes of saints is an office of the Pope in Rome. It examines the life of Christians who are proposed for sainthood, those who have practiced heroic virtue in their lives. The canonization process is many-tiered and may take years as the person's life, death, writings, and more are analyzed. Canonization is preceded by beatification. The person is called blessed and may be honored on a local basis. It's important to remember, though, that all Christians are called to sainthood and that anyone who is with God is, in fact, a saint.

FEATURES/LESSON IDEAS

A Offer some additional biographical information on Thomas Merton:

> Merton was born in France in 1915. His parents were artists. His mother, a Quaker, died when Thomas was ten. Merton and his father then settled in a small village in France where almost everyone was Catholic.

> Later a writer and teacher of English at Columbia University in New York, Merton was baptized at age twenty-three. After a short time he decided to enter a monastery at Gethsemani, Kentucky and become a Trappist monk. From his cell at the monastery, Merton wrote on many themes, particularly on a life of poverty, being a monk, and working for peace.

> Merton was accidentally electrocuted in 1968 while on retreat in India. His many writings remain popular today, including his autobiography, *The Seven Storey Mountain*.

Ask the teens to brainstorm and list some qualities of being a saint. Then, ask them to write a short story on what they would have to do to become a saint.

B Provide some information on an upcoming or recent World Youth Day. Read part of the text of the Pope's message to youth. *Optional*: Call on a teen or youth minister from your area who has attended a World Youth Day to give a short presentation on the experience.

C Allow for the teens to widen their experience of the Church. Arrange for the group to participate in a diocesan-sponsored event related to youth: for example, a retreat, rally, liturgy, or religious education congress.

PRAYER EXPERIENCES

A Help a teen to prepare to read 1 Corinthians 12:12-26 prior to the prayer service. Then gather everyone in a circle. Give each person an unlit candle. Begin by saying, "As a Church we celebrate our unity within our diversity. We appreciate our individual and unique gifts as we gather and remain part of the Body of Christ."

Offer a statement affirming the unique gift(s) of someone in the circle. For example, "I pray for Lori, who brings the gifts of enthusiasm and humor." Then go to the person and light his or her candle. The person with a lit candle will then offer a prayer of affirmation for someone else in the circle. Continue until all the candles are lit.

Finally call on the reader to read the passage from 1 Corinthians thoughtfully.

B Prayerfully read the statements of the Apostles' Creed (see page 116 of the Candidate's Handbook). Pause after each statement and lead the singing of "We Believe" by Christopher Walker (OCP, 1983). The words of the refrain are: "We believe in one God. We believe in one Lord. We believe in one Spirit."

C Assign the prayer of St. Ignatius Loyola (page 116 of the Candidate's Handbook) as a personal prayer reflection. Have the teens write a one-line personal reflection for each line of the prayer.

NAME _____

KNOWING OUR CHURCH
Answer as many of the items as you can.

1. The name of your diocesan bishop:

2. The name of your pastor:

3. The name of the director of religious education for your parish:

4. The name of the president of your parish pastoral council:

5. The year your parish was founded:

6. Some information about the patron/patroness of your parish:

7. The total number of families at your parish:

8. The average amount of money given each Sunday at your parish:

9. The name of one special organization active at your parish:

10. The name of your diocesan newspaper:

11. The street address of your parish:

12. The parish phone number:

13. The schedule of Sunday Masses at your parish:

14. The regular schedule of confessions at your parish:

15. The names of the holy days of obligation celebrated in the United States:

MAJOR TEACHINGS OF THE COUNCIL OF TRENT
Read and review the main teachings of the Council of Trent (1545-1563),
often called the "Catholic Reformation."

Scripture and Apostolic Tradition are equally important.
God's ongoing revelation can be interpreted and understood by the Magisterium, the Pope and bishops who are successors to the apostles. This means that God's revelation did not end with the last page of the Bible.

Justification comes from faith, but good works bring merit as well.
Martin Luther insisted that justification—the passing from sinfulness to the state of grace—is completely unmerited. The council agreed, but drew on the letter of James (2:14-17) to remind Christians of the importance of good works as the expression and fulfillment of faith.

The doctrine of transubstantiation was reaffirmed.
The words describe the Church teaching that Jesus is really present under the appearances of bread and wine at Eucharist.

The Mass is a true sacrifice.
The Mass is a renewal of Christ's sacrifice on the cross. The Mass is an event one and the same as Christ's sacrifice at Calvary. Jesus gave the apostles the power to offer this sacrifice and pass it on through the sacrament of Holy Orders.

The sacrament of Penance is the normal means to receive forgiveness for sins committed after Baptism.
Although it is not necessary to confess venial (lesser) sins sacramentally, Catholics are required to confess serious sins at least once a year.

There are seven sacraments, all instituted by Christ.
For the first time, marriage was named a sacrament. The council listed seven sacraments, Baptism, Confirmation, Eucharist, Penance, Matrimony, Holy Orders, and Anointing of the Sick.

There is a place for purification for Christians who die with venial sins.
Those who die in God's grace, but who are still imperfectly purified, undergo purification so that they might receive eternal salvation. Souls in purgatory benefit from the prayers of those on earth.

Praying the Rosary
Review these directions for praying the Rosary.
Pray at least a decade of the Rosary with a group or on your own.

Beginning
1. Begin on the crucifix and pray the Apostles' Creed.
2. On the first bead, pray the Our Father.
3. On the next three beads, pray the Hail Mary.
4. On the fifth bead, pray the Glory Be.

Body
Each decade (ten beads) is prayed as follows:
1. On the single bead separate from each decade, announce the mystery (e.g., "The First Joyful Mystery, the Annunciation").
2. Pray one Our Father.
3. On each of the ten beads, pray one Hail Mary while reflecting on the mystery.
4. Pray one Glory Be at the end (there is no bead for this).

Conclusion
Pray the "Hail, Holy Queen" at the end of the Rosary.

HAIL HOLY QUEEN
Hail, holy Queen Mother of Mercy,
our life, our sweetness, and our hope.
To thee do we cry,
poor banished children of Eve.
To thee do we send up our signs,
mourning and weeping in this valley of tears.
Turn then, most gracious advocate,
thine eyes of mercy toward us;
and after this our exile,
show unto us the blessed fruit of thy womb, Jesus.
O clement, O loving, O sweet Virgin Mary.
Pray for us, O holy Mother of God,
that we may be made worthy of the promises of Christ.
Amen.

6 Morality

(see pages 119-143 of the Candidate's Handbook)

BACKGROUND

Jesus always did what was pleasing to the Father. As a Christians, this, too, is our task, to make choices that can lead us to become "perfect just as your heavenly Father is perfect" (Mt 5:8).

Jesus' parable of the narrow gate (Mt 7:13-14) clearly presents the two choices facing humans:

> Enter through the narrow gate; for the gate is wide and the road broad that leads to destruction, and those who enter through it are many. How narrow the gate and constricted the road that leads to life. And those who find it are few.

The freedom to choose between good and evil, right and wrong, or life and death is what makes humans moral. Morality involves putting our faith and religion into practice.

The most essential factor in making good decisions is to follow Christ, and to put Christ first in all moral choices. St. Francis de Sales put it this way: "One of the most excellent intentions that we can possibly have in all our actions is to do them because our Lord did them."

The lessons for this chapter help provide teens with criteria for judging the morality of human acts. Explanations are given on the moral object chosen, and the intention and circumstances of a moral act.

Also defined is *conscience*—our "most secret core and sanctuary" in the words of the Second Vatican Council—and how it helps us distinguish between sin and virtue.

Our primary moral compass remains Jesus, who followed the commandments of the old covenant and shared with us the Beatitudes at the Sermon on the Mount as a response to our natural desire for permanent happiness.

A review of the Beatitudes and Ten Commandments with explanations of each are also part of the lessons of this chapter.

Sample Schedules

Model I: Focused Preparation (one 3-hour session)
Suggested Session Plan

Warm-Up/Breaktime (about 40 minutes)
Refer to pages 119-120 of the Candidate's Handbook.
- Use Warm-up/Breaktime Exercise "C" (page 122). Make sure to allow for large-group follow up. List what the teens name as "most important" on the board or newsprint.
- Introduce the session theme, morality. Define the moral life based on the introductory material in the Candidate's Handbook.
- Use Warm-up/Breaktime Exercise "D" (page 123).

Lesson 1: The Morality of Human Acts (about 25 minutes)
Refer to pages 120-123 of the Candidate's Handbook.
- As a means of introduction, use the resource "Questions for Right and Wrong" (page 132). See The Morality of Human Acts "B" (page 123).
- Follow up this discussion based with The Morality of Human Acts "C" (pages 123-126). It is vital for the candidates to understand how the moral object, intention, and circumstances play a role in the morality of an action.

Prayer Experience (about 15 minutes)
- Use Prayer Experience "B" (page 131). *Suggestion:* Choose a guest speaker to talk about love, including sharing a personal story about love.

Breaktime (about 20 minutes)
- Allow a brief time for a stretch, drink of water, etc.
- Use Warm-up/Breaktime Exercise "A" (page 122).

Lesson 2: Choosing Right from Wrong (about 40 minutes)
Refer to pages 123-127 of the Candidate's Handbook.
- *Note:* The lesson should focus on understanding sin as well as on the meaning of conscience and why conscience is the final arbiter in making a moral decision.
- Adapt Choosing Right From Wrong "A" and "C" (pages 125-126) as ways to present the material in the section.
- Play a part of a video that highlights making a moral choice. See Choosing Right From Wrong "F" (page 126). A more current example is *Changing Lanes* (popular release) that focuses on the moral and ethical decisions that result from a car accident. Ask the teens to note how conscience plays a part in the decision-making of the characters involved.

Lesson 3: Our Moral Compass: Jesus, the Commandments, and the Church (about 30 minutes)
Refer to pages 127-136 of the Candidate's Handbook.
- *Note:* This lesson examines major sources for Christian morality: the life and teachings of Jesus (especially the Beatitudes), the Ten Commandments, and Church precepts.
- Use Our Moral Compass: Jesus, the Commandments, and the Church "C" (page 127) to introduce an understanding and practice of living the Beatitudes.

- Use Our Moral Compass: Jesus, the Commandments and the Church "H" (pages 128-129) to further a deeper understanding and practice of the Ten Commandments.
- Assign the teens to work with a partner to memorize the Church precepts (pages 135-136 of the Candidate's Handbook). See also, Moral Compass: Jesus, the Commandments, and the Church "I" (page 129).

Features/Conclusion (about 10 minutes)
- Share some information on St. Maria Goretti and Alessandro Serenelli (see pages 139-141 of the Candidate's Handbook) and Features "A" (page 130).
- Conclude by reciting together with the candidates an Act of Faith or Act of Hope (pages 141-142 the Candidate's Handbook).

Individual Home Assignments
- Have the teens write an essay "What Freedom Means to Me" based on the definition of freedom from the *Catechism of the Catholic Church* (1731-1734).
- Ask the teens to apply the Beatitudes to a current news story. See Our Moral Compass: Jesus, the Commandments, and the Church "D" (page 127).
- Assign several discussion questions from Chapter 6 of the Candidate's Handbook for journal writing.
- Remind the teens to continue working on the "50 Questions" (pages 243-247).

Sponsor/Candidate Activities
- Pass out a set of "Virtues Discussion Questions" (page 133) to each sponsor/candidate pair for discussion.
- Discuss together stories from the news to which the criteria for determining morality can be applied.
- Share and discuss the FAQs, pages 138-139 of the Candidate's Handbook.

MODEL 2: EXTENDED PREPARATION (TWO 1-HOUR SESSIONS)
Suggested Session 1 Plan

Warm-Up (about 10 minutes)
Refer to pages 119-120 of the Candidate's Handbook.
- Introduce the topic of the next two sessions, morality, based on the introductory material in the Candidate's Handbook.
- Use Warm-Up/Breaktime Exercise "B" (page 122).

Lesson: The Morality of Human Acts (about 40 minutes)
Refer to pages 120-123 of the Candidate's Handbook.
- Introduce the relevancy of the object, intentions, and circumstances in making moral decisions.
- Use The Morality of Human Acts "D" (page 124).
- Use The Morality of Human Acts "E" (page 124). *Note:* In the interest of time, have the teens work in small groups. Assign one of the categories listed to each group.

Conclusion/Prayer (about 10 minutes)
Refer to pages 139-142 of the Candidate's Handbook.
- Use Features "C" (page 130).
- Conclude by reciting together the Act of Faith (page 141 of the Candidate's Handbook).

Individual Home Assignments
- Ask the teens to write about a good choice they have recently made and how the "what" question determined that it was indeed good (see The Morality of Human Acts, "D," page 124).
- Ask the candidates to bring the items suggested in Prayer Experience "A" (page 131) to the next session.

Sponsor/Candidate Activities
- Study together the theological virtues, cardinal virtues, Beatitudes, Ten Commandments, and precepts of the Church. Reflect on how each can help us in making moral decisions. Together, apply these helps to a moral decision in the news.
- Assign Our Moral Compass: Jesus, the Commandments, and the Church "G" (page 128). Provide the art materials for the teens to make a simple tassel.

Suggested Session 2 Plan
Lesson: Choosing Right from Wrong (about 25 minutes)
Refer to pages 123-127 of the Candidate's Handbook.
- Use Choosing Right From Wrong "B" (page 125). Display the poster(s) in the meeting room.
- From the material in the Candidate's Handbook, make sure to offer a clear definition of sin and the role of conscience in making a moral decision.
- Use Choosing Right From Wrong "C" (page 125).

Lesson: Our Moral Compass: Jesus, the Commandments, and the Church (about 20 minutes)
Refer to pages 127-136 of the Candidate's Handbook.
- Assign the activity suggested in Our Moral Compass: Jesus, the Commandments, and the Church "A" (page 126).

- Use Our Moral Compass: Jesus, the Commandments, and the Church "B" (pages 126-127). During the time for sharing, have the teens attempt to draw on the moral helps (Jesus, commandments, precepts) in giving their reasoning for making good choices.

Prayer Experience (about 15 minutes)
- Use Prayer Experience "A" (page 131). In addition to the symbols, ask the teens to share the tassels they have made with their sponsors. Where will they put them so that they can serve as reminders of God's commandments?

Individual Assignments
- Use Our Moral Compass: Jesus, the Commandments, and the Church "D" and "E" (page 127).
- Use the assignment suggested in Features "B" (page 130).
- Assign for journal writing some or all of the discussion questions listed in Chapter 6.
- Remind the teens to continue to work on the "50 Questions" (pages 243-247 of the Candidate's Handbook).

Sponsor/Candidate Activities
- Provide the questions in Our Moral Compass: Jesus, the Commandments, and the Church "I" (page 129) as the basis for a conversation between candidate and sponsor.
- Apply the suggestion in Our Moral Compass: Jesus, the Commandments, and the Church "J" (page 129) to a group project with other sponsors and candidates. Arrange for a day to hold and complete the event.

MODEL 3: CONCENTRATED PREPARATION (ONE 90-MINUTE SESSION)
Suggested Session Plan

Warm-Up (about 20 minutes)
Refer to pages 119-120 of the Candidate's Handbook.
- Use Warm-Up/Breaktime Exercise "B" (page 122).
- Introduce the subject of the session, morality, by defining moral life as being responsible for what you do and say, your inaction as well as your action, and the motives for your behavior.

Lesson Plan (about 40 minutes)
Refer to pages 120-127 of the Candidate's Handbook.
- Use The Morality of Human Acts "B" (page 123). Do allow time for a round up of responses to which moral questions are most important to the teens.
- Offer a presentation on what makes a moral human act based on the statement "The morality of a human act depends primarily and fundamentally on the object rationally chosen by the deliberate will."
- Explain how a person's conscience affects a moral decision. Use Choosing Right from Wrong "A" (pages 124-125).
- Present a definition of sin from the Candidate's Handbook. Use The Morality of Human Acts "C" (pages 123-124).
- Ask the candidates to name several helps for making moral decisions. Make sure to list on the board: **Jesus, the Beatitudes, the Commandments, Precepts of the Church.**

Break (about 5 minutes)
- Allow a brief time for a stretch, drink of water, etc.

Lesson Plan continued (about 20 minutes)
Refer to pages 127-136 of the Candidate's Handbook.
- Continue the lesson using Our Moral Compass: Jesus, the Commandments, and the Church "C" (page 127).
- Introduce the Church precepts (pages 135-136 of the Candidate's Handbook). Have the candidates discuss the questions in Our Moral Compass: Jesus, the Commandments, and the Church "I" (page 129) with a partner.

Conclusion/Prayer (about 5 minutes)
- Briefly review the content of the session by referring to some or all of the FAQs (pages 138-139 of the Candidate's Handbook).
- Recite together the Act of Hope (pages 141-142 of the Candidate's Handbook).

Individual Assignments
- Ask the teens to summarize three moral choices cited from a news story including the moral object, the intention of the person(s) making the decision, and the circumstances. In summary, have the teens decide if the moral choice made was good or bad. *Option*: Use Our Moral Compass: Jesus, the Commandments, and the Church "B" (pages 126-127).
- Ask the teens to memorize the Ten Commandments. Check at a future session.
- Assign several of the discussion questions in Chapter 6 for journal writing.
- Assign questions 26-30 of the "50 Questions" (pages 245-246).

Candidate/Sponsor Activities

- Pass out a set of "Virtues Discussion Cards" (page 133) for each candidate to discuss with his or her sponsor.
- Ask the candidates and sponsors to apply the Beatitudes to a current news story. See Our Moral Compass: Jesus, the Commandments, and the Church "D" (page 128).

INTRODUCTION
Warm-up/Breaktime Exercises

A Have the group sit in one large circle. (If the group is larger than twenty, sit in two or more circles.) Place a soda bottle in the middle of the circle for a game of "spin the bottle." In this game, however, the person who spins the bottle must exchange compliments with the person at whom the bottle points. Encourage the teens to be as specific in their compliments as possible and to refrain from compliments on the other person's physical appearance. Instead, compliment the person for who he or she is, how he or she behaves, his or her talents, etc.

B Have the teens respond to a variety of important life issues. Read a statement having to do with an important issue. The teens respond by holding up one to five fingers. Share with them this scale:

- 5 fingers mean you totally agree with the statement
- 4 fingers mean you agree somewhat
- 3 fingers mean you are not sure
- 2 fingers mean you disagree somewhat
- 1 finger means you totally disagree with the statement

Read the following statements one at a time, pausing to allow the teens to hold up their fingers. Give everyone a chance to look at the variety of responses. Then choose a few participants who voted in different ways to explain their responses.

Statements
1. When it comes to war, I believe in "an eye for an eye."
2. If I believe something is right, then it is right.
3. As long as my actions don't hurt anyone else they are morally acceptable.
4. Mortal sin kills my relationship with God.
5. All mortal sins must be confessed in the sacrament of reconciliation.
6. I believe there is a hell.
7. God punishes me when I am bad.
8. Our nation is not morally obliged to share its wealth with any other nation or people.

Add other questions as you wish.

C Give each teen one 8 1/2" x 11" piece of colored construction paper, four small equal-size rectangles of white paper, one triangular piece of white paper, pens, and glue.

Tell the teens they are going to build a "house" with the four rectangles serving as the foundation, the triangle as the roof. The house will represent their lives, with four foundation pieces representing what's most important in their lives.

Ask the teens to print the four most important parts of their own lives, one on each strip (e.g., family, friends, school, work, health, peace, love). Next, have them rank them 1 to 4, placing the most important piece on the bottom as the foundation of the house. When completed, have them glue the rectangles on the construction paper. The triangular roof goes on top with their name.

Allow time for the teens to discuss their foundations for life with a partner or in small groups. Then call on volunteers to name the most important part of their lives. Print their responses on the board and discuss with the entire group.

Extend the exercise by asking the teens to read Matthew 7:24-27. When they have done so, discuss with the teens whether they have built their house on rock or sand.

D Define living a moral life as being responsible for

- what you do and say,
- your inaction as well as your action,
- the motives for your behavior.

Help the teens concretize each of these aspects of the definition with examples from their own lives and the lives of their peers.

Divide the class into small groups. Pass out copies of newspapers, news magazines, and other popular magazines to each group. Have them search for and discuss articles that represent examples of moral and immoral behavior. After time for the small group discussions, call on representatives from each group to share their examples with the entire class.

THE MORALITY OF HUMAN ACTS/ LESSON IDEAS

A Share with the teens a definition of freedom from the *Catechism of the Catholic Church*:

> Freedom is the power, rooted in reason and will, to act or not to act, to do this or that, and so to perform deliberate actions on one's own responsibility. By free will one shapes one's own life. (1731)

Ask the teens to share examples of what freedom might mean to people in the following situations:

- a high school senior about to turn eighteen years old,
- a single mom with three children under age seven,
- a sixty-five-year old man caring for his wife who suffers from Alzheimer's,
- a recent college graduate ready to embark on a career,
- a thirteen-year-old whose parents are out of the house on a Saturday afternoon.

Note the differences in the various examples of freedom discussed above. Then have the participants write a journal entry or brief essay entitled "What Freedom Means to Me."

B Distribute the worksheet "Questions for Right and Wrong" (page 132 of this Manual). Ask the teens to use the scale to mark how important each question is to them when they are making a decision.

When completed, call on the teens to share which question is most important to them in making a moral decision. Write on the board and tally "votes" to determine which question is most helpful to the class.

C Determining the content or matter of a moral decision helps us to determine whether the matter is good or bad. Doing so can usually be accomplished by asking a question of the matter beginning with "what"; for example, "What will we be doing?" or "What is the action involved?"

Actions that fail this question—for example, perjury, rape, lying, murder, or blasphemy—are always wrong, no matter the intentions or circumstances involved.

Share the following scenarios with the teens. Ask them to name the moral object involved, asking a "what" question for each scenario.

- Larry did not have a chance to study for a test so he feigned sickness in order to spend the day at home. (cheating, lying)

- After Grandpa's second heart attack he was told he must give up cigarettes if he hoped to survive. Grandpa continued to smoke, saying "You only live once." (care for personal health related under category of fifth commandment, killing)
- Marge's son had a big report to turn in at school so she took paper and a folder from her work's supply cabinet to give to him. (stealing)

Say, in conclusion, "The morality of a human act depends primarily and fundamentally on the object rationally chosen by the deliberate will."

D Ask each teen to write down a good choice he or she has recently made. For example,
- She visited her grandmother.
- He brought in the neighbor's trash cans.
- He babysat his young niece.
- She studied for her math exam.

The "what" question would determine that each of the above is a good action. Make sure the teens can apply the "what" question to their own examples. Then, ask them to write below the good choice several intentions he or she had for making this choice, the answer to the "why" question ("Why did I do this?").

Call on the teens to share their examples and the intentions. Ask the other participants to comment on whether or not each intention makes the choice more or less good.

E Individually, have the teens create scenarios where a wrong or sinful choice was made under one of the categories of cheating, gossiping, lying, alcohol use, and sex.

Next, have the teens work in pairs to discuss each scenario and to apply the who, where, when, and how questions to show how circumstances cannot make good nor right any action that is evil.

Call on a participant to come before the entire class to be "on the spot." Ask him or her to share the scenario and the answers to the who, where, when, and how questions. Then, ask: "How do the circumstances contribute to increasing or diminishing the good or evil of this particular act?"

Repeat by calling other teens to be "on the spot."

Choosing Right from Wrong/Lesson Ideas

A Help the teens to a deeper understanding of *conscience* and its role in moral decision making. Give a presentation on conscience making the following points:
- A person's conscience must be developed as he or she grows into adulthood. This development comes with an accumulation of and reflection on experience and information. A definition of adult-level conscience can be thought of in three stages.
- First, conscience is a general awareness that there is a difference between right and wrong. This stage does not make a determination about whether a particular act is right or wrong. It simply acknowledges that there is a right and wrong.
- The second stage does involve the judgment of a particular action as morally good or bad. At this stage the person gathers information in order to make the best choice about the action. For example, Catholics consult scripture, Church law, and Church Tradition. They also consult family, friends, and other trusted teachers.

- The third level is the choice itself. An adult-level conscience internalizes what was learned and makes decisions based on them. This is the hardest part of conscience development. A person may know the difference between right and wrong, but can he or she act on it?

With the teens, apply the points on the stages of conscience development to a particular moral decision, e.g., underage drinking, cheating on schoolwork, viewing pornography on the Internet.

B Divide the class into small groups. Give each group several different color markers and a large piece of poster paper. Ask them to discuss, and then print on the paper, several rules or sayings that can help in good decision-making (e.g., "Never talk behind someone's back" or "Settle conflicts peacefully").

When completed, have the groups post their papers on the wall and share some or all of their rules or sayings. Conclude by sharing and discussing three rules that apply to making moral choices in every situation (CCC,1789):
- One may never do evil so that good may result from it;
- the Golden Rule: "Do to others whatever you would have them do to you" (Matthew 7:12);
- love always proceeds by way of respect for one's neighbor and his conscience, i.e., when you sin against someone you wound his or her conscience and you sin against Christ.

C Present several possible reasons for why people sin. Have the participants add reasons of their own to the list. For example:
- "I made a mistake." A person chooses something he or she thought was good, only to find out that the consequences were really bad. With this understanding, review the definition of sin and the differences between a sin and a mistake (see pages 123-125 of the Candidate's Handbook).
- "I chose a lesser good over a greater good." For example, a person cheats on a test to get a good grade (the lesser good), giving up his or her honesty (the greater good). Remind the teens of the rule above that "one may never do evil so that good may result from it."
- "I chose something good for me but bad for you." For example, a fifteen-year-old thinks it's good for him to take his dad's car for a cruise, but it is bad for his dad, the safety of others on the road, etc.
- "I choose something that seems good now but will be bad later." Drinking, drugs, and sex all fit under this type of reasoning.
- "I choose to do something bad just because it is bad." The teens can likely list many examples of peers and adults who seem to chose bad things for this reason. Revenge, blackmail, and gossiping may fit under this category of sinfulness.

In small groups or as part of a class discussion, have the teens come up with the following: 1) a definition of sin; 2) top three reasons why their peer group sins; and 3) what they personally can do about sin in their lives.

D Provide an overview of the theological and cardinal virtues (see also pages 125-127 of the Candidate's Handbook). Print the following names of the virtues on the board and share the following information:

The theological virtues are:
- **Faith.** This is the virtue in which we say "I believe in God and in all that God has revealed to me."
- **Hope.** This is the virtue that responds to our desire for pure and eternal happiness and keeps us from being discouraged during times of loneliness and despair.

Morality

- **Love.** This is the greatest of all virtues and is also called charity. As St. Paul put it, "if I . . . do not have love, I . . . gain nothing" (1 Cor 13:3).

The cardinal virtues are:
- **Prudence.** This is a virtue associated with wisdom or common sense. Prudence is the virtue that guides a good conscience.
- **Justice.** This virtue consists in a person's constant will to treat his or her neighbor fairly.
- **Fortitude.** This virtue is associated with courage to handle the difficulties that arise when one is trying to do good.
- **Temperance.** This moral virtue moderates the attraction of pleasures like food, drink, and sex.

E Have the teens meet in small groups with each small group a fair distance away from the others. The groups should sit on the floor and form a circle. Pass out one set of "Virtues Discussion Questions" (see page 133) to each group. The cards should be cut on the dashed lines and placed in packs. Instruct the groups to: 1) place the cards face down in the center of the circle; 2) designate a person to pick the top card.

Next, the person who chose the card reads it to himself or herself and then decides who in the group should answer the question. The person addresses the question to the one who is chosen. This second person answers the question for the whole group.

The process repeats itself. The person who answered the question picks the second card from the pack, reads it, and asks the question of someone else in the group.

F Show all or part of a classic or current video that highlights moral choice, and the moral virtues. One possibility is *To Kill A Mockingbird*, the famous movie adaptation of Harper Lee's bestseller about a distinguished small town lawyer who risks his career and his life to defend a black farmhand from the charge of raping a white girl. The lawyer battles bigotry in court and takes the time to explain to his children the tremendous significance of the trial.

Our Moral Compass:
Jesus, the Commandments, and the Church/Lesson Ideas

A In small groups, assign the reading of the parable of the Good Samaritan (Lk 10:25-37). Then have each group update the parable using contemporary characters and situations. Allow time for the groups to practice before calling on them to enact their version of the parable before the whole class.

B Ask the teens the question "What are some loving and moral responses?" for each of the following situations (also on page 128 of the Candidate's Handbook) to be completed either individually, with a partner, or in a small group:
- Your friend had her laptop computer stolen. It had her outline and about half of her history research paper on it.
- You got invited to the Homecoming Dance (held after the Friday night football game). Your best friend didn't get asked.
- Your mom has some business to attend to in the school office. On her way across the school grounds she runs into you and some friends of yours she has never met.

- A boy who has been picking on you since grade school has just been assigned to be your lab partner for the semester.
- You find yourself in a grocery line behind a teacher who you believe graded you unfairly in the previous semester.
- The kids at your school all sit together by race in the lunchroom. A new student who is of a race different from you sits down at your lunch table.
- You've invited some friends home after school. When you turn the radio on, an elderly neighbor lady calls you on the phone and says, "Turn it down."
- You are second string on your team. A friend of yours asks your opinion of the first string player who's ahead of you.

Allow time for selected participants to share their responses, their partner's responses, or samplings of their small group's responses to the whole class. Also, have the teens suggest some other situations from their own life that require loving and moral responses (see page 136 of the Candidate's Handbook).

C Related to a study of the Beatitudes, mark a continuum on the floor or wall that covers the entire length of the room using these placards: agree strongly, agree, agree somewhat, disagree, disagree strongly. Then read the following statements. Tell the teens to stand near the place on the continuum that most closely approximates the way they feel about the statement. After everyone is near a place, randomly walk around the room interviewing teens of differing levels of agreement on why they feel as they do.

Statements
- I am dependent on God for all my needs and to fulfill all my dreams.
- I empathize with others who are suffering.
- I try to avoid anger at all costs.
- I believe that good can come from suffering.
- I am bothered by the inequity in the distribution of wealth in the world.
- I could forgive someone who killed one of my family members.
- I am a person of peace.
- I speak up when something is not fair.
- I am up front with people.
- I am not two-faced.
- I believe it is impossible for the world to avoid violence and war.
- I would die for my belief in Jesus Christ.

Have the teens read the two versions of the Beatitudes (Mt 5:3-12 and Lk 6:20-23), compare the differences, and list something they learn from the margin notes in scripture on the reasons for the different versions.

D Have the teens apply the Beatitudes to a current news story. Ask them to answer the question: "What do the Beatitudes suggest would be a proper response to this issue?"

E Watch Jesus' preaching of the Sermon on the Mount from the *Jesus of Nazareth* series video, tape 8 (Franco Zeffirelli, popular release).

F Ask the teens to pair up with a partner and practice memorizing the Ten Commandments using the exact wording found below and on pages 131-134 of the Candidate's Handbook.

Morality

The Ten Commandments

    I. I, the Lord am your God. You shall not have other gods besides me.

    II. You shall not take the name of the Lord, your God, in vain.

    III. Remember to keep holy the Sabbath day.

    IV. Honor your father and your mother.

    V. You shall not kill.

    VI. You shall not commit adultery.

    VII. You shall not steal.

    VIII. You shall not bear false witness against your neighbor.

    IX. You shall not covet your neighbor's wife.

    X. You shall not covet your neighbor's goods.

When both partners have memorized the Ten Commandments, have them form two parallel lines, facing each other. As other pairs finish, have them join either line facing their partner.

After everyone has memorized the Commandments, have the first person in line 1 recite the first commandment. If said exactly right, the first player in line 2 recites the second commandment, then the second player in line 1 recites the third commandment, and so on. With an incorrect response, the very next person in the opposite line begins again with the first commandment.

Continue until the class has said the entire Ten Commandments perfectly once or more than once.

G Read Numbers 15:37-41 to the teens. The passage quotes the Lord speaking to Moses and telling them to put tassels on the corner of their garments, and fastening them with a violet cord to remind them to keep all the commandments.

Have the teens make a simple tassel. Arts and crafts stores can provide simple tassel kits and instructions. Or, simply have the teens tie two or three different colors of 12" strips of yarn together on one end and "weave" them to the bottom before tying them off. Encourage them to use their tassels bookmarks for their bibles or to put them some place as a reminder to keep God's commandments (e.g., their locker, their backpack, etc.).

H Call on one teen to come before the class and be interviewed with questions related to applying the Ten Commandments in day-to-day living. Ask the teen one or two of the following questions. Then call on another teen to answer the same or different questions.

Questions

- How do the Ten Commandments play a part in your moral decision-making? Give an example.
- What are some other gods you have been tempted to worship in your life?
- How do you respond when someone around you uses God's name in vain?
- Describe behavior you consider appropriate and inappropriate for Sunday.
- How do you honor your parents now? How do you think you will honor them when you are an adult?
- How strong is the commitment to save sex until marriage among your peers?
- How does society promote an attitude of disrespect for the body and for sexual behavior?
- When was a time you told a lie that did damage to another person? How did you repair that damage?
- What does it mean to dress modestly?
- How is cheating in school an offense against the seventh commandment?

- How can you practice loyalty and commitment in relationships now to help you prepare for the same when and if you are married?

I Ask the teens to read the information on the Church precepts (pages 134-136 in the Candidate's Handbook). Then have them close their books and write the five laws from memory. Check for accuracy. Then, discuss with the participants the following questions or ask them to write their answers in their journals:

1. What are some ways to spend Sunday in addition to going to Mass?
2. When do you regularly go to confession?
3. What does it mean to be in a "state of grace"?
4. What are the holy days of obligation in the United States?
5. What are the days Catholics are required to fast and abstain from certain types of food?

J Ask the teens to brainstorm ways they can support their parish with gifts of time, talent, and money. Use one of the suggestions for raising money (e.g., car wash, bake sale, etc.) as part of a spontaneous way for the teens to make a monetary gift to the parish or to one of the parish charities. Or use one of the suggestions for using time and talent as a group (e.g., a "clean up" day of the parish grounds; offering teens' help with painting part of the parish building, inside or out; providing free child care at an important parish event, etc.).

REFERENCES/FAQ

References from the *Catechism of the Catholic Church* for the Frequently Asked Questions include:

What is grace? (CCC, 1996-2005)
Grace is God's favor to us. It is the free and undeserved help that God gives to us so that we can respond to him and share in his friendship and eternal life. Grace is a participation in the life of God.

Are Christians always obliged to obey civil law and authorities? (CCC, 1902-1903)
Christians must obey their upright conscience in all matters. If civil law and authorities are opposed to the teachings of the gospel, the fundamental rights of persons, and the moral law, then a Christian must in good conscience disobey the civil law or authorities.

How far can I go sexually? (CCC, 2337-2350)
It's important to remember that God intends sexual intercourse for marriage. It is also important to note that sex is a progressive experience. Open-mouthed kissing, any type of petting, or intimate touching of another's private parts are part of the natural progression to intercourse and should be reserved for marriage. Before marriage, it is best to limit yourself to hugs, light kissing, and hand holding.

Is masturbation a sin? (CCC, 2352)
Again, sexual pleasure sought outside of marriage is opposed to Church teaching and is "an intrinsically and gravely distorted action." Sexual activity is meant to be relational, within the context of marriage. If a person willingly masturbates contrary to God's law, the conditions are present for it to be a mortal sin. Other factors can lessen a person's culpability: for example, immaturity, force of acquired habit, anxiety, or other psychological or social factors.

How can I tell if I made the right decision in the area of morality? (CCC, 1776-1794; 1801).
If your conscience has been well formed through study of scripture, prayer, an examination of conscience, and you have been assisted by the gifts of the Holy Spirit and the witness and advice of others, including the authoritative teaching of the Church, and you do *not* follow your conscience, you will often experience guilt. In this case, guilt can be productive. It reminds you of what you know to be right. Also, some rules of morality apply to every decision that you make: evil may never be done to produce a good result, the Golden Rule ("do to others as you wish done to you") always applies, and loving decisions always involve showing respect for others.

FEATURES/LESSON IDEAS

A Play all or part of the video *St. Maria Goretti: Fourteen Flowers of Pardon* (60 minutes; available from Vision Video catalog). It tells the story of the life and death of Maria Goretti and her forgiveness of Alessandro Serenelli. It includes historic photographs, interviews with Maria's mother, and film footage of the canonization ceremony.

B Assign more reading about Allesandro Serenelli and Maria Goretti from www.mariagoretti.org.

C Present a lesson on chastity, drawing especially from material in the *Catechism of the Catholic Church*, #2331-2359.

D Organize the teens into small groups. Ask them to develop, rehearse, and present a public service announcement for teens that encourages them to remain chaste.

E Read or have the teens read John 14:6-7 (see page 141 of the Candidate's Handbook). Ask them to reflect and then write a list of ten personal pledge statements for their lives that they will attempt to enact to be more like God the Father.

PRAYER EXPERIENCES

A Ask the teens to bring three items to class that symbolize 1) something they have faith in, 2) something they hope for, and 3) something they love. The items could be photos, letters, valuable possessions, or any other things the teens can explain.

Place the items randomly on a table.

Begin by praying together the "Act of Faith" (see pages 141-142 of the Candidate's Handbook for the Acts of Faith, Hope, and Love). Then call on teens to randomly show and explain their item that symbolizes something (or someone) they have faith in.

Continue in the same way, praying and sharing the Act of Hope and Act of Love.

B Remind the participants that love is the greatest of all virtues. It is the virtue that lasts when faith gives way to sight and hope gives way to possession; it lasts forever, into eternity.

Share a personal story about love, focusing on your love for another person, a person's love for you, or God's love for you.

Create a large poster from a piece of newsprint with the words "Love is . . ." printed in the middle in marker. Leave several markers near the poster. Play a song with lyrics that speak in a positive, Christian way of love. While the song is playing, have the teens move freely to the poster and print one or two adjectives that describe love for them.

After the song has ended, gather the teens near the poster. Stand in silent reflection for at least two minutes. Then, conclude by having the teens recite together the Act of Love (page 142 of the Candidate's Handbook).

NAME _____

QUESTIONS FOR RIGHT AND WRONG

Directions: For each question, circle the number that indicates how often you use it to help you make a moral decision.

4=most of the time
3=sometimes
2=rarely
1=never

1.	How will it look?	1	2	3	4
2.	What would Jesus do?	1	2	3	4
3.	What's in it for me?	1	2	3	4
4.	What would my mother say?	1	2	3	4
5.	What is the right thing to do?	1	2	3	4
6.	Will I get caught?	1	2	3	4
7.	What is everyone else doing?	1	2	3	4
8.	Is there a law against it?	1	2	3	4
9.	How would I like to be treated?	1	2	3	4
10.	What should I do?	1	2	3	4
11.	How much is it worth?	1	2	3	4
12.	What will I get out of it?	1	2	3	4
13.	Do I have to do it?	1	2	3	4
14.	Who will know if I don't do it?	1	2	3	4
15.	What do the commandments say?	1	2	3	4

NAME _____

VIRTUES DISCUSSION QUESTIONS

1. What do you do when you hear someone gossiping?

2. Tell about your plan for life.

3. Name and describe someone you would count as wise.

4. Tell about a lesson you learned from a past mistake.

5. When was a time you were treated unfairly?

6. How do you show respect for the rights of others?

7. What does it mean to give someone his or her "rightful due"?

8. If others were to describe your "reputation" how would that sound?

9. Tell about a time you gave someone else the benefit of the doubt.

10. Tell about someone who treated you fairly.

11. Describe a person you know who has courage.

12. What is the most difficult challenge you face in the area of peer pressure?

13. Tell about one of your fears.

14. When was a time you faced a problem without running away from it?

15. How can the virtue of temperance help you in one area of your life?

16. Tell about a time you accepted delayed over instant gratification.

17. Why will faith and hope be unnecessary in heaven?

18. What is something you hope for?

19. Why is love the virtue that lasts into eternity?

20. What do you believe in more than anything else?

Social Justice

(see pages 145-163 of the Candidate's Handbook)

BACKGROUND

Catholic social justice involves the body of doctrine that attempts to understand how societies work and what moral principles and values ought to guide them. This social doctrine of the Church developed in the nineteenth century—it was a gospel response to the many economic, labor, and social issues brought about by the Industrial Revolution. The texts of Catholic social doctrine began with the writings of Pope Leo XIII and have continually been developed from council documents and various letters and statements of Popes and bishops to the present.

To put it simply, Catholic teaching on social justice is a body of doctrine the Church has developed, with the Holy Spirit's guidance, to apply the gospel of Jesus Christ to all the conditions of human life. It is rooted in the communal and social nature of God, who is a Trinity of persons, Father, Son, and Spirit. Likewise, we are God's family who live in community.

As the *Catechism of the Catholic Church* teaches, the Church's social teaching has three aspects:

1. It proposes principles for reflection.
2. It provides criteria for judgment.
3. It gives guidelines for action.

It is important for teenagers to learn the principles, criteria, and guidelines of Catholic social justice because at Confirmation, they are called to be a witness of the gospel to all the world.

The 1998 document *Sharing Catholic Social Teaching: Challenges and Directions—Reflections of the U.S. Catholic Bishops* highlights seven principles of Catholic social teaching: the life and dignity of the human person, family/community participation, the balance of rights and responsibilities, the preferential option for the poor, work and workers, solidarity, and stewardship. While one chapter is much too short to cover all of these principles, it does provide an opportunity to focus on the first and main principle: the right to life and its connection with human dignity. Under separate headings, the chapter also covers the preferential option for the poor, prejudice and racism, consumerism, the environment, and violence versus nonviolence.

Finally, the chapter provides a starting point for the third aspect—guidelines for action—asking the teens specifically, "What can you do?" in this area, especially as they continue to prepare for the sacrament of Confirmation. For more information on this practical aspect of Christian stewardship, refer to the United States Bishop's 1992 Pastoral Letter, *Stewardship: A Disciple's Response*. This document defines discipleship and names some of its implications.

Sample Schedules

Model I: Focused Preparation (one 3-hour session)
Suggested Session Plan

Warm-Up (about 20 minutes)
Refer to pages 145-146 of the Candidate's Handbook.
- *Note:* This session may be combined with a Christian service project undertaken by those preparing for Confirmation.
- Introduce the main topic of the session, social justice, from the introductory material in the Candidate's Handbook. Pay special attention to the major themes of *Sharing Catholic Social Teaching: Challenges and Directions—Reflections of the U.S. Bishops.* See Warm-Up/Breaktime Exercise "A" (page 142).
- Adapt Warm-Up/Breaktime Exercise "B" (page 142) to fit the opening of the session. If you are not able to have the teens actually participate in one of the social/service projects described, spend some time reviewing with them service project requirements for your Confirmation program and checking on the progress they are making towards completion.

Lesson 1: The Right to Life (about 60 minutes)
Refer to pages 146-149 of the Candidate's Handbook.
- Begin a discussion on the "right to life." Use The Right to Life "A" (page 142).
- Continue with a focus on the topic of sexuality. Lead a discussion on the desirability of saving sex until marriage. See The Right to Life "C" (page 143).
- Show the video *Sex, Lies, and Truth* (30 minutes). See The Right to Life "D" (page 143) for more information.

Breaktime/Lesson 1 continued (about 30 minutes)
- Use The Right to Life "E" (page 144). Adapt this "peaceful demonstration" to fit the time and setting of the session. It is optimal that the event be staged during the day. Make sure to arrange for poster materials the candidates can use to proclaim pro-life messages.

Lesson 2: Human Dignity (about 30 minutes)
Refer to pages 150-154 of the Candidate's Handbook.
- Focus the lesson on the issues of poverty, prejudice, and racism.
- Use Human Dignity "A" (page 144).
- Use Human Dignity "C" (pages 144-145).
- After defining and differentiating between prejudice and racism, have the teens complete preparation and demonstration of the exercise suggested in Human Dignity "E" (page 145).

Lesson 3: Other Social Justice Issues (about 20 minutes)
Refer to pages 154-157 of the Candidate's Handbook.
- Focus on defining as many of the social justice issues as possible in this section of the Candidate's Handbook.
- Use Other Social Justice Issues "A" (pages 145-146).

Lesson 3 continued/Prayer Experience (about 20 minutes)
- Adapt a nature walk (see Other Social Justice Issues "C," page 146) to fit your setting and the time you have available. While on the walk, pause to do one of the following: 1) read and

reflect on God's Grandeur (see page 151) or pray the World Peace Prayer (page 162 of the Candidate's Handbook).

Individual Assignments

- Ask the teens to explore the Catholic Campaign for Human Development web site for ideas to fight poverty. Ask them to choose and participate in one of the ideas and report on what they are doing. (See Human Dignity "B," page 144).
- Have the teens write a progress report on the Christian service project(s) they are involved in. Make sure to remind them of completion dates for the projects that may come before reception of Confirmation.
- Continue having the teens work on relevant questions from the "50 Questions" pages 243-247. Questions 36-40 relate directly to this chapter.

Candidate/Sponsor Activities

- Work together on the resource "Areas of Responsibility" (page 150). See The Right to Life "B," (page 143).
- Have the candidates name and discuss their goals in the areas of vocation, education, career and family (see The Right to Life "F," page 144).
- Watch a video together that depicts the struggles related to racism and prejudice.
- Discuss and comment on the issues raised by the FAQs (pages 158-159).

MODEL 2: EXTENDED PREPARATION (TWO 1-HOUR SESSIONS)
Suggested Session 1 Plan

Warm-Up (about 10 minutes)
Refer to pages 145-146 of the Candidate's Handbook.
- Introduce the topic of the next two sessions, social justice, based on the introductory material in the Candidate's Handbook.
- Use Warm-Up/Breaktime Exercise "C" (page 142).

Lesson: The Right to Life (about 40 minutes)
Refer to pages 146-149 of the Candidate's Handbook.
- Connect the discussion on inalienable human rights to the basic right of humans to life itself.
- Use The Right to Life "A" (page 142).
- Expand on the right to life to include other human rights. Use The Right to Life "B" (page 143).
- Arrange for each candidate to have a copy of Pope John XXIII's *Peace on Earth* encyclical. Have the teens work alone to complete the assignment in The Right to Life "G" (page 144).

Conclusion/Prayer (about 10 minutes)
Refer to pages 159-162 of the Candidate's Handbook.
- Use Features "D" (page 148). In re-examining the teens' work in the area of Christian service, consider planning a group project that can be enacted outside of one of the two Social Justice sessions.
- Recite together the prayer of Mother Teresa (page 162 of the Candidate's Handbook).

Individual Home Assignments
- Ask the candidates to visit the web site suggested in The Right to Life "H" (page 144) of this Manual and report on one concrete activity they can participate in to promote social justice that they gleaned from the site.
- Assign the teens to research the right to life issue related to abortion and write short essay answers to the first two questions on page 149 of the Candidate's Handbook.
- Continue assigning completion of questions from the "50 Questions" (pages 243-247).

Candidate/Sponsor Activities
- Encourage the candidates to do a community outreach service project, ideally separate from a long-term project the candidate has been working on. Refer again to The Right to Life "H" (page 144) and also the list of sample projects on pages 237-241 of the Candidate's Handbook.
- Discuss together the questions on family life from Warm-up/Breaktime Exercise "A" (page 142).

Suggested Session 2 Plan

Lesson: Human Dignity (about 35 minutes)
Refer to pages 150-154 of the Candidate's Handbook.
- Use Human Dignity "A" and "B" (page 144) in combination. After the teens complete the "family of four exercise," present several directives and suggestions for combating poverty from the U.S. Bishop's *Economic Justice for All.*
- Use Human Dignity "D" (page 145).

- Play all or part of a video depicting the struggles against racism. See Human Dignity "F" (page 145).

Breaktime/Lesson: Other Social Justice Issues (about 10 minutes)
- Pass out the resource "God's Grandeur" (page 151). Have the teens practice a dramatic reading (see Other Social Justice Issues "B," page 146).
- Allow a chance for a brief stretch and restroom break.

Lesson: Other Social Justice Issues continued/Prayer (about 15 minutes)
Refer to pages 154-157 of the Candidate's Handbook.
- Call on two teen volunteers to present their personal interpretations of God's Grandeur. Follow up by touching on some of the environmental issues mentioned in this section of the Candidate's Handbook.
- Briefly introduce the subject of conflicts and conflict resolution (see Other Social Justice Issues "F," page 146). Have the teens copy the list of common conflicts named into their journals.
- Pray together the World Peace Prayer (page 162 of the Candidate's Handbook).

Individual Home Assignments
- Have the teens write in their journals peaceful ways to resolve the common conflicts listed during the session.
- Ask the teens to outline a social justice program for themselves that will extend past their time of Confirmation preparation (see page 157 of the Candidate's Handbook).
- Have the teens read and report on the Catholic Heart Workcamp (see Features "B" page 148).

Candidate/Sponsor Activities
- Ask the teens to share their interpretation of God's Grandeur (page 151) with their sponsors.
- Assign Features "C" (page 148). Ask both candidates and sponsors to suggest a counterpoint to the list. Allow time at a future session for the sharing of ideas.
- Review together the FAQs (pages 158-159) and research additional responses from the *Catechism of the Catholic Church*.

MODEL 3: CONCENTRATED PREPARATION (ONE 90-MINUTE SESSION)
Suggested Session Plan

Warm-Up (at least 25 minutes)
Refer to pages 145-146 of the Candidate's Handbook.
- Adapt Warm-Up/Breaktime Exercise "B" (page 142) to fit the context of the session. (If you have been able to conduct the session in connection with a service project, make the service project itself and its follow up the featured part of the session.) In lieu of the actual participation in the project, lead a discussion of 1) the candidate's ongoing service projects and 2) the development of a plan to continue with service and outreach after receiving the sacrament of Confirmation.
- Use Warm-Up/Breaktime Exercise "C" (page 142).

Lesson Plan (about 30 minutes)
Refer to pages 146-154 of the Candidate's Handbook.
- For the Right to Life section of the Candidate's Handbook, focus the presentation on the basic right to human life and how the topic of sexuality relates to that basic right (see The Right to Life "C" page 143).
- Arrange for a speaker from the National Right to Life (or similar local agency) to speak with the teens about issues like abortion, adoption, and chastity. Also, encourage the speaker to present ways the teens can offer their support to the Right to Life cause.

Breaktime (about 5 minutes)
- Allow a brief time for a stretch, drink, or bathroom break.

Lesson Plan continued (about 15 minutes)
Refer to pages 154-157 of the Candidate's Handbook.
- Focus on the issue of peace and the qualifications that make up the traditional just war argument of the Church.
- Use Other Social Justice Issues "E" and "F" (page 146).

Prayer Experience (about 15 minutes)
Refer to page 162 of the Candidate's Handbook.
- Related to the theme of peace, use Prayer Experience "A" (page 148).

Individual Home Assignments
- Ask the teens to peruse the National Right to Life website (see The Right to Life "H," page 144) and write a proposal for completing a related project.
- In the same way, have the students name a recycling project they can participate in (see Other Social Justice Issues, "D," page 146).
- Have the teens continue working on the "50 Questions" assignment (pages 243-247).

Candidate/Sponsor Activities
- Provide two copies of the resource "Areas of Responsibility" (page 150). Have the candidates answer individually and then discuss their responses (see The Right to Life "B," page 143).

- Work together to memorize the corporal and spiritual works of mercy (see Human Dignity, "C," page 144-145). The lists also appear in the Candidate's Handbook on page 152 (see Other Social Justice Issues "B," page 146).
- Take a nature walk together. Stop and reflect on Hopkins' *God's Grandeur* (page 151).
- Adapt Features "C" (page 148).

INTRODUCTION

Warm-up/Breaktime Exercise

A Begin a discussion on family values. Point out that families teach healthy values by acting kindly to one another, sharing responsibilities, respecting one another's individuality, and showing affection for one another. Families promote unhealthy behaviors with their indifference, hostilities, and lack of communication.

Call on the teens to write their answers to each of the following questions:
1. What is my parents' most important rule for me?
2. What does my family value most?
3. What is the best advice ever given to me by one of my parents?

Ask the teens to break out with a partner and discuss their responses to each question. Then call on any teen who wishes to share a response before the whole group to do so.

B Conduct this session, or at least the opening of the session, as part of a class social/service project. For example, the teens might begin a 24-hour fast at the session, prepare and provide meals for the homebound or a homeless shelter, or offer a "free garage sale" in which they collect items with all donations being handed over to a community agency that supports the poor. For other service ideas, see pages 237-241 of the Candidate's Handbook.

C Share this dictionary definition of *rights*: "something that is due to a person by law, tradition, or nature." A right is a claim a person can make on others and on society to achieve goals consistent with being a free, thinking person.

Ask the teens to brainstorm a list of what they consider to be inalienable human rights.

The Right to Life/Lesson Ideas

A Share with the teens the major themes of the 1998 document *Sharing Catholic Social Teaching: Challenges and Directions—Reflections of the U.S. Bishops.* They are:
- Life and Dignity of the Human Person
- Call to Family, Community, and Participation
- Rights and Responsibilities
- Option for the Poor and Vulnerable
- The Dignity of Work and the Rights of Workers
- Solidarity
- Care for God's Creation

Provide background information on these principles from http://www.nccbuscc.org/sdwp/projects/socialteaching/socialteaching.htm#themes. This site includes the entire document.

Also, reference the U.S. Bishop's document *Disciples as Stewards.* Share these main implications of stewardship as outlined by the document:
- Mature disciples make a conscious decision to follow Jesus, no matter what the cost.
- Christian disciples experience conversion, life-shaping changes of mind and heart and commit their very selves to the Lord.

- Christian stewards respond in a particular way to the call to be a disciple. Stewardship has the power to shape and mold our understanding of our lives and the way in which we live.
- Jesus' disciples and Christian stewards recognize God as the origin of life, giver of freedom, and source of all things.

B Ask the participants to name the various responsibilities that go along with the following human rights (see the list of rights on pages 148-149 of the Candidate's Handbook). For example,
- *Right to Private Property.* (respecting the property of others; caring for your own possessions; working to earn money to purchase possessions)
- *Right to Emigrate and Immigrate.* (welcoming immigrants; learning and accepting the culture and ways of your new home)
- *Right to Participate in the Political System.* (voting; supporting candidates who reflect your values and beliefs; running for office)
- *Right to One's Reputation.* (acting morally; not gossiping about others)
- *Right to Choose One's Own State in Life.* (working honestly to achieve goals; choosing a state in life that is good and moral; contributing to one's own family)
- *Right to Worship God.* (pray; go to Church; support the Church; respect others' right to worship in their own way)

Pass out the worksheet "Areas of Responsibility" (page 150). Ask the teens to write one name or key word in each box. Then, in small groups or with the entire group, go around and have them talk about what kind of responsibility they have in each of these areas and how much time, energy, and care they spend on it.

C The topic of sexuality and decisions related to teens and sex is one that demands much more than a short lesson. *Sex and the Teenager* by Sr. Kieran Sawyer (Ave Maria Press, 1999) offers a complete course on teens and sexuality. The following material is taken from that text. Ask the teens to name several reasons why saving sex until marriage is the good and right decision. Then share these others:

After marriage,
- the choice to be sexually intimate has been carefully thought through,
- the rights of both parties have been taken into consideration,
- both are prepared to accept the responsibility for a child who might be conceived, and to welcome that child with love,
- sex is an expression of the couple's commitment to one another and to a real-love relationship,
- their life together is central to the long-range goals of both,
- sexual intimacy is even a kind of sacrament—a deep religious experience that helps the couple get closer to God.

D Choose and play one of the following videos covering the subjects of chastity and pro-life:

Pro-Life Doctors Speak Out (American Portrait Films, www.amport.com/prolife.htm, 17 minutes). Excellent presentation on the medical facts on abortion given by three leading pro-life doctors.

Sex, Lies, and Truth (Focus on the Family, www.family.org 30 minutes). Looks at the price paid by having sex outside of marriage. There are two versions of this video. The Christian version includes personal testimony on how faith has helped well-known personalities remain chaste.

Teens and Chastity (The Center for Learning, www.centerforlearning.org, 43 minutes). Well-known chastity educator Molly Kelly speaks on issues of teen pregnancy, AIDS, the myth of safe sex, and the rewards of chastity.

Social Justice

E Arrange for a peaceful demonstration for the right to life. Gather with the teens at a busy street corner to call attention to the pro-life message. The teens should space themselves in both directions of the intersection in the shape of a cross. Each teen can create a poster with a pro-life message that drivers can read while passing by. *Optional*: Spend some time promoting this event and invite others in the parish and community to join the teens in forming the "sidewalk cross for life."

F Ask the teens to write five goals for their lives in areas like vocation, education, career, and family. For each goal have them write one thing they can do now to prepare for those goals.

G Have the teens read Pope John XXIII's encyclical "Peace on Earth" ("Pacem in Terris") at: http://www.vatican.va/holy_father/john_xxiii/encyclicals/documents/hf_j-xxiii_enc_11041963_pacem_en.html.

Ask each person to list one right mentioned in the encyclical that is not included on pages 148-149 of the Candidate's Handbook and to write one responsibility that corresponds with that right.

H The National Right to Life Committee has a teen organization (National Teens for Life). It offers activities that train and involve its members in speaking in schools and to youth groups, volunteering in crisis pregnancy centers, peer counseling, debating, and helping adult Right-to Life members work to pass pro-life legislation. An annual National Teens for Life convention is held in the summer months. For more information, see www.nrlc.org/outreach/teens.html.

HUMAN DIGNITY/LESSON IDEAS

A Present the teens with this scenario: a family of four (two parents, two school-age children) makes $2,050 in monthly income (after taxes). Assign the teens to develop a monthly budget for the family that includes the following expenses: housing, utilities, phone, health insurance, food, clothing, education, recreation, and other (teens designate). The teens may work individually on the exercise or in a small group. *Optional*: Pass out newspaper classifieds on rental costs to the teens so that they can complete the assignment for their own neighborhood or region. Call on volunteers to share final budgets and reflections on the exercise.

B The 1986 United States Bishops' letter *Economic Justice for All* offers several suggestions and the following specific directives to help fight poverty, enhance human dignity, and increase participation by all in the economic life. They are:
1. The well off must change their attitudes to the poor.
2. We must support full and equal employment as well as a just wage.
3. Society must empower the poor to help themselves.

The Catholic Campaign for Human Development (http://www.usccb.org/cchd/youth.htm) has a special section devoted to ways youth can participate in the anti-poverty campaign sponsored by the United States bishops. One of the annual events is an essay contest for youth that asks them to address the condition of poverty along with possible solutions. Share this information with the teens.

C Play a memorization game to help the teens remember both the corporal and spiritual works of mercy. Divide the class into groups of seven. Give each person a number, 1 to 7. Have them work to recite the corporal works of mercy in the following order, each person saying one work:
1. Feed the hungry.
2. Give drink to the thirsty.

3. Clothe the naked.
4. Visit the imprisoned.
5. Shelter the homeless.
6. Visit the sick.
7. Bury the dead.

Ask the teens to rearrange themselves into new groups, making sure each group has a person for numbers 1 to 7. Call on the new groups to recite the corporal works of mercy in order. Finally, ask volunteers to recite all seven corporal works of mercy in front of the class.

Repeat the exercise for the spiritual works of mercy in the following order:
1. Counsel the doubtful.
2. Instruct the ignorant.
3. Admonish sinners.
4. Comfort the afflicted.
5. Forgive offenses.
6. Bear wrongs patiently.
7. Pray for the living and the dead.

To follow-up, ask the teens to suggest a plan to put each of the works of mercy into practice.

D Define prejudice and racism. Prejudice is a prejudgment based on insufficient data. It is a favorable or unfavorable feeling toward a person or thing prior to, or not based on, actual fact or experience. Racism is a particularly evil form of prejudice. It is a belief that one race or ethnic group is superior to another.

E In small groups, have the teens develop role plays that depict typical situations of prejudice and racism that they and their peers face (e.g., parents protest mix-race dating, students of different races sit in opposite areas of the school lunchroom, players of different races participate together on the same athletic teams). Also include peaceful ways to resolve the situation.

F Show a video related to the struggles of the Civil Rights movement of the 1960s in the United States. An excellent choice is the biography of Martin Luther King Jr. from the *A&E* network's Biography series. It is available through www.amazon.com. *Optional*: Invite a person from the community who grew up in a time marked by racism to give a short presentation detailing society's and his or her own changing attitudes from that time on.

OTHER SOCIAL JUSTICE ISSUES/LESSON IDEAS

A Divide the teens into pairs. Give each person five strips of scrap paper. Tell them to number the strips on one side of the paper from 1 to 5. Then, ask them to write their five most important possessions (not including family members, but pets are okay to name) on the opposite side, one per sheet. They should do this silently, then place the scraps face down with numbers showing on the floor or table.

Facing each other, tell the teens to take the number 5 scrap from their partner's pile. Ask the teens to imagine that this possession has really been taken away from them and to discuss with their partners:
• why this possession is important to them,
• how they feel about having it taken away,
• how they will be able to get along without it in the future.

Repeat the same process for items 1 to 4.

Finally, ask the teens to discuss the consumer practices of society, their community, and family, and to name ways they can work toward a style of life more directed to "being" than "having."

B Pass out the resource "God's Grandeur" (page 151) which is a copy of the poem by Gerard Manley Hopkins. Ask the teens to read the poem reflectively and then practice a dramatic reading in their own interpretation. Call on volunteers to share their dramatic reading with the class.

To follow-up, read the first creation story (Gn 1:1–2:4) aloud to the teens. Chart the progression of creation from the story: light, sea/sky, land/vegetation, sun/moon/stars, animals, humans. Remind the class that humans are God's ultimate creation, and that humans are to have "dominion" over creation. Discuss this concept. Point out that dominion is more in line with stewardship than power.

C Take the class on a "nature walk." This walk can take place close to where you regularly hold your class or in a place more typical of nature like a park, forest, shoreline, or mountain trail. Conduct the walk in silence but allow the teens the opportunity to pause and do one of the following: write in their journal, take photos, sketch a scene. If the walk is in an urban area, call on the teens to take note of the signs of the God's world that are still present: the sky, clouds, grass, insects, birds, wind, water, etc.

D View the Sierra Club web page (www.sierraclub.org) for many stewardship ideas, including recycling projects. One that you might be able to begin during a class period is the recycling of small batteries. Send the participants out in the neighborhood in pairs or small groups to knock on doors and ask neighbors for their old batteries of all sizes. Reward winners (most total batteries, most AA batteries, etc.) with a small prize. The Sierra Club lists recycling outlets for collected batteries.

E Share the conditions for a just war with the teens from the resource on page 152. Ask them to apply these conditions to the war on terrorism declared by the United States in 2001 or to another war from history and to report on their findings.

F Ask the teens to share common conflicts they or their peers face in daily life. With the large group, brainstorm ways each of these conflicts can be handled peacefully.

G Note the third assignment on page 157 of the Candidate's Handbook. Work with the class, small groups, or individuals to develop constructive service projects in the spirit of those mentioned in the Candidate's Handbook. *Optional*: Invite older teens who were recently confirmed to share service projects they worked on, including how they prepared and the benefits they received from working on that project.

References/FAQ

References from the *Catechism of the Catholic Church* for the Frequently Asked Questions include:

Why shouldn't we have the right to choose how and when we die? (CCC, 2258-2269, 2276-2277)
Death is not a right. Death claims us; we do not claim death. Only God has absolute control over life and death. We have the responsibility to preserve and care for life. Suicide and euthanasia are contrary to this duty.

If the Bible permits justice in terms of "an eye for an eye," then why is the Church opposed to capital punishment?(CCC, 2266-2267)
Jesus himself ruled out revenge as a motive for punishing those who commit crime. The Church speaks out against the death penalty because of its respect for life, even the life of a convicted criminal. Opposing the death penalty helps testify to the dignity of humanity and tells society we can break the cycle of violence. By keeping the criminal imprisoned, the person is not only kept from doing harm to others, he or she keeps the possibility of redeeming himself or herself. Finally, traditional Church teaching does not exclude recourse to the death penalty if it is the only possible way of protecting society against the criminal.

Many people say, "I am opposed to abortion except in the case of rape and incest." Why is this not an acceptable stance according to Church teaching?(CCC, 2270-2275)
Crimes like rape and incest are always tragic to the women victimized. However, a child conceived in such a situation did not commit the crime and bears no guilt. Life remains a greater good in this situation than death. Committing a second wrong would not make this right. A better option in this rare but sad situation would be adoption.

Why are some people so prejudiced?(CCC, 2223-2224, 2227)
Psychological studies reveal that no one is born prejudiced. They also reveal that the home is the main place for learning prejudice. Parents pass on their own prejudices to their children. Schools, neighborhoods, and church groups can also be places where prejudices are reinforced.

What is affirmative action? Where does the Church stand on it?(CCC, 1935, 2433)
Affirmative action programs are set up to correct past discrimination against minorities and women by setting quotas for things like admission to college or hiring for certain jobs. The American bishops have supported the idea of affirmative action programs when the effects of past institutional discrimination persist.

Can rich people go to heaven? (CCC, 2544-2547)
Yes, Jesus came to save everyone, though he did say that it is difficult for rich people to enter the kingdom of heaven. The key issue is not whether or not a person is rich, but whether or not he or she is greedy. The rich person who counteracts greed by serving the poor and treating the poor as "another self" accomplishes much. Of course, it's important to remember that who is saved and who is not saved is entirely up to God.

Features/Lesson Ideas

A Play the video "Voices of Appalachia" (52 minutes, available from Focus on the Family). It is a documentary of life in Appalachia, tracing the lives of a high school senior, a factory worker, a former battered wife, and a couple struggling to purchase their own home amidst the poverty of the area.

B Read and share more information on the Catholic Heart Workcamp from www.heartworkcamp.com. Also included on the web page is information on how your parish can participate in this service experience along with testimonials from many teens who have already participated.

C After reading the feature "How to Ruin Your Children" (pages 160-161 of the Candidate's Handbook), have the teens rewrite the list under the title of "How to Benefit Your Children" with positive statements related to each of the items.

D Re-examine with the teens the "Sample Service Project Ideas" on pages 237-241 the Candidate's Handbook. Encourage the teens to work individually or in groups on a new project they have not yet considered.

Prayer Experiences

A Give each person a blank sheet of paper and a marker or pen. Ask them to draw a small circle in the middle of the paper and to print the name of a family member or a word for a family situation that needs God's peace brought to it. Next, ask them to draw a larger circle around the first circle. In this circle tell them to write the names of people or situations in their local school, parish, or town that need God's peace brought to them. Finally, have them draw a third, larger circle and list names of people or situations in the world at large that need God's peace brought to them.

After some time for reflection, have the teens sit in a large circle. Pass a lighted candle around the circle. As each person is holding the candle, ask them to pray aloud for one of the people or situations they wrote on their papers.

Conclude by reciting the World Peace Prayer with the teens (also on page 162 of the Candidate's Handbook).

> Lead us
> from death to life,
> from falsehood to truth,
> from despair to hope,
> from fear to trust.
> Lead us
> from hate to love,
> from war to peace.
> Let peace fill our hearts,
> let peace fill our world,
> let peace fill our universe. Amen.
>
> —WORLD PEACE PRAYER

B Lead a prayerful reading of Matthew 25:31-46, the judgment of nations. Call on teens to share their reflections on who are the hungry, ill, lonely, and imprisoned in their peer group and the world at large and ways they can reach out to them.

C Give each teen three strips of paper. Have them finish the following sentences, one on each strip:

- A time I experienced God calling me was. . . . "
- The worst poverty I know of is. . . ."
- I can serve others by. . . . "

Collect the finished strips. Randomly read a sampling of each type of finished sentence to the group.

Pray the following words of Mother Teresa (also on page 162 of the Candidate's Handbook) in conclusion:

> Make us worthy, Lord, to serve our fellow men and women throughout the world who live and die in poverty and hunger. Give them, through our hands, this day their daily bread, and by our understanding love, give them peace and joy. Amen.

NAME _____

AREAS OF RESPONSIBILITY

person or relationship	team or organtization
job or task	goal
ideal or value	cause

GOD'S GRANDEUR

Read the poem slowly and reflectively. Then practice a dramatic reading that you can share with others.

The world is charged with the grandeur of God.
    It will flame out, like shining from shook foil;
    It gathers to a greatness, like the ooze of oil
Crushed. Why do men then now not reck his rod?
Generations have trod, have trod, have trod;
    And all is seared with trade; bleared, smeared with toil;
    And wears man's smudge and shares man's smell: the soil
Is bare now, nor can foot feel, being shod.

And for all this, nature is never spent;
    There lives the dearest freshness deep down things;
And though the last lights off the black West went
    Oh, morning, at the brown brink eastward, springs—
Because the Holy Ghost over the bent
    World broods with warm breast and with ah! bright wings.

—GERARD MANLEY HOPKINS

Just War Conditions

According to Church teaching and tradition the following conditions must be present before a government can declare war and use lethal force:

Just cause. There must be a real, lasting, grave attack by an aggressor on a nation. If lives of innocent people are threatened, if there is a need for self-defense, there would be a just cause.

Legitimate authority. A war can only be declared by the government, or those with legitimate authority to represent the common good of the people.

Comparative justice. The rights and values of the war must be so important that they justify killing.

Right intention. The war must be waged with the best of reasons and a commitment to post-war reconciliation with the enemy.

Probability of success. The odds of a successful military campaign must be weighed against the human cost of the war.

Proportionality. The damage inflicted must not be greater than the good that is expected to result from the war.

Last resort. War must be a last resort, justifiable only if all peaceful efforts have been tried and there are no alternatives.

Once the war has been engaged, other principles apply. For example, civilians may not be the object of direct attack. Minimum force to obtain military objectives must remain in place. Political and military leaders must always see that peace with justice is the only justifiable goal to be achieved by the use of arms.

Liturgy and Sacraments

(see pages 165-181 of the Candidate's Handbook)

BACKGROUND

Catholics believe that God the Father interacts and is present with us in many ways through our physical world. God chooses to be present with us in ways that we can comprehend. God uses everything around us to draw us into the Paschal mystery of Christ and into the mystery of the relationship of the three Persons of the Trinity.

We do not know all of the ways that God reveals himself to us and is present to us. But we do know that God is present to us in the sacraments. Sacraments are sacred and visible signs of God's loving grace made present to the world.

The first or prime sacrament is Jesus Christ. Jesus is God-in-the-flesh. It is in his Paschal mystery—the life, death, resurrection, and ascension of Christ—that God is most clearly revealed.

The Church itself is a sacrament. As Christ is no longer physically present with us, the Church is Christ's instrument on earth.

As a sacrament, the Church is *efficacious* in nature meaning that it not only points to the reality of our salvation, but it also causes it. This happens mainly through the invisible graces of the seven sacraments—Baptism, Confirmation, Eucharist, Penance, Anointing of the Sick, Matrimony, and Holy Orders.

This unit covers the sacraments and liturgy. It is based on material in Part Two, "The Celebration of the Christian Mystery" from the *Catechism of the Catholic Church*.

Special attention is paid to the Eucharist, the "sacrament of sacraments," including a historical development of the Eucharist and an explanation of its various parts.

SAMPLE SCHEDULES

MODEL I: FOCUSED PREPARATION (ONE 3-HOUR SESSION)
Suggested Session Plan

Warm-Up (about 30 minutes)
Refer to pages 165-166 of the Candidate's Handbook.
- Introduce the main topic of the session, liturgy and sacraments, based on the opening material in the Candidate's Handbook and emphasizing the unifying nature of the liturgy and how sacraments symbolize a higher reality.
- Related to the topic of unity, use Warm-Up/Breaktime Exercise "A" (page 161).
- Related to the symbolic nature of the sacraments, use Warm-Up/Breaktime Exercise "D" (page 161).

Lesson 1: The Prime Sacrament (about 40 minutes)
Refer to pages 166-168 of the Candidate's Handbook.
- Focus on the topics of sign and symbol, Jesus' presence in the sacraments, and the Paschal mystery in the liturgy.
- Begin with The Prime Sacrament "C" (page 162), a definition of signs and symbols. Follow with a more specific example using The Prime Sacrament "D" (page 162).
- Define and/or review the meaning of the Paschal mystery. See The Prime Sacrament "B" (page 162).
- Use The Prime Sacrament "E" (page 163) to help the candidates with an understanding of Jesus' real presence in the sacraments.

Breaktime (about 20 minutes)
- Use Warm-Up/Breaktime Exercise "B" (page 161). *Note:* Prior to the session arrange for the teens to bring an item that represents something important in their lives or some current event in the news.

Lesson 2: The Church as Sacrament (about 30 minutes)
Refer to pages 168-172 of the Candidate's Handbook.
- Present a brief explanation of the Church as sacrament.
- Use The Church as Sacrament "A" (pages 163-164).
- Discuss the matter and form of the sacraments. Use the Church as Sacrament "C" (page 165).
- Do a review of the material in this section. Use The Church as Sacrament "E" (pages 166-167).

Lesson 3: Eucharist: Sacrament of Sacraments (about 30 minutes)
Refer to pages 172-177 of the Candidate's Handbook.
- Use Eucharist: Sacrament of Sacraments "B" (pages 167-168).
- Cover the history of the Eucharist. *Recommendation*: Use the video suggested in Eucharist: Sacraments of Sacraments "C" (page 168).
- Review the FAQs from pages 178-179 of the Candidate's Handbook.

Prayer Experience (about 30 minutes)
- Use Prayer Experience "A" (page 171).

Individual Assignments

- Assign The Church as Sacrament "B" (page 164). Have the teens write their responses in their journals.
- Have the candidates write written responses to some or all of the discussion questions in Chapter 7.
- Assign questions 31-35 from the "50 Questions" (page 246 of the Candidate's Handbook).

Candidate/Sponsor Activities

- Adapt Eucharist: Sacrament of Sacraments "A" (page 167). Discuss together the talking points listed in the activity.
- Assign Features "C" (page 171). Ask the candidates and mentors to read together the scripture accounts of the institution of the Eucharist and then discuss.
- Attend a Sunday or weekday Mass together. Meet after Mass to share reflections on the readings. Also, discuss reasons for regularly going or not going to Mass (see Eucharist: Sacrament of Sacraments "D," page 168).

MODEL 2: EXTENDED PREPARATION (TWO 1-HOUR SESSIONS)
Suggested Session 1 Plan

Warm-Up (about 15 minutes)
Refer to pages 165-166 of the Candidate's Handbook.
- Use Warm-Up/Breaktime Exercise "D" (page 161). Connect the activity with the symbolic elements and nature of the sacraments.

Lesson: The Prime Sacrament (about 20 minutes)
Refer to pages 166-168 of the Candidate's Handbook.
- Use The Prime Sacrament "B" (page 162). Stress the presence of the Paschal mystery in the sacraments, especially Eucharist.
- Use The Prime Sacrament "C" (page 162).
- Continue to a discussion of Jesus' presence in the sacraments. Use The Prime Sacrament "E" (page 163).

Breaktime (about 10 minutes)
- Use Warm-Up Breaktime "C" (page 161). Connect your talk to Jesus' presence in the sacraments. Explain how the spirit of teen's from past years continues to remain present in your youth programming.

Lesson: The Church as Sacrament (about 15 minutes)
Refer to pages 168-172 of the Candidate's Handbook.
- Briefly explain why the Church is also known as a sacrament. Draw from the information in the text.
- Use The Church as Sacrament "C" (page 165).
- Have the candidates close by reciting together the "Prayer to the Redeemer" (page 181).

Individual Assignments
- Assign The Church as Sacrament "B" (page 164).
- Ask the candidates to complete all of the discussion questions as journal assignments from the sections The Prime Sacrament and The Church as Sacrament (page 168 and page 172).
- Assign questions 31-35 of the "50 Questions" (page 246).

Candidate/Sponsor Activities
- Discuss together reasons teens do and do not go to Mass. See Eucharist: Sacrament of Sacraments "D" (page 168). Encourage teens to pledge themselves to attending Mass regularly as they prepare for Confirmation.
- The candidates and sponsors should share back and forth the occasions of the first time or most memorable time they participated in each sacrament as applicable.

Suggested Session 2 Plan

Lesson: The Church as Sacrament review (about 20 minutes)
Refer to pages 168-172 of the Candidate's Handbook.
- Check and review the candidate's home assignments from the previous session.
- Use the Church as Sacrament "D" (page 166) to continue the review.

Lesson: Eucharist: Sacrament of Sacraments (about 25 minutes)

Refer to pages 172-177 of the Candidate's Handbook.

- Use Eucharist: Sacrament of Sacraments "B" (pages 167-168).
- Use Eucharist: Sacrament of Sacraments "E" (page 168).
- Review the FAQs on pages 178-179 of the Candidate's Handbook. Ask the teens to submit other questions they have about the liturgy or sacraments. Provide answers or references for the answers to their questions. Also refer to and discuss the feature "Matter Matters" (page 00 of the Candidate's Handbook).

Prayer Experience (about 15 minutes)

Refer to page 181 of the Candidate's Handbook.

- Use Prayer Experience "A" (page 171).

Individual Home Assignments

- Ask the teens to share their reflections on the past or upcoming Sunday readings with their sponsors.
- Assign Features "C" (page 171).
- Remind the candidates to continue answering the "50 Questions" (pages 243-247).

Candidate/Sponsor Activities

- Use Eucharist: Sacrament of Sacraments "D" (page 168). Encourage the sponsors to share why they attend Mass and why they did or did not attend Mass as a teenager.
- Use Features "B" (page 171). Discuss the listed questions.

MODEL 3: CONCENTRATED PREPARATION (ONE 90-MINUTE SESSION)
Suggested Session Plan

Warm-Up (about 20 minutes)
Refer to pages 165-166 of the Candidate's Handbook.
- Use Warm-up/Breaktime Exercise "B" (page 161).
- Provide an overview of the session theme, sacraments, using the material on pages 165-166 of the Candidate's Handbook as well as the FAQ's on pages 178-179 of the Handbook.

Lesson Plan (40 minutes)
Refer to pages 166-168 of the Candidate's Handbook.
- Cover the material in The Prime Sacrament (pages 00-00) that focuses on Paschal mystery, signs and symbols, and Jesus' presence in the sacraments using "B," "C," and "E" (pages 162-163).
- After the main presentation, use The Prime Sacrament "D" (page 162).

Breaktime (about 5 minutes)
- Allow for a short stretch and time for refreshments.

Lesson Plan continued (about 20 minutes)
Refer to pages 168-172 of the Candidate's Handbook.
- Use The Church as Sacrament "A" (pages 163-164). Allow time for sharing.
- Use The Church as Sacrament "D" (page 166).

Conclusion/Prayer (about 5 minutes)
- Lead the "Prayer to Our Redeemer" (page 181 of the Candidate's Handbook).
- Plan for the teens to participate together in a Sunday Mass. See Prayer Experience "B" (page 171).

Individual Home Assignments
- Ask the teens to attend a weekday Mass and write a prayerful reflection on their experience.
- Assign Features "C" (page 171).
- Assign the sacrament-related questions number 31-35, from the "50 Questions" (page 246 of the Candidate's Handbook).

Candidate/Sponsor Activities
- Adapt Eucharist: Sacrament of Sacraments "A" (page 167).
- Use Eucharist: Sacrament of Sacraments "D" (page 168). The teens should complete the journal entries as an individual assignment.
- Review the FAQs from page 178-179 of the Candidate's Handbook.

INTRODUCTION
Warm-up/Breaktime Exercise

A Line the class up in two parallel lines facing each other. Give one person a soft, spongy ball. Ask them to say their name and throw the ball to a person in the opposite line with whom they have something in common. They should say something like, "John and I both live on Pearl Street" or "Mary Beth and I both have fathers named Ed." Continue in this way back and forth until the group has exhausted all possibilities. Note the many things the group has in common as you proceed through the other lessons of this chapter.

B Create a "time capsule" representing the people in the class. Call on each person to write a short autobiography of themselves, telling not only the details of their past but also their dreams for the future. Also ask them to bring an item that represents for them something important in their lives right now, or some current event taking place in the world, nation, or community.

When completed have the teens place all the items in a large container (e.g., a 10 gallon bottled water container or a box cooler). Seal the top of the container with tape or foil and place it in a remote place in the room.

(This activity is different from some time capsule exercises as you should not "bury" the capsule for uncovering in some far distant time. Instead, this capsule can be retrieved and the items reexamined at the end of the course.)

Make the connection between how the items that are in the capsule share a part of the teen's presence, both individually and collectively, and how the sacraments are outward signs of God's presence.

C Create a photo display or a short video presentation featuring parish teens who prepared for Confirmation or participated in youth ministry in previous years. Give the teens a chance to look at the display or view the video. Then gather the group and tell them about some of the teens who were in the program before them. Include specific examples of how their faith developed and grew from the time you first knew them until now.

D Divide the class into small groups standing around tables. Pass out a large newsprint and markers to each table. Tell the teens you are going to read a list of events or life experiences and that as you read the list the teens are to use a marker to draw or write a symbol or word that represents it on the newsprint.

When you have finished reading with the following list, have the teens go around the circle, point to a word or symbol not their own, and ask the person who wrote it or drew it to explain its meaning.

Follow up by explaining that "symbolic mementos of this kind can help others to understand who you really are."

Experiences
- an award you won
- a time you were sad
- a friendship
- something that surprised you
- a happy event
- a major disappointment
- a person who taught you an important lesson

THE PRIME SACRAMENT/LESSON IDEAS

A Take the class outside and show them a shovel handle sticking up from the ground (the spade buried below). Ask them to guess what it is. After they guess shovel, point out that the handle points beyond what we can see and that Jesus is like that. He points beyond what we can see to the mystery of the Holy Trinity.

B Provide a brief definition of the Paschal mystery:

The Paschal mystery refers to Christ's saving actions through his passion, death, resurrection, and ascension. It is through Christ's death that our death was destroyed; it is through his resurrection that our life will be restored. The liturgy celebrates the Paschal mystery of our salvation. Christ continues his work of redemption through the liturgy. Through the liturgy Christians are incorporated into the mystery of Christ.

Our lives are patterned on the dying-rising cycle. Help the teens to recognize this cycle in their own lives. Share an example of how this dying-rising cycle has been a part of your life. Ask them to share or write their own example from their own experience. All of them, for example, have given up grade school for high school. Then, ask if anyone can share a religious or spiritual example (e.g., how they have given up a sinful behavior for a good or righteous one).

C Review a definition of sign and symbols.

A **sign** is anything that points to something else, for example, objects, words, actions, or even people. For example, when a football referee holds two arms straight up he is telling the teams and fans that a touchdown was scored.

A **symbol** is a special sign that goes beyond just pointing to something. Symbols point to something deeper and call to mind feelings within us. For example, the nation's flag can elicit deep feelings of patriotism. A wedding ring can represent all the years, experiences, ups and downs of a marriage.

Remember, all symbols are signs. But not every sign is a symbol. Sacraments are special one-of-a-kind symbols. Sacraments are symbolic actions that externalize an experience of God.

D Tell a detailed story of a love relationship between a husband and wife that includes the following elements. Make the story come to life. Use names and incidents.
- hand holding
- a wedding ring
- husband opening car door for wife
- a kiss good-bye in the morning
- wife calling on the phone to let her husband know she will be late
- husband washing the dinner dishes
- wife leaving husband a love note with his lunch

Have the teens try to name the symbolic actions in the story. Point out that any love relationship includes 1) time spent together, 2) special one-time only symbolic actions, and 3) daily, repeated symbolic actions.

Compare this example with our relationship with God. Our relationship with God should include time spent together (prayer), special one-time symbolic actions (sacraments like marriage and Holy Orders), and oft-repeated symbolic actions (sacraments like Eucharist and Penance that are celebrated every day).

E Read a letter you received from a friend. Ask the teens, "What does it mean to say that my friend is present in the letter?"

Also, excuse yourself from the room. Before you leave, place another adult "in charge" of keeping the class in order. Return after a couple of minutes. Ask: "What does it mean to say that I was present in Mr./Mrs. _____."

Talk about the ways Jesus is present in the sacraments (see pages 167-168 of the Candidate's Handbook).

1. Jesus is present in the heart of the individual Christian who celebrates the sacrament.
2. Jesus is present in the community gathered in his name.
3. Jesus is present in the words of the scriptures.
4. Jesus is present in the priest, his official representative.
5. Jesus is present, at Eucharist in the consecrated bread and wine.

F Show the video *Eucharist: Celebrating Christ Present* (available from St. Anthony Messenger Press at www.americancatholic.org). The video tells the story of Assunta, a devoted grandmother and parish sacristan who is busy getting her church ready for the celebrations of Holy Week as well as helping her daughters plan a traditional Italian Easter dinner. When she is suddenly hospitalized, the family faces the question of who can carry on the traditions of faith and family, mirroring how Christians remember Christ in the celebration of Eucharist.

THE CHURCH AS SACRAMENT/LESSON IDEAS

A The Church as a sacrament is reflected in the following sign and the scripture passage from Matthew 5:16: "Just so, your light must shine before others, that they may see your good deeds and glorify your heavenly Father.

Share other images of the Church. For example:

The Church is community. Jesus said, "I am the vine, you are the branches. Whoever remains in me and I in him will bear much fruit, because without me you can do nothing" (Jn 15:5).

The Church is servant. The Church must serve others as the Lamb of God did when he gave up his life for all.

Provide art paper, drawing utensils, magazine photos, glue, and other supplies. Have the teens work to develop their own symbol for the Church. Ask them to include a scripture passage with the image.

Allow an opportunity for the teens to display their images in the meeting space.

B Assign the teens to read Chapter 1 of the Second Vatican Council document on the Church, *Lumen Gentium*. The document can be accessed at: http://www.vatican.va/archive/hist_councils/ii_vatican_council/documents/vatii_const_19641121_lumen-gentium_en.html

Ask the teens to 1) tell how the Church is defined as sacrament and 2) name other images of the Church described in this text.

C Distribute the worksheet, "Matter and Form of the Sacrament" (page 172 of this Manual). Print the following information on the board or newsprint. Discuss the proper matter and form of each sacrament as the teens fill in the information on their worksheet.

Sacrament	Matter	Form
Baptism	pouring of water	"I baptize you in the name of the Father, and of the Son, and the Holy Spirit. Amen."
Confirmation	anointing with oil	"Be sealed with the Gift of the Holy Spirit."
Eucharist	bread and wine	"This is my body . . . this is my blood," with the rest of the eucharistic prayer.
Reconciliation	sorrow and confession of sins	"I absolve you from your sins."
Anointing of the Sick	anointing with oil and imposition of hands	"Through this holy anointing may the Lord in his love and mercy help you with the grace of the Holy Spirit. . . ."
Holy Orders	laying on of hands by bishop on the candidate	Prayers of consecration.
Matrimony	exchange of marriage vows	Presence of two witnesses and priest or deacon who hears the couple's intention and consent.

D Play a game quizzing the teens on various words and phrases associated with the seven sacraments. Divide the class into two teams. Call a representative from Team 1 to the front. Read one of the words or phrases listed below for any sacrament (e.g., "last rites"). If the person is able to name the sacrament associated with last rites ("Anointing of the Sick") Team 1 gets a point. If incorrect, allow a representative from Team 2 to try to answer correctly. Continue alternating back in forth between teams. Play to a designated score (e.g., 15 points) or until all words or phrases have been exhausted.

Baptism
Church membership
first sacrament of initiation
original sin removed
infants eligible to receive it
pouring of water
new life of grace

Confirmation
gifts of the Holy Spirit
second anointing
sponsor
completion of Baptism
sealing with the Holy Spirit
second sacrament of initiation

Eucharist
transubstantiation
communion
real presence
Sunday requirement
bread and wine
Last Supper

Reconciliation
penance
forgiveness
contrition
absolution
face to face
confession of sins

Anointing of the Sick
viaticum
last rites
extreme unction
healing
sickness
death

Holy Orders
priesthood
priests, deacons, bishops
Magisterium
ordination
ministry
representative of Christ

Matrimony
sexual fidelity
two become one
parenthood
wedding
marriage
love commitment

E Share and explain this quotation on the sacrament by St. Thomas Aquinas:

> A sacrament is a sign that commemorates what precedes it—Christ's Passion; demonstrates what is accomplished in us through Christ's Passion—grace; and prefigures what the Passion pledges to us—future glory.

Ask the teens to read more about the relationship between the Paschal mystery and the sacraments from the *Catechism of the Catholic Church* (1113-1130).

Review these teachings concerning the sacraments (also on page 171 of the Candidate's Handbook):

- The sacraments presuppose faith. The Church's faith precedes the faith of the person who is seeking membership in the Church.
- The sacraments act *ex opere operato*, meaning it is God's power, not the worthiness of the minister or recipient, that is acting in and through the sacraments.
- For believers, the sacraments are necessary for salvation.
- Three of the sacraments—Baptism, Confirmation, and Holy Orders—confer a sacramental seal which is permanent; therefore these sacraments cannot be repeated.
- The sacraments will be celebrated until the end of time.

EUCHARIST: SACRAMENT OF SACRAMENTS/ LESSON IDEAS

A With the entire class, gather and mix the ingredients for a bread recipe. (There are many web sites with bread recipes including www.breadrecipe.com).

Bake the bread, let it cool, and serve a slice to the teens at the end of the current session or at the beginning of the next session.

Ask the teens to write or share about:
- one lesson they learned from making or sharing the bread;
- a meal they will always remember;
- at least two traditions their family has in conjunction with mealtime;
- how they associate the sharing of a meal with Eucharist.

B Distribute the worksheet "Last Supper Institution of the Eucharist" (page 173 of this Manual).

Read the passage from Luke 22:14-20 with the participants (also on page 180 of the Candidate's Handbook). Pause at each *boldface* word or phrase to explain more of its meaning. Use the notes below.

Notes

This Passover. Passover to the Jews meant much the same as Fourth of July means to us. It was an occasion to celebrate freedom. Had Jesus been speaking to people in the United States today, he might have said, "This is a new Fourth of July." What would that mean? (Call on participants to comment.)

Gave thanks. Jesus would have recited the *berekah*, the great prayer of the Jewish people, a thanksgiving to God for all of the gifts God had given them. The word "eucharist" itself means "thanksgiving."

Broke it [the bread]. Breaking bread was a symbol of love and friendship to the Jews. To break bread with someone was to show that you loved them like a member of your own family.

Body. This was not a biological term to the Jews, but a personal term. People *were* their bodies. When Jesus said, "This is my body" he meant: "This is me, my person."

Do this in memory of me. The Jews of Jesus' time believed that after death a person stayed alive in the nether world as long as someone on earth remembered them. That's why they recited the names of their ancestors as part of their religious feasts (see Luke 3:23-38, the genealogy of Jesus). Jesus is asking his disciples to repeat this holy meal as a way of keeping him alive in the world after his death. Whenever we gather to "do this," Jesus promises to be present in our midst.

New Covenant. The Jews had a covenant with Yahweh that held that Yahweh would be their God and offer his protection and they would be his people and obey his laws. In this passage, Jesus is making a new covenant: God will love us as a parent loves a child and we will love and serve God as sons and daughters.

Blood. Blood to the Jew meant life. It had much the same sense to them that the word "heart" has to us today. Think of the common phrase, "I love you with all my heart." In Jesus' time it would have made sense for a person to say, "I love you with all my blood."

Blood which will be shed for you. Solemn agreements were sealed in blood; the blood of a lamb was sprinkled on both parties of the agreement as a sign that they were entrusting their lives to one another. Jesus offers his blood to seal the new contract between God and us. (Remind the teens of the scene in *Tom Sawyer* when Tom and Huck seal an agreement with their blood.)

C For a clear but brief overview of the historical development of the sacrament of Eucharist, play the video *Worshipping Wilma* (part of *The Changing Sacraments* series, available from St. Anthony Messenger Press at www.americancatholic.org). The video also includes break points with an outline of the major events in history.

D Brainstorm two lists with the teens regarding Mass attendance of their peers. For the first list, ask: "Why do teenagers not go to Mass?" Print the responses on the board or newsprint. For example:
  1. too early in the morning,
  2. it's boring,
  3. my parents don't go,
  4. I have to work,
  5. I don't have a ride.

For the second list, ask: "Why do teenagers go to Mass?" Again, print all of their responses. For example:
  1. my parents make me,
  2. it's a sin to miss,
  3. I owe God at least one hour per week,
  4. I am an altar server,
  5. I feel good after I go.

Finally, ask the teens to write a journal entry entitled either "Why I Go to Mass" or "Why I Do Not Go to Mass" incorporating some of the reasons on the board in their personal response.

E Provide the teens with the scripture references to the first reading and gospel for the upcoming Sunday. As they read the passages, ask them to note common themes among the two readings.

Next, have the teens write a brief homily on the two readings, instructing them to:
• make references to the common theme,
• note the context of one or both passages (using the notes in the Bible),
• connect the theme to the experiences of teenagers today.

Call on volunteers to present their homilies to the class.

F Make copies of one of the Eucharistic prayers (*recommendation*: Eucharistic Prayer II or III). Ask the teens to underline the following parts:

- offering of thanks to the Father, through Christ, in the Holy Spirit for all his works;
- asking the Father to send the Holy Spirit (or blessing) on the gifts of bread and wine so that they may become the body and blood of Christ through the words of Christ at the Last Supper, making him present under the species of bread and wine;
- recalling the passion, resurrection, and return of Christ;
- offering intercessions for the living and the dead.

G Ask the candidates to reference Pope John Paul II's 1998 Apostolic Letter *Dies Domini* on keeping the Lord's Day holy (available at http://www.cin.org/jp2/diesdomi.html) and list at least three reasons and three ways the Pope names for keeping Sunday holy.

REFERENCES/FAQ

References from the *Catechism of the Catholic Church* for the Frequently Asked Questions include:

Why are there seven sacraments? (CCC, 1113, 1117)

While God is present everywhere and God's mystery and grace cannot be contained, there are certain places where God is "more" present. For example, it is easy to recognize God's presence in experiences of love, mercy, compassion, and justice. Over time the Church understood that not only did Jesus commission certain actions to be repeated over time, but that he was also present with them in these events. These are the seven sacraments. It was at the Council of Florence in 1439 that the Church declared that there are seven sacrament which "both contain grace and confer it upon all who receive them worthily."

Why do you have to confess your sins to a priest? (CCC, 1461-1467)

The priest is both the representative of Christ and the Church. Confessing to a priest is a way to experience first hand the forgiving touch and saving love of Jesus. Reconciling with the Church is important so we can reclaim our functions within the body of Christ.

What are the rules for receiving communion? (CCC, 1355)

Anyone who wishes to receive communion must be in a state of grace. If you are aware of a mortal sin you have committed, you must receive absolution for the sin in the sacrament of Penance before going to communion. Also, you must abstain from food or drink (with the exception of water and medicines) for at least one hour before receiving communion.

Why do Catholics believe that Jesus is really present in the bread and wine and that they are not just symbolic of his presence? (CCC, 1373-1381)

Jesus said, "Whoever eats my flesh and drinks my blood has eternal life. . . . For my flesh is true food, and my blood is true drink. Whoever eats my flesh and drinks my blood remains in me and I in him" (Jn 6:54-56). This is the scriptural basis for the Catholic belief. Catholics hold that at the time of the consecration (when the priest repeats Jesus' words from the Last Supper, "This is my body" and "This is my blood) the substance of the bread and wine change into the reality of Jesus.

Why can't I receive communion in another Christian church? Why can't my friend who is Christian but not Catholic receive communion at my church? (CCC, 1398-1401)

The very word *communion* has to do with unity, both in our beliefs about Jesus Christ and with one another. It would not be honest for a person to receive communion if he or she did not hold the same beliefs as Catholics do about Jesus; for example, that he is really present in the bread and wine. For the same reason a Catholic cannot receive communion at a Protestant Church. There are exceptions to this rule. For example, sometimes a bishop will give permission for non-Catholic parents to receive communion at the wedding of their Catholic child.

Am I really required to go to Mass every Sunday? (CCC, 2180-2183)

Yes, Catholics are required to go to Mass every Sunday and holy day of obligation unless excused for a serious reason, like an illness. This is one of the Church laws and it is broken without good reason only under the penalty of sin. There are good reasons for this rule. For one, Christ is present at the Eucharist and actively anticipating our being there. Secondly, our absence creates a void, just as missing any one part of a larger body would.

Features/Lesson Ideas

A Provide more information on the use of gluten in communion hosts:

In 1995, the Congregation for the Doctrine of the Faith stated that low-gluten altar bread is valid if the hosts "contain the amount of gluten sufficient to obtain the confection of bread, that there is no addition of foreign materials, and that the procedure for making such hosts is not such as to alter the nature of the substance of the bread."

Canon law also teaches that if a communicant is unable to consume even the smallest particle of gluten, he or she should receive communion under the form of wine only.

B Ask the teens to bring in photos or videos from their First Communion day. Allow the opportunity for sharing. Ask the teens to describe their feelings prior to and on the day of their First Communion. Ask:
- How has your excitement for Eucharist waned in the years since?
- How has your understanding of Eucharist deepened?
- What can you do to grow in understanding of Eucharist and renew your feelings of excitement at receiving Eucharist?

C Have the teens read and compare the other three accounts (besides Lk 22:14-20) of the institution of the Eucharist: Matthew 26:26-29; Mark 14:22-25; 1 Corinthians 11:23-25). Call on volunteers to point out the minor points of difference.

Prayer Experiences

A Give each person a Bible and a set of "Eucharist Scripture Passages" from the resource on page 174. Tell the teens that in each passage Jesus offers some explanation for the Eucharist, which he will reveal, finally, at the Last Supper.

Ask the teens to go to a place where they can be by themselves and read each passage. On the back of each strip, have them write one sentence that expresses an insight they have about Eucharist based on the particular passage.

Play some instrumental background music. Allow at least 20 minutes for the teens to read, reflect, and write.

When the time is complete, gather the teens again in a circle. Go around the circle and ask the teens to share one or two insights on Eucharist.

Conclude with a dramatic reading of the Emmaus story (Lk 24:13-35) or the meal with fish (Jn 21:1-14).

B Arrange for the class to attend a Sunday Mass together, taking on some of the liturgical roles for which they are qualified (e.g., bringing up the gifts, ushering, hospitality). After communion, a teen who has been prepared can lead the "Prayer to Our Redeemer" (page 181 of the Candidate's Handbook) as a meditation.

NAME _____

MATTER AND FORM OF THE SACRAMENTS

Sacrament	Matter	Form
Baptism		
Confirmation		
Eucharist		
Reconciliation		
Anointing of the Sick		
Holy Orders		
Matrimony		

LAST SUPPER INSTITUTION OF THE EUCHARIST

When the hour came, he took his place at table with the apostles.

He said to them, "I have eagerly desired to eat *this Passover* with you before I suffer, for, I tell you, I shall not eat it [again] until there is
   fulfillment in the kingdom of God."

Then he took a cup, *gave thanks*, and said,
"Take this and share it among yourselves; for I tell you [that] from this time on I shall not drink of the fruit of the vine until the kingdom of God
   comes."

Then he took the bread, said the blessing,
broke it, and gave it to them, saying,
"This is my *body*, which will be given for you;
do this in memory of me."

And likewise the cup after they had eaten,
saying, "This cup is the *new covenant* in my *blood*,
which will be shed for you."

—LUKE 22:14-20

Eucharist Scripture Passages

John 2:1-12

Matthew 15:32-39; 16:5-11

John 6:1-14

John 6:22-71

John 15:1-11

Holy Spirit and Confirmation

(see pages 183-203 of the Candidate's Handbook)

BACKGROUND

Confirmation is often called the "sacrament of the Holy Spirit." For this reason it is important for teens to study the Third Person of the Holy Trinity at the time of their preparation for the sacrament of Confirmation.

At Confirmation, the bishop anoints the forehead of each candidate with chrism, saying, "Be sealed with the gift of the Holy Spirit." Confirmation celebrates the presence of the Holy Spirit in the life of the person being confirmed and in the Church that has nurtured his or her faith. Also, the presiding bishop calls on God the Father and God the Son not only to send the Holy Spirit upon the candidates, but also to bestow on them the seven gifts of the Spirit: wisdom, understanding, right judgment, courage, knowledge, reverence, and wonder and awe in God's presence.

The lessons of this chapter deal first and foremost with providing an understanding of the Holy Spirit, the last of the Persons of the Trinity to be revealed. (In fact, it was at the Council of Constantinople in 381 that the Church clearly proclaimed the divinity of the Holy Spirit, that the Holy Spirit is God, the Lord and Giver of Life.) The lessons trace the Church's understanding of the Holy Spirit, beginning with several examples from scripture leading to Christ's sending of the Spirit at Pentecost.

How is the Spirit shared? The lessons focus on the effects of grace received at Confirmation, which brings a special outpouring of the Holy Spirit. In Confirmation, the graces of Baptism are perfected. Like Baptism, Confirmation is given only once because it imprints on the person a spiritual mark or indelible character that cannot be removed.

Finally, the lessons focus on the traditional seven gifts of the Spirit, looking at some of the ways these gifts apply and are an aid in the life of the confirmed Catholic.

Sample Schedules

Model I: Focused Preparation (one 3-hour session)
Suggested Session Plan

Warm-Up (about 30 minutes)
Refer to pages 183-185 of the Candidate's Handbook.
- Introduce the main topics of the session—the Holy Spirit and its special role in the sacrament of Confirmation.
- Use Warm-up/Breaktime Exercise "A" (page 181).

Lesson 1: The Holy Spirit (about 45 minutes)
Refer to pages 185-190 of the Candidate's Handbook.
- Present some information on the Holy Spirit. Use The Holy Spirit "C" (page 183).
- Use The Holy Spirit "D" (page 185).
- Just prior to the break use The Holy Spirit "B" (pages 182-183).

Breaktime (about 20 minutes)
- Allow time for a stretch and refreshments.
- While the teens are on break, play the video on reconciliation suggested in Warm-up/Breaktime Exercise "D" (page 182). Encourage the candidates to watch the video, using it as a follow-up to the presentation on forgiveness during the Warm-up part of the session.

Lesson 2: The Sacrament of Confirmation (about 40 minutes)
Refer to pages 190-193 of the Candidate's Handbook.
- Use The Sacrament of Confirmation "A" (page 184).
- Give a presentation based on the outline in The Sacrament of Confirmation "C" (pages 184-185).
- Use either The Sacrament of Confirmation "G" or "H" (page 186). If using, "G," allow teens to share their essays in small groups or with a partner.

Breaktime (about 5 minutes)
- Allow a brief time for a stretch, drink, and rest room break before the next lesson.

Lesson 3: Gifts of the Spirit (about 35 minutes)
Refer to pages 193-197 of the Candidate's Handbook.
- Introduce the seven gifts of the Holy Spirit. After the introduction, have the teens close their books. Check to see how many can recite the seven gifts back to you.
- Use Gifts of the Spirit "B" (page 186). Prearrange with the speakers the focus of their talk. Allow about four minutes for each presentation.

Conclusion/Prayer (about 5 minutes)
- Briefly review the session.
- Offer a final prayer using Acts 8:14-17 and the Opening Prayer from the rite of Confirmation (page 202 of the Candidate's Handbook).

Individual Home Assignments

- Assign the worksheet "Commitment to Faith" (page 191). Tell the candidates to work on the resource alone, then plan to discuss their work with their sponsors.
- Have the teens research and report on the issue of what is the proper age for Confirmation (see The Sacrament of Confirmation, "E," page 185).
- Assign Features "D" (page 188).
- Assign questions 41-45 of the "50 Questions" (page 247 of the Candidate's Handbook).
- Assign any discussion questions from the Candidate's Handbook that were not completed as part of the session.

Candidate/Sponsor Activities

- Discuss the items on the "Commitment to Faith" resource (see above).
- If possible attend a celebration of Confirmation together at a neighboring parish (see The Sacrament of Confirmation, "F," page 186).
- Review the FAQs, pages 198-199 of the Candidate's Handbook.

MODEL 2: EXTENDED PREPARATION (TWO 1-HOUR SESSIONS)
Suggested Session 1 Plan

Warm-up (about 15 minutes)
- Introduce the topic of the next two sessions from the Background information on page 175 and from pages 183-185 of the Candidate's Handbook.
- Use Warm-up/Breaktime Exercise "B" (page 181).

Lesson: The Holy Spirit (about 40 minutes)
Refer to pages 185-190 of the Candidate's Handbook.
- Introduce the topic of the Holy Spirit.
- Show the video suggested in The Holy Spirit "E" (page 184).

Conclusion/Prayer (about 5 minutes)
- Explain the Individual Home Assignments as needed.
- Pray together "Come, Holy Spirit" (pages 201-202 of the Candidate's Handbook).

Individual Home Assignments
- Assign the teens to write definitions of the various meanings of the term grace. See Warm-up/Breaktime Exercise "C" (page 182).
- Assign the worksheet "The Holy Spirit in Scripture" (page 189). See The Holy Spirit "C" (page 183).
- Use some or all of the discussion questions about the Holy Spirit (page 190 of the Candidate's Handbook) for journal assignments.

Candidate/Sponsor Activities
- Discuss together the Individual Home Assignments given above.
- Share the features "W.I.N." and "Symbols of the Holy Spirit" (pages 199-200 of the Candidate's Handbook).
- Assign one or more of Features "A," "B," and "C" (pages 187-189).
- Discuss the FAQs, pages 198-199 of the Candidate's Handbook.

Session 2 Plan
Prayer Experience (about 10 minutes)
- Use Prayer Experience "A" (page 188).

Lesson: The Sacrament of Confirmation (about 30 minutes)
Refer to pages 190-193 of the Candidate's Handbook.
- *Note:* If you are able to arrange for the bishop to visit with the candidates, devote the remainder of the session to his visit. See The Sacrament of Confirmation "D" (page 185). If the bishop is unable to visit, proceed as follows.
- Review some of the scriptural origins of the sacrament of Confirmation. See The Sacrament of Confirmation "A" (page 184).
- Use The Sacrament of Confirmation "C" (pages 184-185).

Lesson: The Gifts of the Spirit (about 20 minutes)
Refer to pages 193-197 of the Candidate's Handbook.
- Use Gifts of the Spirit "A" (page 186).

Individual Home Assignments

- Assign the essay from The Sacrament of Confirmation "G" (page 186).
- Assign the essay from Gifts of the Spirit "D" (page 186).
- Continue working through questions 41-45 from the "50 Questions" (page 247 of the Candidate's Handbook.

Candidate/Sponsor Activities

- Work together on the worksheet "Commitment to Faith" (page 191).
- If possible, use The Sacrament of Confirmation "F" (page 186).

MODEL 3: CONCENTRATED PREPARATION (ONE 90-MINUTE SESSION)
Suggested Session Plan

Warm-Up (about 30 minutes)
Refer to pages 183-185 of the Candidate's Handbook.
- Introduce the main topic of the session, The Holy Spirit and Confirmation, as well as briefly covering the different meanings of grace (see Warm-up/Breaktime Exercise "C," page 182).
- Use Warm-up/Breaktime Exercise "B" (page 183).

Lesson Plan (about 50 minutes)
Refer to pages 185-197 of the Candidate's Handbook.
- Use The Holy Spirit "A" (page 182).
- Cover the eight ways the Spirit is present in the Church (see The Holy Spirit "B," pages 182-183).
- Introduce the scriptural origins of Confirmation (see The Sacrament of Confirmation, "A," page 184).
- Review the meaning of the people, words, and symbols associated with Confirmation (see The Sacrament of Confirmation "C," pages 184-185).
- Use Gifts of the Spirit "A" (page 186).

Prayer Experience (about 10 minutes)
- Use Prayer Experience "C" (page 188). Call on two or three volunteers to share their prayer to the Holy Spirit in conclusion.

Individual Home Assignments
- Assign the worksheet "The Holy Spirit in Scripture" (page 189). See The Holy Spirit "C" (page 183).
- Assign the essay suggested in The Sacrament of Confirmation "G" (page 186).
- Assign the essay suggested in Gifts of the Spirit "D" (page 186).
- Use any or all of the discussion questions in Chapter 9 for journal entries.
- Continue to work on the "50 Questions" (pages 243-247 of the Candidate's Handbook), particularly numbers 41-45.

Candidate/Sponsor Activities
- Assign the worksheet "The Commitment to Faith" (page 191) for completion and discussion.
- As possible, use The Sacrament of Confirmation "F" (page 186).
- Review together the FAQs, pages 198-199 of the Candidate's Handbook.

INTRODUCTION
Warm-up/Breaktime Exercises

A Arrange for two teens (not in the current class) who are known to be "sworn enemies" over a resolvable issue like membership in different peer groups, liking the same boyfriend/girlfriend, an argument that happened so long ago that it is hard to remember what its source was, etc. to speak with the class.

Make sure to tell each speaker that 1) they will be telling the story of their conflict with the other person publicly, but separately; 2) that they are to do so in the spirit of reconciliation and forgiveness; and 3) that they will be expected to participate in a public display of reconciliation and forgiveness (foot washing ceremony) at the conclusion of both presentations.

Begin the activity by reading the story of Jesus' washing of the disciples feet from John 13:1-20 and the story of reconciliation and forgiveness between teenagers on pages 183-185 of the Candidate's Handbook.

Call on the first teen speaker to address the class. (The second teen speaker should be outside of the room.) The speaker should address the following issues related to his or her relationship with the second speaker:

- how long they have known each other,
- when, if ever, their relationship was good or civil,
- what happened to damage the relationship,
- why he or she would like to reconcile now.

When completed, ask the second speaker to follow the same format with the first speaker now absent from the room.

With both speakers in front of the group, review the contents of their presentations. Conclude by saying something like, "As you both are willing to forgive one another and reconcile, we all support your decision with our prayers."

Play some appropriate background music. Have the two teens sit in front of the class and take turns washing each other's feet.

Conclude by leading a prayer for the two teens and the success of their new spirit of friendship and cooperation. Together with the entire class, pray the following prayer to the Holy Spirit (also on pages 201-202 of the Candidate's Handbook).

COME, HOLY SPIRIT

Come, Holy Spirit, fill the hearts of your faithful
    and kindle in them the fire of your love.
Send forth your Spirit, O Lord,
    and renew the face of the earth.
O God,
on the first Pentecost
you instructed the hearts of those who believed in you
by the light of the Holy Spirit:
under the inspiration of the same Spirit,
give us a taste for what is right and true

and a continuing sense of his joy-bringing presence

and power,

through Jesus Christ our Lord.

Amen.

B Call on teens to share (in small groups or with the entire class) examples of people who have been, for them, models of faith. These examples could be parents, grandparents, older neighbors or other relatives, teachers, coaches, employers, and the like. To carry the discussion further, ask the teens to share one specific incident in which they learned a lesson in faith from that person or an incident that is indicative of that person's Christian faith.

C Help the teens to understand the various meanings of the term *grace*. Print the boldface terms on the board or newsprint. Offer the following explanations.

Sanctifying grace. This is the gift of God's life, the gift of divine life in those who have been reborn in Baptism in union with the Holy Spirit. Sanctifying grace results in the presence of the gift of the Holy Spirit in a person. Through sanctifying grace, we are connected in the intimacy of the Blessed Trinity. Sanctifying grace perfects the soul and enables it to live with God and to act by his love.

Habitual grace. This is the permanent disposition to live and act in keeping with God's call.

Actual graces. These are God's help to do good and avoid evil in the concrete circumstances of everyday life. Actual graces refer to God's interventions in our lives, whether at the beginning of our conversion or in the course of our life thereafter.

Sacramental graces. These are gifts proper to each of the sacraments.

Special graces. Also known as "charisms," special graces like virtues are those the Spirit gives to certain members of the Church for the common good in serving and building up the Church. The gift of miracles or of tongues are other examples of such charisms.

D Play the *Edge TV* video on Reconciliation (available from Pflaum www.hitimepflaum.com.) This five segment, 45 minute presentation includes stories of young people finding hope by reconciling differences between themselves, others, and God.

THE HOLY SPIRIT/LESSON IDEAS

A Jesus tells us that we will know the Spirit, "because it remains with you, and will be in you" (Jn 14:17). It is the work of the Holy Spirit to reveal Christ to us. Review the vignettes listed on page 186 of the Candidate's Handbook. Ask the teens to tell how Christ's presence is revealed in each.

Assign small groups to develop role plays that depict Christ's presence being revealed in the words and actions of others. Encourage the groups to leave the role plays open-ended so that the rest of the class can name their recognition of Christ's presence in the story.

Allow time for each group to present their role plays and the rest of the class to offer their comments.

B Divide the class into small groups of four or eight teens. Call on the groups to memorize the ways, listed below (and on page 187 of the Candidate's Handbook) that the Holy Spirit is present in the Church. The small groups should sit in a circle and study the ways. Then, with books closed, the first person says the first way ("in the Scriptures he inspired"), the second person the second way ("in

Church Tradition"), etc. If the group has four members, continue around the circle twice. Anytime someone misses a way, the next person must start over at the beginning. After allowing some practice time, call on small groups to come before the class to recite these eight ways the Spirit is present in the Church.

"The Church is a place where we know the Holy Spirit in:"
—the Scriptures he inspired;
—Church Tradition;
—the Magisterium, which he assists;
—the sacramental liturgy;
—prayer, wherein he intercedes for us;
—the gifts and ministries by which the Church is built up;
—the signs of apostolic and missionary life;
—the witness of saints through whom he shows his holiness and continues the work of salvation.

C Pass out the worksheet "The Holy Spirit in Scripture" (page 189 of this Manual) and give a bible to each teen. Have them work individually on this worksheet. When completed, discuss and check their answers.

Answers
Genesis 1:1-2: The Hebrew word for wind is *ruah*. From the time of creation, the Spirit's creative powers were active and present in the world.

Genesis 2:7: The Spirit also gives life to humans.

Exodus 19:16-19: The Spirit—and God's power—is revealed in thunder, lightening, and fire.

Ezekiel 37:1-14: In the well-known story of "dry bones," it is the Spirit who brings life from death.

Luke 1:26-35: Jesus' conception is brought about by the Holy Spirit who overshadows his mother, Mary.

John 14:16-17: At the Last Supper, Jesus tells his apostles not to be afraid for he is sending them the Holy Spirit.

John 20:21-23: Just as the Spirit brought life to the first humans in Genesis, Jesus brings new spiritual life to the apostles by breathing on them.

D Read or assign for reading the story of the Coming of the Spirit at Pentecost (Acts 2:1-41). Focus especially on Peter's speech (vs. 14-36). Explain that this was, in effect, the first "witness" talk inspired by the Holy Spirit. Define a witness talk as a Christian's inspired personal testimony about his or her faith in Jesus Christ.

Ask the teens to prepare their own short witness talks, focusing on issues like:
• what Jesus means to them,
• the importance of Jesus in their lives,
• how they have come to know Jesus,
• ways they recognize Jesus in others.

Call on selected volunteers to share their witness talks with the entire class.

E Show the video presentation of *The Visitor* (available from Vision Video at www.visionvideo.com) based on Leo Tolstoy's story *Where Love Is*, the story of a cobbler named Martin and his struggle with personal tragedy—the loss of his wife and child. A friend from Martin's past assures him that an important visitor is coming to see him. Ordinary, everyday people become the channels of God's grace and are used by the Spirit to restore to Martin a new joy, hope, purpose in life.

The Sacrament of Confirmation/Lesson Ideas

A Pass out the worksheet "Confirmation in Scripture" (page 190 of this Manual) and a bible to each teen. Have them work individually, or in pairs, to write about the origins of the sacrament of Confirmation in the New Testament. Check the answers against the following:

Answers

Acts 8:14-17 There is a distinction between Baptism (in the name of the Lord Jesus) and the reception of the Holy Spirit. As in Confirmation, the Spirit is conferred through the laying on of hands. Also, this passage points out that it is an apostle who lays on hands. In Confirmation, it is a successor of the apostles, the bishop who is the minister of the sacrament.

Acts 19:1-6 These followers have been baptized with the baptism of John the Baptist. Paul baptized them in the name of Jesus. He laid hands on them and the Holy Spirit came upon them. They received special charisms, or gifts of the Spirit, namely the gifts of tongues and prophecy.

2 Corinthians 1:21-22 The language of this passage describes a similar process of Christian initiation. The Spirit is understood to be the "first installment" on the full benefits of faith God guarantees to all Christians. The mention of a "seal" is representative of the seal that comes with the anointing at Confirmation.

B Reception of the sacrament of Confirmation in the teenage years is associated with growing maturity and adulthood in the Christian faith and Church life. Discuss this premise with the teens.

Assign the worksheet, "Commitment to Faith" (page 191). Allow time for the teens to work individually finishing each sentence. Then, call on one person to sit in a chair before the entire group. Interview the person, asking for his or her comments regarding commitment in one or two areas. Then call a second person to the front and continue in the same way for as long as you are able.

C Review the meaning of the following important people, words, symbols and actions that make up the Confirmation rite (see also pages 191-192 of the Candidate's Handbook). Write the boldface words on the board or newsprint to accompany the following explanations:

Bishop. The bishop is the official representative of the universal Church, a successor of the apostles. Although the bishop was present symbolically at Baptism through the use of the chrism which he blessed, he was probably not personally present. While the bishop is the ordinary minister of Confirmation, in the cases of adults or older children being confirmed at the Easter Vigil, the pastor or other parish priest is typically the minister of Confirmation. A priest may also confirm when there is danger of death.

Laying on of Hands. This gesture was one way the apostles called on the Spirit to come on new Christians. The laying on of hands is a symbol of commissioning and is also used in the sacrament of ordination. It is also a gesture of healing and is intended in this way in the sacraments of Anointing and Penance.

Anointing with Chrism. As in Baptism, the signing with chrism reminds us of our baptismal call to be priest, prophet, and king. Oil is also used to seal, protect, and bind us together as Christians. When the bishop anoints a candidate he says, "Be sealed with the gifts of the Holy Spirit." The chrism used at Confirmation is blessed by the bishop once a year, on Holy Thursday, at the Chrism Mass.

D Invite the bishop to one of the classes prior to the date Confirmation will be celebrated at your parish (of course, this must be done well in advance). The main purpose of the visit is give the bishop an opportunity to meet more personally with the candidates he will confirm. These are some things you can invite the bishop to do with the group:

- speak with the teens about the history/effects of the sacrament of Confirmation,
- reminisce about his own Confirmation day,
- share his ideas for the commitment a confirmed Catholic should exhibit,
- talk about the meaning of the gifts of the Holy Spirit,
- simply observe the regular content of the class and socialize with the teens throughout the period.

E In 2001, the United States Catholic bishops revised a policy stating that children baptized as infants should be confirmed sometime between the age of discretion (seven years old) and age sixteen. Some dioceses have chosen to celebrate Confirmation at the time of First Eucharist. The primary reason for this is to restore the original Baptism-Confirmation-Eucharist sequence of the sacraments of initiation. Dioceses who have chosen to celebrate Confirmation later, in the teen years, usually hold a view that initiation is a lengthy process in which the Catholic is gradually incorporated into the Church community. In this view Confirmation is seen as a sacrament of Christian maturity. Another pastoral reason for celebrating Confirmation at the later date was explained by one bishop in a letter to his diocese. He wrote:

> A marked drop in religious education attendance by young people throughout the diocese was noticed as soon as the lower Confirmation age was in place. Many pastors reported a fifty to sixty percent drop off. Some places reported that parents and guardians of children saw no need for religious education after Confirmation was received. In some places there were no teenage programs offered which could attract the adolescent as did the Confirmation preparation program. While all these reasons may be contested, they are valid reasons. In the future there could be better religious education or teen ministry programs put in place by parishes and schools. With better education of parents and guardians, religious education could continue after Confirmation. However, the plain fact of the matter is that religious education did not continue and something needed to be done to remedy the situation.
>
> Many teachers reported that it was very difficult pedagogically to bring the young children to make the distinctions between Confirmation and First Eucharist. The fact that the reception of First Reconciliation takes place at the same time complicated the pedagogical task.
>
> The argument that the young child is more innocent and open to the grace of the sacrament of Confirmation is a valid one based on the theology of not placing an obstacle in the way of the grace of a sacrament. However, St. Thomas taught that grace was based on nature in the sense that the better prepared a person was for the reception of a sacrament, the more grace could be received. . . . Adolescence is a time when all the help to spiritual maturity that can be given is needed. Confirmation is an ideal sacrament to help at this time of growth in one's life. (quoted from "Pastoral Reasons for the Change of Administering the Sacrament of Confirmation in the Diocese of Corpus Christi, April 30, 1998)

Ask the teens to research the issue of what age is proper for receiving the sacrament of Confirmation. For example, they may write letters soliciting the opinion of their local bishop and/or the bishops of other dioceses.

Holy Spirit and Confirmation

F Arrange for the teens to attend a celebration of Confirmation at a neighboring parish. Or, encourage them to attend the Easter vigil liturgy at your own parish.

G Assign an essay with the title "I Will Be the Light of Christ to the World." The essay should deal with concrete ways the teen plans to put their faith into action in their lives, at school, home, and work, with their friends, and in their families. "I will be nice to my siblings" or "I will set a good example for my friends" are vague responses. "I will turn the other cheek when my sister insults me, rather than retaliating," or "I will tell my friends, honestly, that I don't like it when they drink at parties, rather than letting them think it doesn't bother me," are more specific and set a clearer course of action.

H If not viewed before in connection with the sacrament of Baptism (Chapter 1), play the video *Godparent Gussie* (part of *The Changing Sacraments* series, available from St. Anthony Messenger Press at www.americancatholic.org).

GIFTS OF THE SPIRIT/LESSON IDEAS

A Make a set of "Gifts of the Spirit Flash Cards" for each teen (see pages 193-194 of this Manual). Allow time for them to study the name and meaning of the gifts individually and an additional few minutes for them to review with a partner. Then, test the teens on the names and meanings of the seven gifts. Ask them to write the name of each gift and a one-sentence description. Check the results.

B Arrange for teens and/or adults to give short presentations on the gifts of the Holy Spirit. Ask them to use the information on pages 193-197 from the Candidate's Handbook as the basis of their talks, as well as to tell how they have applied the gift to their own lives.

C Have the teens use lunch bags to receive mail. Instruct them to print their names on the bags. Then give this assignment: Tell the teens they are to write seven notes telling another person how he or she represents one of the gifts of the Holy Spirit. Have the teens follow these rules:
1. write one letter for each gift of the Spirit,
2. write letters to seven different people.

D Assign an essay, "Seven Gifts of the Spirit." Have the teens address the following questions (also on page 194 of the Candidate's Handbook):
1. What do these gifts mean to me?
2. How are they part of my life?
3. How can I share them with others?

REFERENCES/FAQ

References from the *Catechism of the Catholic Church* for the Frequently Asked Questions include:

Is the Holy Spirit equal to the Father and Son? (CCC, 253-256)
The Holy Spirit is equal to the Father and Son because he is God. Because of the nature of the Blessed Trinity, the Holy Spirit is entirely in the Father and the Son just as the Father is entirely in the Son and the Holy Spirit and the Son is entirely in the Father and the Holy Spirit.

What is the sin against the Holy Spirit, spoken of in Matthew 12:31-32, that cannot be forgiven? (CCC, 1864)
The sin against the Holy Spirit that Jesus speaks of is attributing works of the Spirit of God to Satan, exactly what Jesus' enemies had done when they said Jesus' power over demons came from Satan. God's mercy has no limits. But anyone who deliberately rejects God's mercy, his offer of forgiveness, and the salvation offered by the Holy Spirit by refusing to repent is guilty of the eternal sin.

Why is Pentecost sometimes called the birthday of the Church? (CCC, 767, 1076)
It was at Pentecost, through the coming of the Holy Spirit, that God completed all covenants with humanity. On Pentecost, the Holy Spirit united all of Jesus' disciples into one community of faith, the Church.

Is reception of the sacrament of Confirmation necessary for salvation? (CCC, 1306)
A person who has been baptized, but not confirmed can certainly be saved. But the Church teaches that Christian initiation is incomplete without reception of Confirmation and Eucharist. It follows, according to Church teaching, that all the faithful are obliged to be confirmed at an appropriate time.

At what age does the Church teach that Confirmation should be celebrated? (CCC, 1307-1310)
Canon law teaches that the sacrament of Confirmation should be conferred around the age of discretion (about seven years old) unless the bishops determine there is another more appropriate age or the person is in danger of death. In 2001 the bishops in the United States decreed that Confirmation in the Latin Rite dioceses of the United States will be between "the age of discretion and about sixteen years of age."

Why are children who are baptized at Easter also confirmed?(CCC, 1291, 1298)
Any child who has reached the age of discretion is considered to be sufficiently mature in the matters of faith and capable of nurturing a personal faith life and following his or her conscience. For that reason, their initiation follows the adult form in which they receive all three sacraments of initiation at the Easter vigil.

Can my parent be my Confirmation sponsor? (CCC, 1255, 1311)
No, the Church sees two distinct and important roles for parents and sponsors. In fact, it is recommended that the Confirmation sponsor be the same as the baptismal sponsor to continue to help your parents nurture your faith life.

FEATURES/LESSON IDEAS

A Ask the teens to write ten answers to the question "What's important now?" related to events in their daily lives for the coming semester. For example,

"What's important now?"

To make the basketball team.

Holy Spirit and Confirmation

"What's important now?"

To earn enough money to afford car insurance.

When completed, call on the teens to go back over their list and make notes about what kinds of things they will need to do to achieve what they deem to be important. Call on volunteers to share sample responses from their lists.

B Read more selections from Coach Lou Holtz's book for teens, *A Teen's Game Plan for Life* (Sorin Books, 2002).

C Provide several forms of art media (e.g., water colors, color pencils, chalks, magazine photos, etc.) to the teens. Ask them to create their own artistic symbol or depiction of the Holy Spirit. Refer the teens to several descriptions of symbols for the Holy Spirit on pages 200-201 of the Candidate's Handbook.

D Have the teens use a Bible concordance to trace how many times the word "Spirit" is used in the gospel of Luke and the Acts of the Apostles.

PRAYER EXPERIENCES/LESSON IDEAS

A Cut and stretch the plastic holder off of a six-pack of soft drinks into one long piece. Tie one end to the middle of a wire coat hanger. Suspend the coat hanger from the ceiling. Place a large bucket of water below the plastic strip. Dim the lights. With a match, light the bottom of the plastic. "Balls of fire" simulating the tongues of fire will drop into the water. Read the Pentecost narrative or sing the Taizé chant *Veni Sancte Spiritus* ("Come Holy Spirit") while the plastic burns.

Conclude by praying the opening prayer from the Rite of Confirmation (also on page 202 of the Candidate's Handbook):

> God of power and mercy,
>
> send your Holy Spirit
>
> to live in our hearts
>
> and make us temples of his glory.
>
> We ask this through our Lord Jesus Christ, your Son,
>
> who lives and reigns with you and the Holy Spirit,
>
> one God, for ever and ever.
>
> Amen.

B Have the teens reflect quietly on passages from scripture that have to do with the Holy Spirit. Ask them to choose a favorite Spirit passage and print it on a bookmark.

C Ask the teens to write a personal prayer directed to the Holy Spirit.

NAME _____

THE HOLY SPIRIT IN SCRIPTURE

For each passage, write a sentence telling what it says about the Holy Spirit.

Genesis 1:1-2

Genesis 2:7

Exodus 19:16-19

Ezekiel 37:1-14

Luke 1:26-35

John 14:16-17

John 20:21-23

NAME _____

CONFIRMATION IN SCRIPTURE

Read the following passages. Briefly summarize each passage and explain what it tells about the origins of the sacrament of Confirmation.

Acts 8:14-17

Acts 19:1-6

2 Corinthians 1:21-22

NAME _____

COMMITMENT TO FAITH
Finish each sentence. What will you do in each of these areas after receiving the sacrament of Confirmation?

I will continue my Catholic education by . . .

I will practice Christian service by . . .

I will participate in liturgy by . . .

I will work continue to follow the commandments, especially in the most difficult area of . . .

I will become involved in the parish ministry of . . .

I will improve my practice of personal prayer by . . .

I will publicly witness to my Catholic faith by . . .

GIFTS OF THE SPIRIT FLASH CARDS

WISDOM

UNDERSTANDING

RIGHT JUDGMENT

COURAGE

KNOWLEDGE

REVERENCE

WONDER AND AWE IN GOD'S PRESENCE

GIFTS OF THE SPIRIT FLASH CARDS

The gift that allows us to look at reality from God's point of view.

The gift that helps us understand more about God
and the larger mysteries of faith.

The gift that helps us make good and free choices,
and develop our conscience in light of Church teaching.

The gift that helps us to be encouraged even when we face our greatest fears.
It gives us the strength to follow our own convictions.

The gift that helps us to know God and note how God is working in our lives.

This gift widens the circle of respect to include care, concern,
and compassion for God and God's creation.

The gift that helps us to delight in God's presence and power
and to be continually amazed at God's love for us.

Your Christian Vocation

(see pages 205-221 of the Candidate's Handbook)

BACKGROUND

Our vocation is the calling or destiny we have in this life on earth and for our life in eternity. God has called all people to love and serve him. The result of fulfilling this primary vocation is eternal happiness.

Within our primary Christian vocation, given to us at Baptism, are several ways for us to live and use our talents to their fullest extent. Teenagers are at a time in their lives when they can rightly consider how they may best use their gifts so that they are personally satisfied and of service to others.

In Church parlance, the term vocation has been commonly associated with the sacrament of Holy Orders—the sacrament of Christian ministry—as well as with other "religious" vocations that usually include taking vows of poverty, chastity, and obedience. Though the definition of vocation has expanded to include both the married and those committed to single life, ordained men (bishops, priests, and deacons) and brothers and sisters (men and women who live in religious communities) have made a public commitment to serving God by serving God's people.

In the teenage years, teens are free to dream and imagine themselves in one of the vocations that the Holy Spirit may be prompting them to choose.

The lessons in this chapter help the teens to that end. First, teens are reminded of the opportunity they have to dream up any possible and reasonable goal for their lives. They are offered suggestions for recognizing and naming their personal God-given talents and gifts. They are given a seven-step plan for discerning life choices. This chapter introduces this plan and shows how it is applicable to making choices regarding career.

A Christian vocation extends beyond this world into the next. The course concludes by reminding the teens of their own mortality to help them realize that they only have a limited time to bring their lives to fulfillment. This exercise also helps them not to forget that their ultimate goal is heaven, a final communion with the Blessed Trinity, Mary, the angels, and all the saints.

The Hebrew word "Amen" means "I believe." The lessons of this chapter help the teens to be a talking and walking Amen and to live out completely the faith professed in Baptism and confirmed in the sacrament of Confirmation.

Note: You may wish to combine some or all of the lessons of this final chapter with a concluding Mass or a social outing like a picnic.

Sample Schedule
Model I: Focused Preparation (one 3-hour session)
Suggested Session Plan

Warm-Up (about 30 minutes)
Refer to pages 205-206 of the Candidate's Handbook.
- Briefly define *vocation* based on the material in the text. Relate the topic to Christian vocation and the sacrament of Confirmation.
- Use Warm-up/Breaktime Exercise "A" (page 201). If the group is larger than fifteen, divide the candidates into smaller groups.
- Use Warm-up/Breaktime Exercise "D" (page 201) either as a small group activity or with the entire group.

Lesson 1: Discovering and Using Your Gifts (about 30 minutes)
Refer to pages 206-211 of the Candidate's Handbook.
- This lesson focuses primarily on using one's gifts to plan for a career.
- Use Discovering and Using Your Gifts "A" (pages 201-202). Allow time to discuss some of the teen's ideas for a career.
- Use Discovering and Using Your Gifts "D" (pages 202-203).

Breaktime/Lesson 1 continued (about 25 minutes)
- Allow the chance for a quick stretch, drink of water, etc. prior to the continuation of the lesson.
- Use Discovering and Using Your Gifts "F" (page 203). If time permits, allow the teens to ask questions of the panelists.

Lesson 2: A Call to Love (about 90 minutes)
Refer to pages 211-214 of the Candidate's Handbook.
- Focus the lesson especially on the vocations of marriage and priesthood/religious life. Provide an overview of the topic based on the material in the Candidate's Handbook. Offer short stretch breaks when necessary.
- Use A Call to Love "C" (pages 203-204). Have the teens complete this activity with a partner.
- Use A Call to Love "D" (page 204). The written paragraph assignment can be used as a private journal entry.
- Introduce the vocation of priesthood and religious life. Use A Call to Love "G" (page 204).
- Use A Call to Love "H" (page 205).

Lesson 3: Life in the Trinity/Prayer (about 5 minutes)
Refer to pages 215-217 of the Candidate's Handbook.
- Conclude with the short presentation and prayer from Life in the Trinity "A" (page 205).

Individual Home Assignments
- Assign A Call to Love "E" (page 204). Ask the teens to write the results of their interviews in their journals.
- Complete all "50 Questions" from pages 243-247 of the Candidate's Handbook

Candidate/Sponsor Activities

- Use Discovering and Using Your Gifts "E" (page 203). The sponsors should tell about how a discernment process led to their own career choice.
- Adapt and use Prayer Experience "B" (page 209). Encourage a discussion on how the scripture passages speak of the vocation of love and marriage.
- Have a discussion about the use of drugs and alcohol among teens. See Life in the Trinity "B" (page 205).
- Discuss the FAQs on pages 218-219 of the Candidate's Handbook.
- *Note:* If this is the last one-to-one time planned for candidates and sponsors, make sure they allow time for reflection and thankfulness for the relationship that was forged during preparation for Confirmation.

MODEL 2: EXTENDED PREPARATION (TWO 1-HOUR SESSIONS)
Suggested Session 1 Plan

Warm-Up (about 10 minutes)
Refer to pages 205-206 of the Candidate's Handbook.
- Introduce the main topics of the next two sessions: career planning, marriage, religious life, and Christian vocation in the Trinity.
- Use Warm-Up/Breaktime Exercise "B" (page 201).

Lesson: Discovering and Using Your Gifts (about 20 minutes)
Refer to pages 206-211 of the Candidate's Handbook.
- Discuss what it means to have a "healthy self-concept." Use Discovering and Using Your Gifts "B" (page 202).
- Use Discovering and Using Your Gifts "C" (page 202).

Lesson: Called to Love (about 20 minutes)
Refer to pages 211-215 of the Candidate's Handbook.
- Invite a priest or religious to speak to the group about his or her understanding of 1) our Christian vocation, 2) the traditional vocations to the religious life, and 3) the vocation to marriage. See A Call to Love "F" (page 204).

Prayer Experience (about 10 minutes)
- Adapt Prayer Experience "B" (page 209) for half the amount of time. (Give each candidate only five scripture passages rather than ten.)

Individual Home Assignments
- Assign Discovering and Using Your Gifts "A" (pages 201-202).
- Assign A Call to Love "E" (page 206). Allow time in the next session for the teens to briefly share the results of the survey.
- Assign the essay suggested in A Call to Love "A" (page 203).

Candidate/Sponsor Activities
- Share the discernment process for a career suggested in Discovering and Using Your Gifts "E" (page 203).
- If possible, arrange for the candidates to visit the sponsor's place of employment and discuss aspects of his or her career. (This activity could be conducted as a joint project with a larger group of candidates and sponsors.)

Suggested Session 2 Plan

Warm-Up (about 5 minutes)
- Allow the teens to share some of the results of their survey of married couples (see Individual Home Assignments, above).

Lesson Plan: Life in the Trinity (about 40 minutes)
Refer to pages 215-217 of the Candidate's Handbook.
- Focus the entire lesson on alcohol and drug use among teens.
- Use Life in the Trinity "B" (pages 205-206).
- Use Features "A" or "B" (pages 207-208)

Prayer Experience (about 15 minutes)
- Use Prayer Experience "A" (page 208).

Individual Home Assignments
- Assign the essay suggested in Life in the Trinity "C" (page 206).
- Complete the "50 Questions" assignment (pages 243-247 of the Candidate's Handbook).

Candidate/Sponsor Activities
- Ask the candidate to share the essay he or she wrote on heaven (see Individual Assignments, above).
- Discuss the FAQs, pages 218-219.
- Reserve time for the candidates and sponsors to write each other letters of appreciation for the time spent together during the Confirmation preparation program.

MODEL 3: CONCENTRATED PREPARATION (ONE 90-MINUTE SESSION)
Suggested Session Plan

Warm-Up (about 20 minutes)
Refer to pages 205-206 of the Candidate's Handbook.
- Introduce the main topic of Chapter 10, career and vocation choices, as well as the Christian vocation to life in the Trinity.
- Use Warm-Up/Breaktime Exercise "D" (page 201).
- Offer a brief discussion on maturity. Use Warm-Up/Breaktime Exercise "C" (page 201).

Lesson Plan (about 35 minutes)
Refer to pages 206-211 of the Candidate's Handbook.
- Continue the discussion on careers and career planning. Use Discovering and Using Your Gifts "A" (pages 201-202).
- Use Discovering and Using Your Gifts "D" (pages 202-203).
- Use Discovering and Using Your Gifts "E" (page 203). Make sure to allow follow up in the large group to allow volunteers to share some of their career aspirations.

Breaktime (about 5 minutes)
- Allow time for a stretch, refreshments, visit to the bathroom, etc.

Lesson Plan continued (about 25 minutes)
Refer to pages 206-217 of the Candidate's Handbook.
- Combine A Call to Love "E" and "F" (page 204). Arrange a vocations panel that addresses more than one type of vocation. Include a person with a vocation to the single life as well. Allow time for the panel to take questions from the teens.

Conclusion/Prayer (about 5 minutes)
- Have the candidates stand and recite together the Prayer of Blessed Elizabeth of the Trinity (page 221 of the Candidate's Handbook). See Life in the Trinity "A" (page 205).

Individual Home Assignments
- Use A Call to Love "A" (page 203).
- Complete the "50 Questions" (pages 243-247).

Candidate/Sponsor Activities
- Encourage the teens to talk over possible career choices using the discernment model described in Discovering and Using Your Gifts "E" (page 203).
- Arrange a time when several candidates and sponsors can watch and then discuss the video *Mother Teresa* (see A Call to Love, "B," page 203).
- Discuss and compare ideas about what heaven is like.
- Review the FAQs, pages 218-219 of the Candidate's Handbook.
- If this is the final one-to-one meeting, leave time for an expression of thankfulness and appreciation between sponsors and candidates.

INTRODUCTION
Warm-up/Breaktime Exercises

A Ask the teens to bring photos of themselves when they were freshmen (or photos from at least two years prior). Sit with the group in a circle. Call on volunteers to pass their old photo around while they describe their "freshman selves" in third person. For example, "He had a hard time making friends" or "She thought she knew everything." Also, ask the person to describe how he or she is different now from when the photo was taken.

B Make a set of flash cards. Put numbers on them to represent five-year age intervals beginning at twenty-five and ending at eighty. Briefly define *vocation* as a call to marriage, religious life, or committed single life and *career* as a job that expresses one's talents and creativity. Call a volunteer to the front of the room. Ask him or her to pick from the "age" flash cards and to describe the career and vocation he or she imagines living when actually that age. Call on other teens to repeat the exercise.

C Discuss maturity and what it entails. Offer the following descriptions (write them on the board or newsprint). Then ask the teens to add other descriptions of maturity to the list:

- **A mature person has the ability to give as well as to receive.**
- **A mature person is empathetic; can perceive how another person is feeling.**
- **A mature person can establish and keep relationships with others.**
- **A mature person is comfortable with himself or herself.**
- **A mature person is emotionally, spiritually, and physically fit.**
- **A mature person is able to meet his or her needs in a healthy way.**

D Print the following sentence starters on the board or newsprint:

1. **I would like to be a person who. . . .**
2. **Right after high school I plan to. . . .**
3. **If I could achieve one dream for the future it would be. . . .**
4. **I am happiest when. . . .**
5. **I see myself as the kind of Catholic who. . . .**
6. **I would describe my faith as. . . .**
7. **I would consider a religious vocation if. . . .**
8. **My idea of the "perfect" marriage is. . . .**

Prepare a set of eight flash cards, with the numbers 1 to 8. Choose two people. Ask them each to pick a flash card. The number they choose is the sentence they are to finish before the group. The person who picked first shares first. The person who picked second has a chance to think about how he or she will finish the sentence. Collect the cards. Before the second person shares, allow a third person to pick a number, and so on.

Discovering and Using Your Gifts/Lesson Ideas

A Pass out six 3" x 5" pieces of paper to each teen. Tell them to write six different answers to the same question—"Who am I?"—one on each paper. (For example, "I am a person who is good at soccer" or "I am a person who enjoys spending time with my family and friends.")

After allowing time for writing, tell the teens to draw a star next to any of the items that tells something they like to do. Then ask them to draw another star by any item that tells something they are good at. They may have two stars on the same paper.

Your Christian Vocation

Point out to the teens that examining what they like to do and what they are good at can give them a good idea of what they can do for a career.

Pass out one more slip of paper. Ask the teens to write an idea about how they might combine what they like and what they are good at into a career. On the other side of the paper, ask them to speculate on "who might pay them for this career"; i.e., what type of living they could expect to make in this area.

B Conduct a discussion about having a healthy self-concept based on maintaining a balance between feelings of narcissism and worthlessness (see pages 207-208 of the Candidate's Handbook).

Share the expression "believing your own lies." People who fall in this category often boast, saying things like "the team couldn't have won without me" or "all the guys/girls are in love with me." Call on volunteers to share their observations about people they know who have this attitude. Ask: "How does this attitude effect the person who has it and those around him or her?"

Next, point out another type of person who falls into the trap of believing their own lies, related to the extreme of worthlessness. These type of people tend to believe that they are too fat or too thin, the worst students, friendless, and of no value to anyone else. Ask volunteers if they know someone who seems to believe in his or her own worthlessness. Ask what effect that belief has on the person and on those around him or her.

Point out that the opposite of believing one's own lies is to believe in the truth. Go around the classroom. Ask each teen to share one truthful statement about himself or herself that best represents who he or she is. For example, "I am an outgoing person who is comfortable in new situations" or "I am truly knowledgeable about sports."

Finally, ask the teens to brainstorm what types of actions and attitudes result from a healthy self-concept. Write the suggestions on the board or newsprint. For example:
*   **better chance for lasting friendships/relationships,**
*   **easier to do an assessment of one's vocation and career choices,**
*   **more comfortable in confronting new challenges,**
*   **more likely to be happy.**

C Ask the class to brainstorm a list of putdowns common among their peers (e.g., "you don't have any game" or "get a life""). Print the list on the board or newsprint. The list may become more absurd as you go.

Next, have the teens work in pairs to come up with creative "comebacks" to some of the putdowns on the list. The comebacks should not be derogatory in themselves, but rather should claim in confidence the person's healthy self-concept (e.g., "I love my life. Do you love yours?").

D Pass out the worksheet "Thinking About Career Choices" (page 210 of this Manual) and ask the teens to work on it individually, marking each item according to the scale listed.

When they have finished, divide the class into groups of four or five teens. Ask them to go around the group, sharing one item they marked as most important and why they marked it as they did. Then have them go around again and tell about an item they marked least or less important and tell why they did.

Next, in the same format, ask the teens to discuss the following questions one at a time:
*   Which factor have you spent the most time thinking about?

- How much have your parents influenced your career choice?
- What are some things you can do to find out more about your chosen career?

E Ask the teens to apply the discernment steps below (also on pages 209-210 of the Candidate's Handbook with an explanation) to a career they are contemplating. After time for reflection, have them share with a partner their career plan and how each step might help them to prepare.

Discernment Steps
1. Dream
2. Temper with Realism
3. Plan
4. Seek Advice
5. Pray
6. Act on Your Decision
7. Evaluate

Also, ask the teens to think about and share a second career option and to imagine a scenario in which they might realistically end up in this career.

F Arrange for adults from the parish community to participate in a career panel. Invite three or four adults (men and women) in a variety of careers to speak with the teens. Encourage them to include some or all of the following points in their presentations:
- background on their career (how long they've been in it; what they like about it; what their daily work schedule is like; how it helps them to live out God's plan for their lives);
- planning (the steps they took as a teenager to plan for their career);
- things teens can do today to plan for a career;
- the importance of dreaming lofty goals.

A Call to Love/Lesson Ideas

A Share this quotation of St. Augustine with the teens:
Love is itself the fulfillment of all our works. There is the goal; that is why we run: we run toward it, and once we reach it, in it we shall find rest.

True love in any form is caring, accepting, honest, nurturing, and forgiving.

Ask the teens to write a short essay titled "My Call to Love" explaining how they envision themselves incorporating true love into a vocation that God calls them to and they accept.

B Play all or part of the video *Mother Teresa* (82 minutes, available from Vision Video at www.visionvideo.com). The video was shot over five years in ten different countries, depicting how Mother Teresa transcends political, religious, and social barriers to do works of love based on her deep faith in Christ.

C Have the teens brainstorm a list of questions they should ask themselves about a potential marriage partner prior to making the commitment to being married. List and discuss the questions. Some examples are listed below:
- How does my partner treat me?
- How does my partner treat others (family, friends, people in customer service, etc.)?
- Is this person someone I will be proud to marry in front of family and friends?

Your Christian Vocation

- Does this person have similar values?
- Is this person someone I want to have and raise children with?

D Randomly divide the class into pairs of girls and boys. Ask the teens to work individually to fill-out the "Marriage Issues Survey" (page 211 of this Manual). After they have both finished, ask the teens to discuss each item with their partner.

To sum up, call the group together. Call on volunteers to share what they consider to be the "most important" issue and the "least important" issue before going into a marriage. Make sure to hear a variety of opinions.

Finally, ask the teens to write a paragraph explaining which issues they would have to come to agreement on with a potential marriage partner before they could possibly consider marriage and what possible steps they could take to resolve any disagreements.

E Arrange an opportunity for the teens to interview at least two or three married couples. If the activity is to be done during class time, invite some married couples to be present and available for interviews in a panel setting. Another option is to have the teens work on this activity at home and come to class prepared with the results of the interview. In either case, the teens should find out from the couple:

- the circumstances having to do with "how they met,"
- how the subject of marriage was first brought up between them,
- how they understand marriage to be a lifelong commitment,
- their opinion of what teens can do now to prepare for marriage,
- how God and faith plays a part in their marriage.

F Invite a priest and/or religious to visit the class. Ask the person(s) to share the following information about his or her vocation:

- the occasion or "call" that led them to seek out ordination or religious life,
- the preparation that took place before ordination and/or making final vows,
- the joys of religious life,
- how his or her gifts are at the benefit of the entire Church.

Allow the opportunity for the teens and visitors to engage in a question and answer session.

G Distribute five strips of paper and a pencil to each teen. Print the following sentence starters on the board. Ask the teens to finish one sentence on each strip of paper.

- **Some things that attract me to the lifestyle of a priest or religious are. . . .**
- **A priest whom my family and I admire is _____ because. . . .**
- **I think more teenagers would answer the call to religious life if. . . .**
- **The gospel counsels of poverty, chastity, and obedience are important to all Christians because. . . .**
- **A time I thought about being a priest or religious was. . . .**

When completed, sit with the teens in one large circle. Ask them to arrange the strips from 1 to 5, with 1 being the sentence they are most willing to share with others, 5 being the sentence they are least willing to talk about. Then go around the circle calling on teens to share their sentence. Ask appropriate follow-up questions as time permits.

H Show the video *Life Work: Finding God's Purpose in Your Life* (45 minutes, available from Vision Video at www.visionvideo.com). The presentation includes testimonies from Catholics who have found joy in their vocation, including Alan Keyes, Patrick Madrid, and Fr. Bill McDonald. It offers encouragement for anyone to pursue God's unique plan for their lives.

Life in the Trinity/Lesson Ideas

A Remind the teens that our ultimate end is to be in the perfect unity of the Blessed Trinity. Yet, even now on earth, we are to make a home for the Trinity in our lives. How do we do this? Jesus said to his disciples, "Whoever loves me will keep my word, and my Father will love him, and we will come to him and make our dwelling with him" (John 14:23)

Also, pray with the teens the following Prayer of Blessed Elizabeth of the Trinity (also on page 48 of the Candidate's Handbook):

O my God, Trinity whom I adore, help me forget myself entirely so to establish myself in you, unmovable and peaceful as if my soul were already in eternity. May nothing be able to trouble my peace or make me leave you, O my unchanging God, but may each minute bring me more deeply into your mystery! Grant my soul peace. Make it your heaven, your beloved dwelling and the place of your rest. May I never abandon you there, but may I be there, whole and entire, completely vigilant in my faith, entirely adoring, and wholly given over to your creative action. Amen.

B Discuss the issue of teenage use of alcohol, especially related to drinking and driving. First, ask the teens to list several reasons they think teenagers do drink (print on board or newsprint). For example:

peer pressure
influence of family members who use alcohol
makes them feel older
to gain more self-confidence
to relax
to escape problems
to feel happy

With the teens, create a second list of several reasons why teenagers do not drink. For example:

"I don't like the taste."
"I don't need to."
"It's bad for your health."
"My parents would be mad."
"It's illegal."
"It causes problems."
"I want to be in control."

Related to both lists, call on a teen to stand before the group and to be interviewed on issues related to teenage use of alcohol (and drugs). Ask:

- When was a time you said "no" to alcohol? How did you do it?
- How do teens go about getting alcohol?
- How do you insure that you do not get into a car with a driver who has been drinking?
- How have your parents influenced your attitudes towards alcohol?

Your Christian Vocation

- If you were at a party where everyone was drinking and you didn't want to drink, what would you say?
- What is the general attitude of your peers towards alcohol? What is your attitude?

Repeat the exercise by asking other teens to come to the front of the class to be interviewed.

C Have the participants write a short essay that describes what they think heaven is like.

D Tell the teens that they are to imagine that they are going to die shortly and that they are to write a testimony for themselves that will be read at the funeral. The testimony should do more than list their accomplishments. It should sum up what they really believe about creation, God, life, and life after death. After the teens have written the testimony, ask them to choose someone else to read it to the class. Allow time for each person's testimony to be read aloud.

References/FAQ

References from the *Catechism of the Catholic Church* for the Frequently Asked Questions include:

Does everyone have a vocation? (CCC, 358, 825)
A Christian's primary vocation, given at Baptism, is to bring God's love to others. Everyone also has a unique vocation because God has a plan for everyone. A vocation involves understanding God's will for our lives. It involves understanding who we are now and who we will become in the future.

How many years of training does it take to become a priest?(CCC, 1578)
Training for the diocesan priesthood usually involves four years of graduate study after college. Many dioceses also require an extra year of "internship" so that the seminarian (candidate for priesthood) can live and minister at a parish. Finally, the candidate is ordained a deacon for a period of time before being ordained a priest. This period may last anywhere from a few months to a few years.

Does the Church have rules for who you can marry?(CCC, 1625)
Yes. A person cannot marry while married to someone else. Religious, permanent deacons, or priests cannot marry unless they have received a dispensation from their vow of celibacy. Blood brothers and sisters cannot marry, nor can first cousins. Family members who have established legal ties (e.g., step-brothers to step-sisters) cannot marry either. Also, a license from a civil court is necessary for marriage. Some states also require a couple to have a medical examination before marriage.

How does the Church care for the sick and dying? (CCC, 1499-1525)
All the faithful are obliged to care for the sick and dying, through their prayers and visits. Also, the sacrament of Anointing of the Sick is a sacrament of healing in which the healing and loving touch of Christ is extended through the Christian community to those who are seriously ill or dying.

Why does God allow death? (CCC, 1006-1014)
Death was not part of God's original plan for humans. Death was the consequence of the first sin of Adam. However, "Just as all die in Adam, so too in Christ shall all be brought to life" (1 Cor 15:22).

What is meant by "rising from the dead"? (CCC, 997-1001)
At death, the body and soul are separated. The body decays and the soul goes on to meet God. Through the power of Jesus' resurrection, God will grant incorruptible life to our bodies by uniting them with our souls at the end of time.

Do we know when the world will end?(CCC, 673, 1048)
Many religious groups today make predictions about when the end of the world will occur. Several claim the end is imminent. Recall Jesus' words when asked this question by the apostles. He told them, "but of that day or hour, no one knows . . . only the Father" (Mk 13:32). Rather, Jesus expects that we will live every day as if it were our last.

Features/Lesson Ideas

A Arrange for a recovering teenage or young adult alcohol and/or drug abuser to speak with the class. (For recruiting possible speakers, contact organizations like Mothers Against Drunk Drivers, a local counseling or treatment center, Alcoholics Anonymous, or parish support groups.) Possible topics for the presentation can include:

- how he/she got started with alcohol,
- some dangerous situations alcohol use has led to,
- when the line to abuse was crossed,
- regrets for using alcohol,
- difficulties with recovery.

B Play a video or part of a video that deals with alcohol abuse, including the danger of driving while under the influence. Check with local driving schools or high school libraries for the most current videos on the topic.

C C. S. Lewis contrasted hell and heaven in the following way. Share these images with the teens (also on pages 220-221 of the Candidate's Handbook):

In hell they talk a lot about love.
In heaven they just do it.

Hell is an unending church service without God.
Heaven is God without a church service.

In hell, everything is pornographic and no one is excited.
In heaven everything is exciting and there is no pornography.

In hell there is sex without pleasure.
In heaven there is pleasure without sex.

Hell is a bad dream from which you never wake.
Heaven is waking from which you never need to sleep.

Ask the teens to write some other sentences contrasting hell and heaven in the same form as C. S. Lewis used. When completed, ask them to share these images with a partner or in a small group.

PRAYER EXPERIENCES

A Have the teens sit in a circle. Dim the lights. Lead a prayer for teens who are suffering from alcoholism or addictions of any kind. Pray:

Dear God,
alcohol and drugs have hurt many people we know.
We seek your help to encourage them
to seek a right course and become
the people you intend them to be.
We ask this prayer in the name of your Son,
Jesus Christ, our Lord.
Amen.

Pass a candle around the room. Tell the teens when they are holding the candle they should offer a prayer for someone they know who is suffering from addiction. The response is, "Lord, hear our prayer." Also, tell the teens if they wish to pray silently for a person, they may do so when they are holding the candle. In that case, you lead the petition, "For *name's* intention, we pray . . . Lord, hear our prayer."

B Pass out a set of "Scripture Passages on Marriage" (see page 212 of this Manual) to each teen. Ask them to use these strips as bookmarks and place them on the appropriate pages in their bible. When all have completed this task, begin playing a recording of some instrumental background music. Ask the teens to move to a quiet place, alone, look up one passage, and meditate on its meaning for their lives and the possible commitment ahead for them in marriage or another vocation. Allow about twenty minutes. Tell them to move on to other passages when they feel ready. They do not have to get to them all.

When completed, pray the Glory Be (also on page 221 of the Candidate's Handbook):

Glory be to the Father, and to the Son, and to the Holy Spirit: as it was in the beginning, is now, and ever shall be, world without end. Amen.

NAME _____

Thinking About Career Choices

Directions: Mark the items below based on the following scale: 5=very important, 1=not important to me at all.

1. A career where I make a great amount of money   1 2 3 4 5

2. A career where I have contact with the public   1 2 3 4 5

3. A career that offers flexible hours   1 2 3 4 5

4. A career that mostly takes place out of doors   1 2 3 4 5

5. A career that brings fame and prestige   1 2 3 4 5

6. A career that helps others, especially the less fortunate   1 2 3 4 5

7. A career that is fast-paced, has its share of pressure, and is never boring   1 2 3 4 5

8. A career that is future-oriented   1 2 3 4 5

9. A career that allows me to "be my own boss"   1 2 3 4 5

10. A career that allows me to work at home if I choose   1 2 3 4 5

11. A career that allows me to use my talents and skills in a creative way   1 2 3 4 5

12. A career that my parents approve of   1 2 3 4 5

13. A career that other people find "cool"   1 2 3 4 5

14. A career that offers great security   1 2 3 4 5

15. A career that allows me the opportunity to express my faith in God freely   1 2 3 4 5

NAME _____

Marriage Issues Survey

Directions: Mark the issues below based on the following scale: 5=very important, 1=not important to me at all.

1. Spending time with my friends after we're married   1   2   3   4   5

2. Where we will live   1   2   3   4   5

3. How many children we will have   1   2   3   4   5

4. Reserving time for family meals and prayer   1   2   3   4   5

5. Participating in and worshipping in a religious community   1   2   3   4   5

6. Belonging to the same religion or church   1   2   3   4   5

7. The amount of money we have   1   2   3   4   5

8. Both parents sharing responsibility for child-rearing   1   2   3   4   5

9. The responsible use of alcohol   1   2   3   4   5

10. The place where we will spend holidays   1   2   3   4   5

11. The neatness of our home   1   2   3   4   5

12. The understanding of marriage as a commitment until death   1   2   3   4   5

13. Balancing work with family time   1   2   3   4   5

14. Being able to trust one another   1   2   3   4   5

15. Being each other's best friend   1   2   3   4   5

NAME _____

Scripture Passages on Marriage

Matthew 5:1-12	Matthew 5:13-16
Matthew 7:21, 24-25	Matthew 19:3-6
Matthew 22:35-40	Mark 10:6-9
John 2:1-11	John 15:9-12
John 15:12-16	John 17:20-23

1. **Define** *catechumenate.*

    The catechumenate is the process of conversion and study of the faith for the purpose of preparing for the sacrament of initiation. Today, it is a process that may last a year or longer.

2. **What are some differences between the Rite of Christian Initiation for Adults (RCIA) and the Rite of Baptism of Children (RBC)?**

    In the RCIA, all three sacraments of initiation are administered at the Easter Vigil. In the RBC, Baptism is administered to infants, the other sacraments of initiation follow at a later time. In the RCIA, catechesis precedes reception of the sacraments. In RBC, catechesis comes after Baptism. In RBC, the order of reception of the sacraments may be different than the traditional ordering of Baptism, Confirmation, and Eucharist.

3. **Name the elements of the basic rite of Baptism.**

    The basic rite of Baptism consists of either immersing the candidate in water or pouring water on his or her head, calling the person by name, and pronouncing the words, "I baptize you in the name of the Father, and of the Son, and of the Holy Spirit."

4. **How many adults were baptized at your parish at the last Easter vigil?**

    Candidates should inquire from RCIA coordinator for answer.

5. **How many children were baptized in the last calendar year at your parish?**

    Candidates should inquire from parish secretary or record keeper for answer.

6. **What are the central beliefs about God espoused in our Catholic creeds?**

    The central beliefs about God are: There is one God. God is Creator, not created. God is almighty. God is Trinitarian (three persons in the one God).

7. **Name at least four attributes of God.**

    Answers should come from the following: God is eternal. God is unique. God is infinite and omnipotent. God is immense. God is not limited to space and time. God contains all things. God is immutable. God is pure Spirit. God is alive. God is holy.

8. **Name and explain three dogmas about the Holy Trinity.**

1) The Trinity is one. This means there is but one God in three persons. 2) The three persons are distinct from one another (e.g., the Father is not the Son, nor is the Son the Holy Spirit). 3) The divine persons are related to one another. Though intimately related to one another, the three persons have one nature or substance.

9. **Where is the tabernacle placed in your parish ? Why is it placed where it is?**

Answers will vary, however, the teens should understand that the tabernacle is to be placed in a "most worthy place with the greatest honor."

10. **When is the Feast of the Holy Trinity?**

The Feast of the Holy Trinity is on the Sunday following Pentecost.

11. **How did the early Church answer Arius' claim that Jesus only took the "appearance" of a man?**

The Church answered these claims in statements of the Nicene Creed: Jesus is eternally begotten of the Father. Jesus is God from God, Light from Light, true God from true God. Through Jesus all things were made.

12. **Define** *Incarnation.*

Incarnation means "embodied in human form." On the first Christmas God became human in the person of Jesus.

13. **What did Jesus tell his disciples would happen to him in Jerusalem?**

Jesus told his disciples that he would be handed over by some Jewish leaders to the Gentiles who would mock him, spit upon him, scourge him, and put him to death.

14. **How can you come to know Jesus?**

You can know Jesus in many different ways. For example, in yourself (Jesus lives in you), in the Church ("where two or three are gathered in my name"), in the sacraments (especially the Eucharist), in the Bible, through prayer, and in the least of our brothers and sisters.

15. **How do you think you would respond if someone held a gun to your head and asked "Do you believe in Jesus Christ?"**

Answers will vary.

16. **Name and explain three kinds of writing in the Bible.**

Answers may include parables (short stories with a moral lesson), proverbs (wise sayings), history, hymns (e.g., book of Psalms), letters (all of the New Testament epistles), genealogies (lists of ancestors), and prayers (e.g. the Lord's Prayer).

17. **What are the three stages of the composition of the gospel?**

The first stage was the life and teaching of Jesus Christ. The second stage was the spreading of the gospel through the oral tradition. In the third stage, the gospels were written.

18. **How did the Second Vatican Council encourage a renewed interest in the scriptures for Catholics?**

The Second Vatican Council introduced a three-year cycle of readings for Sunday Mass so that nearly all of the New Testament books are sampled and a good selection of the Old Testament will be heard. Also, the Church encourages Catholics to study and pray with the Bible.

19. **What is meant by the term *Septuagint*? *vulgate*?**

The Septuagint is the name for the Greek translation of the Old Testament. The vulgate is the name for the Latin translation of the Bible. It is a word that means "commonly known"

20. **Which of the following translations of the Bible are accepted by Catholics? Protestants? both?**

King James (P)   New Jerusalem (B)   Revised Standard (B)

New American (C)   The Way (P)   Good News (P)

21. **What were the causes of the schism between the churches of East and West and of the Protestant Reformation?**

One cause of the schism between the Churches of East and West was the introduction of the added expression "and the Son" to the article of the Nicene Creed referring to the Holy Spirit ("he proceeds from the Father and the Son") without seeking approval for such a change from a worldwide council of bishops. The Protestant Reformation was caused by the perception of several abuses in the Church. Several of these perceived abuses involved the mixing of spiritual and political issues.

22. **How does the Church answer the criticism that "Catholics pray to saints"?**

Catholics do not pray to saints as if they were God. We ask the saints to intercede for us, to join us in prayer, because we know that their lives have been spent in close communion with God. We also ask the saints for their friendship so that we can follow the examples they have left for us.

23. **Define *infallibility* related to Church teaching.**

Infallibility is the name given to Church teaching in the areas of faith and morals that are "without error." This teaching is based in the fact that Jesus remains with the Church for all time and that such teachings are given with God's assistance. The most common form of infallibility is that given by the Pope when he teaches "from the chair" of St. Peter.

24. **Who is the bishop of your diocese? What do you know about him?**

Encourage the candidates to use the diocesan web page to research this answer.

25. **Define each of these Church structures:**

archdiocese—the dioceses under the jurisdiction of an archbishop ("chief" bishop)

college of cardinals—the body of cardinals that elect a new Pope, assist the Pope in governing the Church, and administer the Church when the Pope is absent

parish—a part of a diocese that has its own church

diocese—the district of churches under the jurisdiction of a bishop

Appendix

deanery—a district of parishes within a diocese

parish council—an official group of parishioners who gather regularly to provide the pastor with wise and prudent advice on pastoral matters

26. **How does the morality of human acts depend on the object chosen, the intention, and the circumstances of the action?**

The moral object is "what" we do. There are objectively good and bad actions. A good intention cannot make a bad action just. A bad intention, however, can make an act evil, that is itself good. Circumstances can effect the degree of merit or blame to an action, although again they cannot make good an action that is in itself evil.

27. **Write the Beatitudes.**

The Beatitudes found in Matthew 5:3-12 are:
Blessed are the poor in spirit, for theirs is the kingdom of heaven.
Blessed are they who mourn, for they will be comforted.
Blessed are the meek, for they will inherit the land.
Blessed are they who hunger and thirst for righteousness, for they will be satisfied.
Blessed are the merciful, for they will be shown mercy.
Blessed are the clean of heart, for they will see God.
Blessed are the peacemakers, for they will be called children of God.
Blessed are they who are persecuted for the sake of righteousness, for theirs is the kingdom of heaven.
Blessed are you when they insult you and persecute you and utter every kind of evil against you [falsely] because of me. Rejoice and be glad, for your reward will be great in heaven. Thus they persecuted the prophets who were before you.

28. **Write the Ten Commandments.**

I. I, the Lord am your God: you shall not have other gods besides me.
II. You shall not take the name of the Lord, your God, in vain.
III. Remember to keep holy the Sabbath day.
IV. Honor your father and your mother.
V. You shall not kill.
VI. You shall not commit adultery.
VII. You shall not steal.
VIII. You shall not bear false witness against your neighbor.
IX. You shall not covet your neighbor's wife.
X. You shall not covet your neighbor's goods.

29. **Write the precepts of the Church.**
1. Attend Mass on Sundays.
2. Confess your sins at least once a year.
3. Receive communion during the Easter season.
4. Keep the holy days of obligation.
5. Observe days of fasting and abstinence.
In addition, Catholics are to provide for the material needs of the Church.

30. How can the sacrament of Penance help you to live a moral life?

The sacrament of Penance, or reconciliation, provides occasions for grace, for the absolution of sins, and the opportunity to be more loving.

31. How is the Paschal mystery like other historical events? How is it different from other historical events?

The Paschal mystery is a unique event in history. Like other historical events, it really happened at a definite time and in a specific location. Unlike other historical events, the Paschal mystery transcends time and place. Because through this event Jesus was able to destroy death and bring about salvation, the Paschal mystery has been present to every generation since. Christ is truly present in these events.

32. Define *transubstantiation*.

The term transubstantiation expresses how the reality (substance) of bread and wine changes into the reality of Jesus' risen and glorified body and blood.

33. According to the Council of Florence, what three things are necessary for a sacrament to be valid?

According to the Council, proper matter, correct words or form, and a designated ordained minister are necessary for the validity of a sacrament.

34. Name the two main parts of the Mass. What takes place in each part?

The liturgy of the Word, where God's word in scripture is proclaimed, and the liturgy of Eucharist, where the bread and wine become Jesus' Body and Blood.

35. Put these parts of the Mass in sequential order:

Penitential Rite (1) Gospel (3) Consecration (8)
First Reading (2) Our Father (9) Communion (11)
Homily (4) Sign of Peace (10) Holy, Holy, Holy (6)
Eucharistic Prayer (7) Offertory (5) Concluding Rite (12)

36. Name and explain three basic human rights.

The most basic human right is the right to life. Other related human rights are: the right to private property, the right to emigrate and immigrate, the right to participate in the political system, the right to one's reputation, the right to choose one's state in life, and the right to worship God.

37. What is meant by the phrase "preferential option for the poor"?

As the bishops have instructed, we are to search out the poor in our midst and care for them.

38. List the corporal works of mercy.

The corporal (bodily) works of mercy are: Feed the hungry. Give drink to the thirsty. Clothe the naked. Visit the imprisoned. Shelter the homeless. Visit the sick. Bury the dead.

39. List the spiritual works of mercy.

The spiritual works of mercy are: Counsel the doubtful. Instruct the ignorant. Admonish sinners. Comfort the afflicted. Forgive offenses. Bear wrongs patiently. Pray for the living and the dead.

40. Outline the Church's basic positions on the justice issues of consumerism, the environment, and war and violence.

Christians are called to turn away from the accompanying greed of consumerism and work instead for lasting gifts that will benefit them God's kingdom, not just this world. The Christian view on the environment comes from the first creation story in the Bible, that God gave humans dominion over creation. Dominion also requires stewardship. According to Church teaching, violence is always the last option. The Church's just-war tradition provides guidelines for situations where violence can be used.

41. List at least four ways Catholics are able to know the Holy Spirit.

Catholics are able to know the Holy Spirit in the following ways: in the scriptures he inspired; in Church Tradition; in the Magisterium, which he assists; in the sacramental liturgy; in prayer, wherein he intercedes for us; in the gifts and ministries by which the Church is built up; in the signs of apostolic and missionary life; in the witness of saints through whom he shows his holiness and continues the work of salvation.

42. What is the essential rite of Confirmation?

The essential rite of Confirmation is the anointing of the candidates with chrism.

43. Name four effects of the sacrament of Confirmation.

Confirmation brings a special outpouring of the Holy Spirit. Other effects of the sacrament of Confirmation are: It roots us more deeply in God's love, leading us to call out to God, "Abba! Father!" It unites us more firmly with Christ. It strengthens our bond with the Church. It gives us the special strength of the Holy Spirit to spread and defend the faith by word and action, to confess the name of Christ boldly, and never to be ashamed of the cross.

44. List the seven gifts of the Holy Spirit.

The seven gifts of the Holy Spirit are: wisdom, understanding, right judgment, courage, knowledge, reverence, and wonder and awe.

45. How many candidates will be confirmed at the next Confirmation at your parish?

Encourage the candidates to ask the Confirmation Leader this question.

46. How is self-concept related to self-esteem?

Self-concept is how you think of yourself. If you look honestly at yourself and feel good about yourself, then your self-esteem will be high.

47. Who administers the sacrament of Matrimony?

The couple administer the sacrament of Matrimony to one another. The priest or deacon serves as an official witness.

48. What does the Church teach about sex outside of marriage?

Sex outside of marriage is a sin.

49. What is meant by the term *religious life*?

Religious are lay men or women or ordained men who live in a religious community and take vows to live out the evangelical counsels of poverty, chastity, and obedience.

50. How is the ministerial priesthood different from the common priesthood?

The ministerial priesthood is different from the common priesthood of the baptized in that it confers a sacred power for the service of the faithful. Ordained ministers—in three degrees of bishop, priest, and deacon—serve the Church by teaching, by leading worship, and by their governance.